DIFFERING VISIONS OF
A LEARNING SOCIETY

Research findings

Volume I

Edited by Frank Coffield

D0279159

The POLICY
P~P
PRESS

E·S·R·C
ECONOMIC
& SOCIAL
RESEARCH
COUNCIL

First published in Great Britain in July 2000 by

The Policy Press
34 Tyndall's Park Road
Bristol BS8 1PY
UK

Tel +44 (0)117 954 6800
Fax +44 (0)117 973 7308
e-mail tpp@bristol.ac.uk
http://www.policypress.org.uk

© The Policy Press 2000

In association with the ESRC *Learning Society Programme*

British Library Cataloguing in Publication Data

A catalogue record for this book is available from the British Library

ISBN 1 86134 230 6 paperback

ISBN 1 86134 246 2 hardback

Frank Coffield was Director of the ESRC's research programme into *The Learning Society* from 1994 to 2000.

Cover design by Qube Design Associates, Bristol.

Photographs on front cover supplied by kind permission of Mark Simmons Photography, Bristol.

Printed and bound in Great Britain by Hobbs the Printers Ltd, Southampton.

Contents

Notes on contributors

Ms Jane Alderton is Senior Lecturer at the Institute of Nursing and Midwifery, University of Brighton. She has published research on knowledge use by nurses and midwives and interprofessional healthcare teams.

Professor Stephen Ball is Professor of Sociology of Education and Director of the Centre for Public Policy Research at King's College London. He is editor of the *Journal of Education Policy* and the author of several books on education policy including *Politics and policy making in education* (Routledge, 1990), *Education reform* (Open University Press, 1994), with Sharon Gewirtz and Richard Bowe, *Markets, choice and equity in education* (Open University Press, 1995) and *Choices, pathways and transactions post-16* (Routledge Falmer, 2000) with Meg Maguire and Sheila Macrae.

Dr Will Bartlett is Reader in Social Economics at the School for Policy Studies, University of Bristol. He has carried out research on social policy, covering health and education reforms, and on comparative economic systems. He has published widely on various aspects of marketisation in Western European welfare states and in the transition economies of Eastern Europe. He is co-editor of *A revolution in social policy: Quasi-markets in the 1990s* (The Policy Press, 1998).

Professor Neville Bennett was Co-Director with Elisabeth Dunne of the ESRC study, 'The Acquisition and Development of Core Skills in Higher Education and Employment', which was one of the projects in *The Learning Society Programme*. He is Professor of Education and Senior Deputy Vice Chancellor at Exeter University.

Clive Carré was Research Fellow on the ESRC study, 'The Acquisition and Development of Core Skills in Higher Education and Employment', which was one of the projects in *The Learning Society Programme*, at Exeter University, working with Elisabeth Dunne and Neville Bennett.

Dr Antje Cockrill is a Research Associate at the Centre for Advanced Social Sciences at Cardiff University, whose interests lie in regional development studies, comparative studies of European education and training systems, and lifelong learning.

Professor Frank Coffield has been Professor of Education in the Department of Education at the University of Newcastle since 1996. He was Director of the ESRC's research programme into *The Learning Society* from 1994 to 2000. In 1997 he edited a report *A national strategy for lifelong learning* (Department of Education, University of Newcastle) and produced in 1999 *Breaking the consensus: Lifelong learning as social control* (Department of Education, University of Newcastle). Four reports on findings from *The Learning Society Programme* have been produced so far: *Learning at work*; *Why's the beer always stronger up North? Studies in lifelong learning in Europe*; *Speaking truth to power: Research and policy on lifelong learning*; and *The necessity of informal learning*, all published by The Policy Press.

Mr Gerald Cole is a Research Fellow at the University of Sussex. He is the author of books on management, and has researched into the teaching of business studies and the assessment of professional competence.

Professor Phil Cooke is Professor of Regional Development and Director of the Centre for Advanced Studies at the University of Wales, Cardiff. Recent books include *The governance of innovation in Europe* (Pinter, 1999), *The associational economy* (Oxford University Press, 1998), and *Regional innovation systems* (UCL Press, 1998).

Professor Brian Davies is Professor of Education at the School of Social Sciences, Cardiff University. His interests lie in the analysis of pedagogic discourse.

Dr Therese Dowswell is a health service researcher with a special interest in the maternity services and the education and training of health services staff. Until recently Therese was a Senior Research Fellow in the Department of Psychology at the University of Leeds. Inspired by participants in recent research projects, Therese is now a student nurse at the School of Health Studies at Bradford University.

Elisabeth Dunne was Senior Research Fellow and Co-Director of the ESRC study, 'The Acquisition and Development of Core Skills in Higher Education and Employment', which was one of the projects in *The Learning*

Society Programme. She is now a Staff Development Officer at Exeter University.

Professor Michael Eraut is Professor of Education at the University of Sussex Institute of Education and directed one of the projects entitled 'Development of Knowledge and Skills in Employment', as part of the ESRC's *Learning Society Programme.* He has published widely in the areas of professional and vocational education and about different kinds of knowledge.

Dr John Fitz is Reader in Education at the School of Social Sciences, Cardiff University. His interests lie in the analysis of educational policy.

Dr Jenny Hewison is a Senior Lecturer in the School of Psychology at the University of Leeds. Her teaching and research interests lie in health psychology, and in learning and behaviour change, with particular reference to staff and patients in the National Health Service.

Ms Cathy Howieson is a Senior Research Fellow at the Centre for Educational Sociology at the University of Edinburgh. She was a member of the team involved in a comparative study of academic and vocational education in England, Wales and Scotland as part of the ESRC's *Learning Society Programme.*

Dr Sheila Macrae is Research Fellow in the School of Education, King's College London, working on a longitudinal study of young people in transition from school to work. She has been involved in a number of other research projects at King's, the Open University and elsewhere, and has a special interest in students with learning and behaviour difficulties.

Dr Meg Maguire is Senior Lecturer in the School of Education, King's College London. She is co-editor of *Becoming a teacher* (Open University Press, 1997) and author of a number of papers on the teaching profession and women teachers. She is deputy editor of the *Journal of Education Policy,* and is currently completing a book on primary schooling in the inner city.

Mrs Bobbie Millar is Academic Secretary in the School of Health Care Studies at the University of Leeds. At the beginning of the research she was Director of Academic Affairs at the Leeds College of Health and became involved in the project because the College provided education and training for a range of healthcare professionals.

Professor David Raffe is Professor of Sociology of Education and Director of the Centre for Educational Sociology at the University of Edinburgh. He has conducted several 'home international' comparisons of the home countries of the UK, comparative studies of European and other OECD countries, and is a co-director (with Michael Young) of the Unified Learning Project, which is part of the ESRC's *Learning Society Programme*.

Professor Teresa Rees, School of Social Sciences, Cardiff University. She has carried out research on the position of women in the labour market and on training programmes in both the UK and Europe. She has acted as advisor to the European Commission on mainstreaming equal opportunities and is Equal Opportunities Commissioner for Wales.

Dr Peter Scott is currently Lecturer in Employee Relations in the Department of Management at Manchester Metropolitan University. He has also worked at the Universities of Bath, Bristol, West of England and the University of Wales, Cardiff, where he was a researcher on the project reported in this volume.

Mr Peter Senker has been a Senior Researcher in the Science Policy Research Unit and, more recently, the Institute of Education at the University of Sussex. He has published widely on the training of engineers and is now a visiting professor at the University of East London.

Dr Ken Spours is a Senior Lecturer in the Lifelong Learning Group at the Institute of Education, University of London. He was a research officer on the 'Unified Learning Project', which was part of the ESRC's Learning Society programme.

Professor Michael Young is Professor of Education and Director of the Post-16 Research Centre at the London Institute of Education. He is a co-director (with David Raffe) of the Unified Learning Project, which is part of the ESRC's *Learning Society Programme*.

Introduction:
A critical analysis of the
concept of a learning society

Frank Coffield

The findings from the Economic and Social Research Council's (ESRC) programme of research into 'the learning society' are presented in two volumes, of which this is the first; and they appear at a most opportune time because the Secretary of State for Education and Employment in England recently raised for discussion issues of vital importance to all democratic societies, namely, how can research evidence be used more effectively in the development and implementation of government policy? And, more generally, what should be the relationship between government and the research community? In essence David Blunkett has issued three challenges to all social science researchers, each of which *The Learning Society Programme* is prepared to be judged by:

- to study issues "central and directly relevant to the political and policy debate";
- to "take into account the reality of many people's lives";
- and to engage open-mindedly with policy rather than be "driven by ideology paraded as intellectual inquiry or critique" (Blunkett, 2000, p 2).

A quick glance at the titles in the table of contents of the seven chapters which follow will reveal that the topics chosen for study amply fulfil the first two criteria laid down by the Secretary of State. Whether the third challenge has also been met is left to the judgement of the reader, but programmes of research have the advantage over 'stand-alone' projects of developing a measure of internal quality control through discussing and debating emergent findings and policy implications.

In the two volumes of findings from *The Learning Society Programme* researchers produce new findings in areas where evidence has been particularly thin (for example skill levels at work); they develop new and useful concepts (such as social capital); they criticise current orthodoxies (the over-reliance on human capital); they analyse the success of approaches which re-engage traditional non-participants in learning (credit-based learning); they re-assess the significance of forms of learning (such as informal learning) which are currently being unduly neglected; they identify significant gaps in our knowledge (social theories of learning); they develop research methods (a new, interdisciplinary approach to the analysis of skills at work); they examine weaknesses and contradictions in existing policies (learning markets); and they make detailed suggestions for the improvement of these policies (which will be summarised in the second companion volume – see Coffield, 2000: forthcoming).

Research offers at least one further service in a democratic society: it produces discomfort and independent, critical research can produce acute discomfort. A genuine partnership between the worlds of policy and research will only prosper if researchers are as involved as politicians in determining the terms on which business is to be conducted. The following ground rules should be added to those suggested by David Blunkett:

- the partnership needs to be one of equals who respect each other's roles, objectives and independence;
- the agenda of what is to be researched and how it is to be studied *cannot* be set by one of the partners, but must be jointly arrived at after public discussion and debate with all relevant parties;
- public funding should also be made available to those who think the unthinkable, who interrogate the fashionable and who ask pertinent (and at times impertinent) questions of the powerful;
- a broad definition of all the types of research to be publicly funded needs to be adopted so that research is not confined to the evaluation of governmental objectives;
- politicians need to accept that there is a form of engaged and constructive criticism which should not be routinely dismissed as cynicism;
- policy makers and politicians need to move beyond the 'cherry-picking' of research, where only those findings which support existing policies or those under development are seized upon.

These conditions are not only basic to all scientific research; they are at the root of all creative endeavour in a vibrant, open and learning society. So in an equal and thriving partnership challenges are issued and taken up by all the partners. Just as researchers are rightly required to remain balanced, open-minded and free of dogma, governments in their turn must "give serious consideration to 'difficult' findings" (Blunkett, 2000, p 2), by which is meant politically inconvenient or unacceptable findings which contradict their most cherished beliefs.

The Learning Society Programme will provide an early test of the government's receptivity to unwelcome findings because some of the conclusions arrived at by projects reflecting on their data challenge some of the fundamental assumptions of current policy. Two brief examples will be given, one from each volume. First, the staff in the National Health Service, who were studied by Jenny Hewison and her colleagues, perceived the positive, upbeat rhetoric of lifelong learning (about providing a series of learning opportunities throughout their careers) as more of a threat than a promise (see Chapter Five, this volume). In other words, the costs of lifelong learning, such as unreasonable demands on those with children for training in out-of-work time, were thought to outweigh its advantages.

Second, the removal of structural barriers to participation in lifelong learning, such as costs, time and lack of childcare, remains a central plank in government thinking. It is therefore likely to be demotivating for politicians and policy makers alike to be told by Gareth Rees and his colleagues in their regional study of participation in South Wales (in the second volume of findings) that the removal of structural barriers is a *necessary*, but not a *sufficient* condition: "... non-participation is largely a product of the fact that individuals do not see education and training as appropriate for them and these views, in turn, are structured by factors which occur relatively early in life" (Rees et al, 1999, p 8). The researchers are referring to such factors as time, place, gender, family and initial schooling which together create "a framework of opportunities, influences and social expectations that are determined independently" (Rees et al, 1999, p 8) of government action. Consequently, policies which concentrate on access and participation are likely to have limited impact unless they are integrated with wider strategies to combat poverty and social exclusion.

Other difficulties which confronted the researchers right from the start of the programme were that aspirations to create a learning society in the UK were severely hampered by widespread and deep-seated disagreement about the characteristics of such a society and the resulting impossibility of simply assessing progress towards a few generally agreed objectives. Moreover, the political and educational discourse surrounding a learning society and lifelong learning was shot through not only by extreme conceptual vagueness but also by 'factual' assumptions and assertions which were unsupported by any hard evidence or which have since been seriously questioned by findings produced by the programme. This programme has therefore helped to counter the seemingly endless production of extended articles and full-length books, devoted to a learning society and lifelong learning but devoid of any empirical evidence. There is space for only one prize example which is typical of the genre. John Towers, who was then Chief Executive of the Rover Group and Chair of the Business Council of the World Initiative on Lifelong Learning, wrote an evangelical Foreword to a well-known book on lifelong learning by Norman Longworth and Keith Davies:

> We at the Rover Group Ltd are proud to be among the world's foremost 'learning organisations' ... we invested in the empowerment of the people who work for us. I am glad to say that this strategy has worked like a dream. People at Rover are infinitely more fulfilled, more mature, more committed and more prepared to take responsibility than they were five years ago.... What we have achieved here lights the way to what can be achieved in every other sphere of life.... Schools, colleges, universities, professional associations – even whole nations – can learn something from our experience. Their strengths too lie in the development of their people. Their future lies in empowering them through improved learning conditions, and in putting the focus on the needs of each individual learner. (Towers, 1996, p ix)

Despite all that has happened to Rover since 1996, politicians from all the main parties and lifelong learning pundits show no signs of learning the appropriate lessons. Their speeches and writings, for instance, continue to advocate the simplistic form of human capital theory exemplified above, whereby responsibility for coping with economic restructuring is passed to individuals. Workers can become enthusiastic and flexible lifelong learners and yet remain powerless to influence the major decisions which transform their lives. For too long lifelong learning has remained an evidence-free zone, under-researched, under-theorised, unencumbered by doubt and unmoved by criticism.

The *Learning Society Programme*

In 1994 the ESRC decided to respond to all the claims and counterclaims about the links between education and wealth creation and between training and competitiveness by commissioning a programme of research which had the full, official title of *The Learning Society: knowledge and skills for employment*. A research specification was written (see Coffield, 1994), the programme was advertised and 326 applications received. Fifty-five projects were selected to form a long short-list and were then invited to submit a fuller research proposal. These were then peer reviewed by a wide range of academics and non-academic users of such research, and sufficient funds (£2.5 million) had been allocated to the programme to commission 13 projects. Subsequently a fourteenth project on 'Innovations in Teaching and Learning in Higher Education' was financed by a number of co-funders[1]. The projects employed more than 50 researchers in teams spread throughout the UK, from Belfast to Brighton and from Edinburgh to Exeter. Each project had a different starting and finishing time and the programme itself ran until the end of March 2000.

During the lifetime of the programme four reports were published on such themes as learning at work[2], studies of lifelong learning in Europe[3], research and policy on lifelong learning[4] and informal learning[5]. Other contributions to the public debate on lifelong learning were produced, which either explored the concept of a learning society[6] or offered constructive criticism of government policy (Coffield, 1999). Each of the 14 projects has also written for the benefit of the general reader a brief two-page summary of their objectives, achievements and outputs and sets of these summaries are available free of charge[7].

The aim of the final two books (of which this volume is the first) is, however, different. It is to present a comprehensive overview in a collection of extended articles of the objectives, methods, main findings, policy implications and publications of each project. The work of up to seven projects is described in each of the two volumes; and the only reason for the choice of the particular projects in this first volume is that they completed before the others. This introduction and its counterpart in the companion volume seek to place the findings of the projects within a broad context of research on a learning society and lifelong learning and within policy debates on these issues. Taken together, these two books should become the first 'port of call' for anyone wishing to learn about the outcomes of *The Learning Society Programme*.

The launching of the programme by the ESRC in the early 1990s showed remarkable prescience in that it coincided with a national and international burgeoning of interest in lifelong learning. The policy discourse in Britain and elsewhere has been strikingly convergent at least "in the general advocacy of the concepts of 'lifelong learning' and the 'learning society' – two terms which seem to have become both ubiquitous and almost indistinguishable" (Green et al, 1999, p 254). The sole difference between the two literatures is that British reports emphasise *learning*, whereas those from supranational organisations, such as the European Commission, the OECD and UNESCO, stress *knowledge*. For example, Jacques Delors' report to UNESCO talks of "a learning society founded on the acquisition, renewal and use of knowledge" (1996, p 24); and the first pillar of that society is a "sufficiently broad general education [combined] with the possibility of in-depth work on a selected number of subjects" (Delors, 1996, p 24). In 1996, the European Commission issued a White Paper, *Teaching and learning: Towards the learning society* and declared 1996 the European Year of Lifelong Learning, with the clear intention of fashioning a "Europe of Knowledge" (CEC, 1997).

Lifelong learning was also driven up the political agenda in most industrialised countries by pressure from powerful groups. For instance, European businessmen (sic) issued "a cry of alarm" about inadequacies in education putting at risk the competitiveness of European industry (see European Round Table of Industrialists, 1995; Cochinaux and de Woot, 1995). Reports continue to pour out from intergovernmental bodies (eg OECD, 1996), from centres and consultants (eg *The Learning Organisation* by Stahl et al, 1993) and from the education ministries of individual countries (eg Ministry of Finland, 1997). If a learning society could be brought into being by the publication of official reports, then the age of enlightenment would already have dawned. Change on the ground has, however, proved to be "slow, fragmentary and contested" (Raggatt et al, 1996, p 6).

The international flurry of papers and conferences on lifelong learning has been replicated in the UK, particularly since the election of a new Labour government in May 1997. Within two years no less than 23 government initiatives in lifelong learning were established (see Fryer, 1999, p 5 for a list), including the *University for Industry*, the *National Grid for Learning* and the *Sure Start* programme which aims to provide integrated support for pre-school children. In addition, a Green Paper, entitled *The Learning Age* (DfEE, 1998) and a White Paper, *Learning to succeed* (DfEE, 1999) have been published, the latter of which seeks to establish a radical new framework for post-16 learning (see Coffield, 2000 for a detailed evaluation). New posts which include the term 'lifelong learning' in the title have also been created across industry, education and politics, but too often lifelong learning has been used simply to rebrand existing centres, courses and students, without any new thinking, new kinds of students or any new pedagogy. Lifelong learning, in fact, is being widely used to give the outward appearance of change. The lifelong learning development plans from local authorities should therefore be required to state explicitly what is new about their proposals.

So if policy and practice are to be radically transformed, if nothing less than "widespread and systematic" cultural change is required (Fryer, 1999, p 8), then there will need to be a body of knowledge adequate to that formidable task. When *The Learning Society Programme* began work in 1994, that body of knowledge did not exist. It would be absurd to claim that 14 medium-sized projects on a small number of topics have produced (or could have produced) all the knowledge necessary to create a learning society within the UK. What is being claimed is that, in a number of key areas, painstaking research has been carried out, important findings have been produced, and these have serious ramifications for policy. What also became clear from the four dissemination conferences held in Scotland, England, Northern Ireland and Wales during 1999 is that the findings from the programme are providing a much-needed curriculum for those professionals who have 'lifelong learning' in their job title, but who have received no specific or additional training to help them appreciate how different their role could become, provided they remain in post. The Labour government appointed Kim Howells the first Minister of Lifelong Learning in England in 1997, George Mudie the second in 1998, and Malcolm Wicks the third in 1999. A year is not a long time in the politics of lifelong learning. In sum, these two volumes seek to demonstrate the value of independent, critical research in an area which is awash with unsubstantiated generalities, armchair musings and banalities without bite.

Ten models of a learning society

One of the achievements of the programme is to have explored critically the concept of a learning society and, by examining the definitions used by the 14 projects, it is possible to discern at least 10 contrasting ways in which the term is being used. These different ways of conceptualising a learning society help to make sense of the confusing and conflictual literature surrounding the term, and they are also used here to structure some of the main findings of the programme. Finally, the Labour government's policies for lifelong learning, as detailed in the White Paper, *Learning to Succeed* (DfEE, 1999), are examined to see which model or combination of models they espouse.

The 10 models are listed below and then introduced briefly with references to other publications produced by researchers within the programme which explain them in more detail:
- skills growth
- personal development
- social learning
- a learning market
- local learning societies
- social control
- self-evaluation
- centrality of learning
- a reformed system of education
- structural change

Teresa Rees and Will Bartlett, whose project on adult guidance is described in Chapter Four of this volume, are to be credited with introducing this approach as they identified the first three models above in their data as implicit but contrasting definitions of a learning society; the other seven were added later, as a result of reflection on the research outcomes from the projects. Individual projects tended to concentrate on particular sub-sets of these models depending on the main focus of their study, but the programme as a whole has provided the useful service of conceptual ground-clearing.

Skills growth

The *skills growth* model is based on the belief that "the improvement of the skills of the labour force is a critical determinant of the international competitiveness of the economy" (Bartlett and Rees, Chapter Four). The trouble, however, is that the alleged link between investment in education and economic performance is a *belief* rather than an established research finding. Despite extensive research, no causal connection has been found and yet the skills growth model remains the central plank of government policy on education and employment (see Coffield, 1999 for a detailed critique). Alan Brown and Ewart Keep, in a review of the relevant literature commissioned especially by *The Learning Society Programme*, conclude that

> ...the kind of very simple linkage that policy-makers assume cannot be proved and probably does not exist. Higher levels of education and training may be a necessary precondition for greater economic success,

but on their own they are not sufficient to ensure that it occurs. (Brown and Keep, 2000: forthcoming, p 22)

Such caution is, however, dispensed with in training manuals for senior managers where, for instance, books such as *Developing a learning culture* talk of "unleashing human capital" and draw the following unwarranted conclusion from the research literature: "Learning and skill development, education and training – the routes to increased knowledge and skills – are the only routes to competitiveness" (Jones, 1996, p 11).

Within *The Learning Society Programme*, Jenny Hewison, Therese Dowswell and Bobbie Millar studied changing patterns of training provision in the National Health Service (NHS) and their findings, presented in Chapter Five, do not support the more naïve interpretation of human capital theory illustrated above. In their own words:

> The majority of [nurses and allied staff] in our sample did not tend to undertake training to increase their knowledge and skills. They did not explicitly express a desire to do their jobs better. In this sense, they did not see their participation as an investment in their productive capacity; they simply wanted a qualification. (Chapter Five, this volume)

In other words, these professionals were engaged in credentialism, that is, gaining training credits in order to protect or improve their current job prospects rather than investing in human capital to increase their future earnings. It takes a qualitative study of the kind conducted by Jenny Hewison and her colleagues to elucidate the real and complex motivations of adult learners and to prevent us confusing investment in human capital with credentialism. The general significance of this distinction has been well summarised by Ralph Fevre: "Policies designed to increase our investment in human capital may actually lead only to an increase in credentialism which ... does nothing to improve our chances of success as a high-skill, high wage economy" (1997, p 25).

The danger of using qualifications as a proxy for competence in the workforce has been well pointed out by Alison Fuller and Lorna Unwin in their study of the UK steel industry. Their survey of over 5,000 employees from 33 firms and five sectors within the steel industry found that the clear majority had either no qualifications or very low level qualifications; and yet the sector had improved both its productivity and profitability:

> ... it is inappropriate to conclude that there is a lack of competence amongst the steel industry's (or other sectors') labour force(s) because the majority of the workforce hold low levels of formal qualifications. (Fuller and Unwin, 1999, p 611)

In addition to detailed qualitative studies, *The Learning Society Programme* also funded a major new survey of the pattern of skills in Britain because the empirical evidence on this crucial issue was particularly thin. This survey of a representative sample of British workers not only developed a new interdisciplinary methodology for the analysis of skills in the workplace which can be used as a benchmark for future comparisons, but it has also produced a wealth of significant findings which can only be touched on here. To give but one example, David Ashton, Alan Felstead and Francis Green, whose chapter appears in the second volume, provide strong evidence that aggregate skill levels have been increasing in Britain, but their most striking finding is that "computer usage has turned out to be a crucial factor in the upskilling of the British workplace" (Coffield, 2000: forthcoming). Nor is it just advanced or complex computing skills which are highly valued in the British labour market, as "the premium for using computers at just 'moderate' levels of complexity (compared to non-users) is 13 per cent for both sexes" (Coffield, 2000: forthcoming). When the rewards for possessing such skills have been shown to be so extensive, there is a clear incentive for individuals to acquire them. Other issues, such as whether the gap between the skill-rich and the skill-poor is widening or closing, will be dealt with in the introduction to the second volume.

Personal development

The second model, *personal development*, aims to promote individual self-fulfilment through greater participation in all forms of learning, both at work and in the community. Individual Learning Accounts (ILAs) are a clear example of this approach which is meant to encourage individuals to take greater responsibility for their own learning and to share the costs of the projected expansion in lifelong learning. A recent evaluation of ILAs in Dorset reports great enthusiasm for them among account holders: "When people make their own choices about learning they are much more likely to enjoy it" (Payne, 2000, p 2). But only 5% of respondents had received any formal guidance. That is why Bartlett and Rees in Chapter Four argue for a guidance element to be incorporated into all

ILAs to ensure that choice in the learning market for individuals is not just increased but also informed. What we still do not know is: can employers (large and small) be persuaded to contribute to ILAs? Can demand for learning be increased by yet another supply-side measure, and are the returns to intermediate qualifications sufficiently high for individuals to risk investing in them? (See Robinson, 1999.)

Again, Jenny Hewison's project on training in the NHS found evidence that only a minority of their sample took courses of further training as a means of personal fulfilment. They warn, moreover, that a shift in policy towards regarding continuous professional development as an individual responsibility may be "counterproductive in that it might systematically disadvantage certain sectors of the workforce previously targeted as training priorities: women and the less well qualified" (Chapter Five, this volume). Such an outcome is likely because further training within the NHS takes place increasingly in the employee's own time and so staff with children are faced with the difficult choice of enrolling on a course and bearing the attendant social, financial and psychological costs or refusing the 'opportunity' of training with possible adverse consequences on their careers:

> ... 'not taking the opportunity' is generally interpreted as a sign of lack of commitment to work. By these means, structural inequalities in access are turned into attributes of individuals. They cease to become problems and become useful selection devices in decisions relating to recruitment, promotion or availability of future training opportunities. (Chapter Five, this volume)

Social learning

Social learning is the third model which stresses that innovation is dependent on collaboration as well as competition because learning at its best and most creative is social rather than individual. The emergent concept of social capital, where the focus of attention is on relationships between individuals and institutions rather than on individual skills, was developed by two projects within the Programme – Sheila Riddell, Stephen Baron and Alastair Wilson studying adults with learning difficulties, and John Field and Tom Schuller examining an apparent divergence between initial and continuing education. The overviews of both these projects are contained in the second volume. John Field and Tom Schuller argue from their empirical work in Scotland and Northern Ireland that social capital adds an important dimension to our understanding of the relationship between education and the economy. The positive aspects of social capital (it offers, for example, ample opportunities for informal learning) have been stressed by many commentators, but Field and Schuller add their counter-intuitive rider that it can be:

> ...inherently narrowing, in that it gives access only to the limited range of resources that happen to be available in any given locale; and characteristically familistic forms of social capital can be particularly limiting and inward-looking, making it more difficult to build bridging ties. (Field and Schuller, 1999, p 11)

Field and Schuller also call attention to the historic legacy of the high percentages of young people who left school not just in Scotland and Northern Ireland but throughout the UK with no or very poor qualifications through the 1960s, 1970s and much of the 1980s. The effects of this polarisation in attainment – those who obtained good qualifications continue to receive more education and training, while the disadvantages for people with poor basic skills intensify as they proceed through adulthood – are likely to be with us for another 30 years, unless the recommendations of Sir Claus Moser's working group are energetically implemented (1999). The economic costs of around seven million functionally illiterate or innumerate adults have been estimated at £10 billion a year (Moser, 1999, p 25), but the research of John Bynner and Samantha Parsons (1997) also underlines the impact of poor basic skills on family life, health and participation in public life. In this model, lifelong learning needs to be more than a means of improving economic performance; it has to become a moral response to the social exclusion of those who benefited least from initial education.

A learning market

According to Basil Bernstein, "Today throughout Europe, led by the USA and the UK, there is a new principle guiding the latest transition of capitalism. The principles of the market and its managers are more and more the managers of the policy and practices of education" (1996, p 87). The discipline of the market was introduced to schools by the Education Reform Act of 1988 and later extended to the post-compulsory sector by the Further and Higher Education Act of 1992. Within a learning market, it is claimed, greater choice and freedom are given to individuals who assume responsibility for their own learning and pursue their self-interest as consumers. By means of developed budgets and formula funding, the providers of learning opportunities are actively encouraged to behave more like businesses, whose performance in the marketplace is assessed annually by targets and outcomes, and by the difference between inputs and outputs. This, very briefly, is the essence of the fourth model.

Stephen Ball, Meg Maguire and Sheila Macrae set out to explore both the dynamics of one local learning market for post-16 year olds in South West London and the market behaviour of the main providers in that area; and their findings are presented in Chapter One. They list the main effects of the market and some are positive, such as the development of systems to improve retention and a greater awareness of students with special educational needs. Other outcomes, however, are less benign: heightened competition between Further Education (FE) colleges and 11-18 schools; the FE colleges felt financially disadvantaged by a different funding regime; and relationships between the two sectors were marked by suspicion so that students were "poorly informed or mis-informed about post-16 alternatives" (Chapter One, this volume). The authors continue by describing the quality of the relationships between these institutional competitors as 'cut throat':

> Markets reward shrewdness rather than principle and privilege the values of competition over professional values. Education markets, like other markets, are driven by self-interest – "the College cannot afford to take a moral stand", as one respondent put it. The self-interest of consumers who choose is set alongside that of producers aiming to thrive, or at least survive. The 'cut throat' quality and values of competition increasingly in play in this market make possible and encourage a variety of dubious actions and tactics. (Chapter One, this volume).

One outcome is what the authors call an 'economy of student worth', where some students (eg white, middle-class girls) are highly valued and competed for, but others (eg black, working-class boys) are less desirable and find their choices constrained. In short, this learning market supported and empowered a few at the expense of the many. In Stephen Ball's own words "The market provides a mechanism for the reinvention and legitimation of hierarchy and differentiation via the ideology of diversity, competition and choice" (Chapter One, this volume).

Market forces were also introduced into the provision of adult guidance services in the mid-1990s and, in Chapter Four, Will Bartlett and Teresa Rees studied their impact on four localities in England and one in Scotland. If job insecurity and mobility are to become more widespread, we will require a sophisticated system of adult guidance to enable job seekers to move flexibly around a more fluid labour market. The researchers conclude that unfortunately the introduction of the market principle has produced a wide disparity of provision, with the availability of competent, unbiased advice dependent principally on the geographical location of the job seeker: "... provision is unequal across localities and unrelated to labour market conditions, a highly unsatisfactory state of affairs" (Chapter Four, this volume).

Despite this growing body of empirical research about the adverse effects of market forces in education, Sir Christopher Ball still believes (without quoting any supporting evidence) that learning opportunities should be marketed and sold to adults just like holidays or soap. Learning, however, is not a commodity like baked beans which can be 'branded', 'marketed' and 'delivered' to 'customers'. It is a transaction which takes place between teacher and learner, where learners are guided through interaction with a more skilled partner to use the intellectual tools of their society[8]. Moreover, whether learning can be 'marketed' and what effects markets have on 'customers' are empirical questions which make the disregard for evidence all the more reprehensible.

Local learning societies

Both of the projects based in Wales[9] argue that there is no such thing as a learning society, and that their findings more accurately reflect regional or even local learning societies. As Phil Cooke and his colleagues put it:

> ... opportunities for, and participation in, post-compulsory training and
> learning are strongly determined by the character, strength and history
> of local labour markets, local employers and the patterns of employment.
> (Chapter Six, this volume)

Wales is well on its way to developing its own distinctive pattern of education, training and skills provision, and that distinctiveness is based on a variety of factors: a separate capacity for policy making, bilingualism, adaptation to local needs and developments, smaller and more closely knit policy networks, less emphasis on institutional competition, an all-Wales credit accumulation scheme for post-compulsory education, a different pattern of secondary education, as well as its own history of education and training.

One consequence of such local learning societies is that national initiatives tend to be seen as rather remote, irrelevant to local needs and imposed from above. So, for instance, Phil Cooke and his colleagues report that the National Targets for Education and Training were having a limited impact in the three sectors (engineering, construction and care) where they were studying multi-skilling in South Wales, because the targets were "perceived to be of little or no relevance to the individual or the enterprise" (Chapter Six, this volume).

It was not, however, just the two Welsh projects which emphasised the power and the role of the locality in making sense of the learning society. Stephen Ball and his colleagues in the first chapter refer repeatedly to the impact of the city economy and of the social and cultural variety in South West London on the patterns of choice and types of transition made by the young people in their sample. Most young people, for example, did not consider all the educational options open to them and chose to remain within the local area, while others from middle-class families who were more knowledgeable and confident considered institutions farther afield than their working-class peers. Race and class were part of what the authors describe in a memorable phrase as the "complex topography of choice":

> The education market in this locality provides the possibility of 'escape' for some, while leaving untouched, and indeed reinforcing, the classed and racialised categorisation of space and spatial separation, and it erects barriers for others. (Chapter One, this volume)

Another project, directed by Pat Davies and John Bynner, and described in volume II, sought to explore the impact of credit-based systems of learning on local learning cultures in London. The Open College Network has proved to be outstandingly successful in attracting large and growing numbers of traditional non-participants. The clear majority of these new learners were women, over 25 years of age, unemployed or unwaged, and from ethnic minority groups; and the total numbers of learners increased steadily from 6,500 in 1992-93 to 30,000 in 1997-98. The explanation of this success story is complex and appears to lie not so much in the attraction of credits (as many participants knew nothing about them before enrolment) as in the ability of the colleges to cooperate in the accreditation of learning that had previously not been regarded as worthy of certification.

This research finding reinforces both the critical role of collaboration among local institutions in bolstering the participation of excluded groups and the practical importance of a broad definition of learning. The research, however, also identified organisations where professional and organisational cultures, for example, in the workplace and in prisons, prevented the development of local learning societies.

Social control

The sixth approach to a learning society, the *social control* model, introduces a sceptical note to the public debate. It suggests that all the fulsome rhetoric about the transformative powers of lifelong learning may be deceptive because easy talk of companies becoming 'learning organisations' disguises a basic conflict of interests between employers and employees, and between the socially included and excluded. Companies which downsize, deregulate, relocate and outsource will find increasing difficulty in engendering long-term commitment within their workforce. Conversely, for an employee, loyalty to an employer or a firm may prove to be an expensive trap because, in the words of Richard Sennett, the short-termism of global capital corrodes trust and mutual commitment: "Detachment and superficial cooperativeness are better armour for dealing with current realities than behaviour based on values of loyalty or service" (1998, p 25).

Confirmation of such a conflict of interests came from Jenny Hewison's project on NHS training. She and her colleagues conclude that 'opportunities for lifelong learning' were viewed by many of the participants in their study as a threat or an obligation imposed by employers rather than as a promise:

> It was not that they lacked motivation to learn, but rather that learning opportunities were often offered on very disadvantageous terms. We argue that many groups of learners will needed to be given a better deal if desired participation rates are to be achieved at an acceptable human cost. (Chapter Five, this volume)

It may therefore be appropriate on occasions to *decline* an invitation to learn because the costs are too high or the benefits too marginal. What must be avoided is explaining away the unwillingness of 'non-learners' to participate in formal education and training as laziness or lack of motivation. "Defensiveness", writes Guy Claxton, "seen from the inside, is always rational" (1999, p 332).

The research finding that more than 25% of the adult population in this country take no part whatsoever in either 'taught' or 'non-taught' learning presents policy makers specialising in lifelong learning with perhaps their most taxing challenge (see Beinart and Smith, 1998). The scale of the task facing reformers can be judged from the attitudes of those officially labelled as 'non-learners': "Respondents who had done no learning in the last ten years ... were asked what might encourage them to do some learning, education or training. Half (50%) said that nothing would encourage them" (Beinart and Smith, 1998, p 29).

Even if the number of teenagers leaving school each year without any qualifications and with damaged identities as learners was to be reduced, those adults who see all forms of learning, including learning at work, as not for them would remain uninfluenced. One possible response, which has begun to be discussed publicly, is to suggest that certain sections of the community have become so alienated through poverty, bad experiences of schooling or unemployment that, in their own best interests, they may have to be more actively encouraged to learn. Alan Tuckett, Director of the National Institute of Adult Continuing Education and Vice Chair of the National Advisory Group for Continuing Education and Lifelong Learning, has been arguing that "marginalised adults may need propelling into [the] liberating possibilities of lifelong learning" by instilling in them a sense of obligation to others and to themselves (see Ecclestone, 1999). The strength of Alan Tuckett's position is that it is a genuine and well-meaning proposal to help those caught on the wrong side of the learning divide who have neither secure, well paid employment nor the skills needed to acquire it. On the other hand, such a drastic step would suggest that policy makers now claim to understand the needs of people better than they do themselves. A move to compulsion would treat non-participants as irrational, impervious to persuasion or incapable of self-help and would discount any suggestion that they reject some of the learning opportunities offered to them because they *deserve* to be rejected. Isaiah Berlin's liberal credo, as summarised by Michael Ignatieff, provides a spirited and principled answer to the policy makers' dilemma:

> ... a liberal politics deals only with what human beings say they want. Their preferences can be argued with and persuasion is possible, but coercion – in the name of what they might prefer, if they could only see it more clearly – is always illegitimate. The revealed preferences of

> ordinary men and women must be the limit and also the arbiter of all
> practical politics. (Ignatieff, 1998, p 226)

The suggestion that a strong element of social control pervades the rhetoric
of the state or of employers may appear a crude exaggeration for effect
and yet John Field claims that the scale of compulsory adult education in
the UK is already extensive:

> ... recent years have seen a quiet explosion in compulsory education
> and training for adults. For the sake of argument, let us leave aside
> programmes for the unemployed such as New Deal, where the coercion
> is obvious. Without anyone much noticing, a great deal of professional
> development and skills updating is carried out not because anyone wants
> to learn or is ready to learn, but because they are required to learn.
> Contract compliance, regulatory frameworks and statutory requirements
> are three of the main culprits. (Field, 1999, p 11)

We may have to abandon the term 'the post-compulsory sector', as
demands for lifelong flexibility and employability on the part of workers
begin to bite. Viviane Forrester, who sees the two terms as close relatives,
defines 'flexibility' as "the right to dismiss workers when, how and however
frequently it pleases the managers"; and she treats its stern brother
'employability' as meaning "being available for every kind of change, for
the whims of fate, in this case those of the employers" (1999, pp 14 and
110).

These combative definitions insert a note of structural conflict into the
predominantly apolitical and ahistorical public discourse on lifelong
learning. As Stewart Ranson argues, the deep organising principle of
British society is not learning, but the capitalist division of labour: "There
is thus no classless universal interest around which a national consensus
on the learning society can be constructed" (1998, p 244).

Self-evaluation

Most of the writing on the learning society treats it as a normative concept,
as a desirable future destination which this country may or may not
reach. It may, however, be preferable to use the concept reflexively to
enable this society to learn about itself and to evaluate progress. Using
the learning society as an *evaluative device* constitutes the seventh model
to be explained. Rather than enumerating all the characteristics thought

to be essential in a learning society, a tactic which is likely to produce an endless and not very helpful list, it may be more profitable to "publish an annual 'state of the nation' report on lifelong learning, bringing together achievements in the different fields, relating to all age groups and including indices of informal learning and acknowledging existing weaknesses" – to quote the first policy recommendation of Field and Schuller (1999).

Such an annual evaluation of progress depends, however, on the existence of valid, reliable and comparable data on lifelong learning. A number of projects, and especially those directed by Pat Davies and John Bynner and by John Field and Tom Schuller, experienced considerable difficulties "extracting a coherent and robust set of data over time ... even in relation to formal education and training. It was virtually impossible in respect of informal learning" (Field and Schuller, in Coffield, 2000: forthcoming). There is an urgent need to develop, in conjunction with our European partners, an agreed set of indicators on lifelong learning which would enable benchmarking and the assessment of progress. Tom Schuller and Caroline Bamford have also usefully explored the problems of measuring social capital where the focus is on relationships rather than individuals (2000).

It is not only the state, however, which needs to evaluate its own achievements, to assess the impact of initiatives and to monitor progress generally; these are essential activities for institutions, partnerships and individuals. There are, however, few levers within the voluntarisitic system in the UK to encourage firms to increase levels of training. Interestingly, the project directed by Elliot Stern found that regulation acted as an important impetus to innovation in continuing vocational training.

> When companies are expected to undertake industrial training or assessments (eg as part of Investors in People) ..., they become aware of employee aspirations, sometimes for the first time, which reportedly has effects on company policies. (Stern et al, 1999 p 16)

The centrality of learning

The eighth model, the *centrality of learning* for a learning society, underlines an intriguing anomaly in the literature on lifelong learning, namely, that one can read acres of print on the topic without ever coming across a discussion or a definition of the concept at the heart of the enterprise, that is, learning. In similar vein, the National Advisory Group for Continuing Education and Lifelong Learning proposes that government should instigate a national campaign to promote 'learning cultures', but the group singularly fails to define or describe what is meant by the term (see Fryer, 1999, passim). This significant silence about learning in all official reports on education, never mind on lifelong learning, prompted the present author to comment as follows:

> In all the plans to put learners first, to invest in learning, to widen participation, to set targets, to develop skills, to open up access, to raise standards, and to develop a national framework of qualifications, there is no mention of a theory (or theories) of learning to drive the whole project. It is as though there existed in the UK such widespread understanding of, and agreement about, the processes of learning and teaching that comment was thought superfluous. The omission is serious and, if not corrected, could prove fatal to the enterprise. (Coffield, 1998, p 4)

The silence has been heard by others, mainly psychologists both inside and outside the Programme. Within *The Learning Society Programme*, Andrew Hannan, Harold Silver and Sue English investigated innovations in teaching and learning in higher education and found "innovators and innovation projects relating to teaching and learning to be often isolated, low status and treated with suspicion" (Coffield, 2000: forthcoming). Moreover, Elisabeth Dunne, Neville Bennett and Clive Carré studied the acquisition of 'key' or 'core' or 'generic' skills by students in higher education and in the first years of employment. They conclude that "employers and policy makers alike have been seduced by the slogans, with scant consideration of their definition, characteristics, transferability or utility" (Chapter Three, this volume). They go further when they claim that the discourse, the training and the policies with regard to 'key skills':

> ... all require an ingredient which to date has been sadly lacking – the utilisation of a defensible theory of learning. Simply put, theories provide the rudder for effective policy implementation. Without it, policy direction is unplanned, random or likely to end on the rocks. (Chapter Three, this volume)

Their chapter imposes some much needed clarity on the conceptual confusion surrounding the term 'key skills', but their empirical findings will be disconcerting for those who believe that "learning should be increasingly responsive to employment needs and include the development of general skills, widely valued in employment", which was one of the principles in the terms of reference of the National Committee of Inquiry into Higher Education (The Dearing Report,1997). Dunne, Bennett and Carré found little evidence, even among university teachers committed to the development of 'key skills', that "their espoused or actual theories of teaching are underpinned by understandings of learning theory, or that they intentionally teach for transfer" (Chapter Three, this volume).

The debate in the UK over 'key skills' has, however, been far too introspective. Ken Spours, Michael Young, Cathy Howieson and David Raffe in Chapter Two analyse different strategies for unifying academic and vocational learning in England, Wales and Scotland, and usefully compare the narrow conception of 'key skills' in these three British systems of education with the much broader and challenging notions in continental systems:

> In both England and Scotland approaches to core/key skills tend to reflect a deficit concept of the learner, and the perceived need to remedy the failures of compulsory schooling. This is in contrast to policies elsewhere in Europe where programmes to promote generic skills are based on analyses of the skill demands of new industries and are exemplified by the German idea of 'work process knowledge' and the Dutch notion of the 'core problems' of different occupational sectors. (Chapter Two, this volume)

It does not have to be like this. There exists a growing body of evidence about how to expand the general 'learning power' of all learners and Guy Claxton has recently brought together the main findings from that substantial research literature. He begins by arguing that:

> ... to create a true learning society we need a new conception of the human mind and its powers of learning: one that has at its heart the learnability of learning itself. With such an image, the imagination of parents, schoolteachers, professors and managers can be freed to focus on the process of learning and on people's development as learners, rather than being mesmerised by 'performance indicators' and qualifications. (Claxton 1999, p 19)

Drawing on the latest research, Claxton (1999) then demonstrates that such a new conception exists and that learning is a much richer concept than most teachers or learners recognise. He moves beyond the cliché 'learning to learn', which tends to bring most discussions on the topic to a halt, by explaining the full "repertoire of learning strategies that compromise the good learner's toolkit" (Claxton, 1999, p 58). Healthy scepticism needs to be added, however, to what he describes as the three main ingredients of 'learning power': resilience, resourcefulness and reflectiveness.

A number of advances in our understanding of learning have also been made within *The Learning Society Programme*, particularly by Michael Eraut and his team at Sussex University, who produced a useful definition of the word 'learning' as used in the phrase 'the learning society':

> ... [it] should refer only to significant changes in capability or understanding, and exclude the acquisition of further information when it does not contribute to such changes. One advantage of this definition is that it can be applied to the group, organisational and societal levels as well as that of the individual person. (Eraut, 1997, p 556).

A further advantage of this definition is that it takes us beyond the anodyne phrase 'We're all learning all the time'. On the other hand, Michael Eraut also argues that it may be a psychological and tactical mistake for government publications such as the *National Adult Learning Survey 1997* (Beinart and Smith, 1998) to describe those adults who do not participate in formal education or training as 'non-learners'.

Eraut and his colleagues report in Chapter Seven on their study of the development of knowledge and skills at work. They begin by criticising the dominant paradigm in education and training policy "which treats learning as a self-conscious, deliberate, goal-driven process which is planned and organised by 'providers' to yield outcomes that are easily described and measured" (Chapter Seven, this volume). Although this paradigm deals adequately with most (but not all) of the learning carried out in formal contexts, Michael Eraut and his colleagues show in some detail that it fails to capture much of the important, informal learning that occurs in the workplace. Their chapter in this volume, and Eraut's other recent published work, for example, in *The necessity of informal learning*, help to remedy that deficiency. Taken together with the other papers produced by this project, they constitute, in the opinion of the editor of this volume, a theoretical advance in our understanding of informal learning, an advance which was acknowledged by other researchers within the Programme who began to use Michael Eraut's terminology and his insights, albeit critically at times.

Michael Eraut has a capacity for the sustained abstract exposition of complex ideas; as a result his articles repay careful study and repeated reading. In the final chapter of this book, for example, he offers clear and useful classifications of different forms of knowledge, of work-based learning, of non-formal learning and of the contexts for learning. He addresses such central questions as: How do people learn at work? What are they learning? How can tacit knowledge be made explicit? His response to the third question is that the process is not as simple as many commentators claim because sometimes "knowers are unaware of their knowledge due to its implicit acquisition; or because they cannot find a representation of it which might enable them to communicate it to others" (Chapter Seven, this volume). Above all, what Eraut and his team have demonstrated is that any theory of a learning society or of a learning organisation must recognise not only the significance of work-based learning and the critical importance of informal learning at work, but also that the attributes and dispositions required for lifelong learning in the workplace can *only* be acquired *in* the workplace. This is theory with highly significant practical implications.

A reformed system of education

Two of the projects argue that further, incremental reform will be required of the present system of education if progress towards a learning society is to be sustained; and this constitutes the penultimate model to be introduced.

First, Pat Davies and John Bynner claim in the second volume that, although credit-based learning has been shown to be effective in widening participation and challenging professional cultures, a *national* credit framework needs to be established to exploit its possibilities to the full. At present, they claim, credit-based learning tends to be marginalised because it contains features of at least the first three models of a learning society – skills growth, personal development and social learning – and so its contribution to improvements on a wide range of fronts has only recently begun to be recognised. There is a further reason for its continuing marginalisation: credit-based learning is a classic case of a bottom-up reform which, as a result, has struggled for years for recognition by national policy makers.

Second, Ken Spours and his colleagues plead in Chapter Two of this volume for a single, more inclusive system for all post-16 learners, adults as well as 16–19 year olds, and for formal and informal learning at work as well as academic learning; this means exploring new possibilities for relating academic and vocational learning. But why should we move to a more unified system? At one level the answer is because "academic learning needs to be more applied and vocational learning needs greater theoretical content to be able to develop both conceptual and technical capability" (Hodgson and Spours, 1997, p 8) in *all* students. At a deeper level, the researchers argue that academic/vocational divisions persist because those following vocational programmes are considered to have a more limited capacity to learn, an assumption that is gaining rather than losing currency. In their own words:

> Unification is not primarily a means to a more efficient system, but a change in purpose, direction and the distribution of resources; in other words it is part of creating a new kind of society based on different assumptions about the potential of human beings. (Chapter Two, this volume)

This argument also serves to move the debate on from an incremental to a more structural model of change which is the theme of the next section.

Structural change

Lifelong learning encourages the exploration of radical ideas and two examples are given here. For Michael Young, a learning society should "embody an education-led economy rather than an economy-led education system" (1998, p 155). For Stewart Ranson, a learning society:

> ... requires more than a quantitative expansion or a mere adaptation of existing systems: rather, it will need a reform of the organising principles of learning: from instrumental and technical rationality to moral and practical principles of the learning society: from learning for economic interest to learning for citizenship. (1998, p 91)

The tenth and last model of the learning society argues that lifelong learning provides the necessary stimulus for *structural change*. Lifelong learning has one supreme advantage which has yet to be realised in practice: it cries out for a synoptic view of education, training and employment to be adopted, and for these three sectors to be treated as *one system* and planned in relation to one another.

Cochinaux and de Woot argue that the various phases within lifelong learning (from pre-school education to adult education) need to become more interdependent, progressively becoming part of one integrated system. They introduce the metaphor of a "lifelong learning chain", where each element influences all the others and "the quality of the chain will be that of the weakest link" (1995, p 53). To mobilise the full potential of the whole, "more and better bridges between the various elements of the system have to be created" (Cochinaux and de Woot, 1995, p 56).

At present, each of the distinctive phases such as pre-school, 5-16, FE, HE, adult and community education, learning at work, and the University of the Third Age is treated as a separate area for policy and acts as a constraint on structural change because each has its own professional staff, pressure groups and priorities and engages in turf wars with its nearest neighbours for resources. Such is the loyalty that each group of professionals has to its own sector that, for example, adult educators, advocating a switch in resource from initial to continuing education, appear not so much as champions of lifelong learning as turf warriors fighting for their particular (admittedly neglected) corner of the market. Such in-fighting is intensified by the environment of competition for institutional advantage and the consequent drive not only to increase student numbers but to attract the more biddable, teachable students. None of these professional groups owes loyalty to the overarching concept of lifelong learning and so a new cadre of professionals who are committed to an holistic interpretation of lifelong learning needs to be brought into being. If lifelong learning is to take off, a new constituency of support needs to be formed to promote the cause of structural reform as lifelong learning is not a particular phase such as HE or FE. And if the present system of education, training and employment is viewed from the perspective of lifelong learning, and the existence of an amalgamated Department for Education and Employment should assist such a stance, then what catches the eye are major discontinuities and unjustifiable inequalities rather than clear progression routes and consistent and compatible policies.

Some examples from *The Learning Society Programme* flesh out this argument. First, although the ESRC considered the research Programme as concerned with the post-compulsory phase, the earliest findings from the projects suggested that it makes little sense to constrict the remit of lifelong learning to this sector. So lifelong learning, as the name implies, was interpreted within the Programme as meaning from the first to the last year of life, from 'womb to tomb' in common parlance.

For instance, the study by Stephen Ball, Meg Maguire and Sheila Macrae of education markets in the post-16 sector in one area of London (see Chapter One), emphasises that such markets cannot be understood without reference to the educational and social experiences of their sample in the previous 13 years:

> A proper understanding of patterns of participation in post-16 education and training must rest upon analysis of the positioning, educational aspirations and learning identities produced by the compulsory sector. Our compulsory system as presently organised is not geared to inclusivity or achieving maximum post-16 participation. Indeed many of the policies currently in play work directly against this goal. A policy for lifelong learning needs to begin at the age of three, not 16. (Ball et al, 1999a, p 33)

Second, Ken Spours et al point out in Chapter Two that the latest government White Paper on lifelong learning, *Learning to Succeed*, reinforces the policy separation between 16-19 year olds and adult learning, by, for instance, insisting on two separate inspectorates for the two phases rather than one combined body. Because of a continuing reluctance to reform A levels in England, "institutional barriers, funding barriers and age barriers persist" (Chapter Two, this volume). Even if all the reforms currently being proposed by government are successfully implemented, the divisive fault lines between those on vocational tracks and those on academic tracks, between those on work-based routes and those in educational institutions, would remain intact. More positively, this project also draws attention to the wide range of strategies being employed within the UK, and across Europe, for breaking down curricular (and other) barriers and boundaries.

One final example is taken from the regional study of participation in education and training conducted in South Wales by Gareth Rees, Ralph Fevre, Stephen Gorard and John Furlong and reported on in the second of these two volumes. Researching the learning careers of individuals throughout the life cycle highlighted for them the importance of *continuities* across the various phases and of interconnected *progression routes* from one phase to the next and on across the life span. Current policies, however, for 5-16 year olds are seriously out of joint with policies for the post-compulsory phase. For instance, the curriculum and pedagogy which are externally regulated by government in primary and secondary schools are more likely to create passive, surface learners rather than the self-regulating, creative and reflective students required by the changed world of work. If one of the aims of initial education is to ensure that all young people become lifelong learners, then the current National Curriculum in schools and the undergraduate curriculum in universities will need to be reformed to include a significant dimension on learning.

Final comments

There is no suggestion in any of the above that the 10 models which have been summarised encapsulate all the possible approaches to a learning society. Both within the Programme and in the relevant literatures, commentators have been generous to a fault with their definitions, visions and policies and a number of examples will be given to indicate the range of options available. Stephen Ball and his colleagues in Chapter One describe an *informal learning society* among those young people post-16, for whom leisure activities and 'living for the weekend' were more significant than education, training and paid employment. Their sub-employment or 'flexibility' was set within the new economies of London, "founded on the exploitation of fashion and music, as commodities in an economy of youth; an economy of appearance and experience, a hedonistic economy" (Ball et al, 1999b, p 2).

Again, a researcher within the Programme, Michael Young, argues that the learning society has become such a contested concept that "the different meanings given to it not only reflect different interests but imply different visions of the future and different policies for getting there" (1998, p 141). He imposes a different order from the one adopted in this introduction on the large variety of conflicting interpretations of the term in his choice of four models: the *schooling* model (high participation in full-time post-compulsory education); the *credentialist* model (qualifying becomes a continuous, lifelong process); the *access* model (individuals have the right to choose where, when and what to study and are given the responsibility for the planning and coherence of their learning. "However, the learner in question is often one who is least equipped for such a responsibility", Young, 1998, p 148); and the *connective* model (divisions between academic and vocational curricula, the nature of qualifications, relations between learning and production and learning itself are all re-conceptualised).

An influential commentator who was not part of the Programme, Richard Edwards, identifies three main strands among the competing discourses surrounding the term 'the learning society', which he labels: an *educated society* (providing "learning opportunities to educate adults to meet the challenges of change and citizenship", 1997, p 184); a *learning market* (the goals of which are economic competitiveness and self-reliance, as discussed above); and *learning networks* (individuals and groups participate in learning to pursue their own goals as members of overlapping networks which can be local, national, regional or global; the challenge here to the notion of an homogeneous, national learning society springs not from the competitive individualism of the market but from the emergence of new forms of sociality, for example technological networks). These brief and inadequate summaries of the ideas of Michael Young and Richard Edwards do not exhaust all the approaches taken to the concept of a learning society, and further typologies can be found in the ideas of, for instance, Ron Barnett (1994) and Peter Jarvis (1999). Moreover, Stewart Ranson and John Stewart add a further dimension when they argue that a learning society can only grow out of a learning democracy; they are highly critical of those advocates of a learning society who confine themselves to writing "... about new forms of learning for individuals rather than about learning for new forms of society" (Ranson and Stewart, 1998, p 253). Sufficient has, however, been quoted for a number of general conclusions to be drawn.

First, it is obvious that any talk of *the* learning society will have to be abandoned; there are simply far too many modern and postmodern readings of the term for any general agreement on one approach or model to be possible. We are all pluralists now. Implementation of new approaches to lifelong learning will, however, be hampered by the lack of consensus on definitions, aims and basic values.

Second, all these different models do not carry equal weight or status. For over 20 years the skills growth model allied to a learning market has constituted the dominant discourse, sweeping all criticism before it. Since the election of a Labour government that dominance has continued, although the language of 'social exclusion' has been imported from Europe, introducing a much needed social dimension to British policy which had become fixated on economic competitiveness.

Third, too many of these models discuss participation and provision without reference to politics, power or sharpening inequalities – as if all learners were alike. Stephen Ball and his colleagues point out that in the central policy texts on lifelong learning (that is, government Green and

White Papers), learners are characterised in an overly simplistic manner as individual, rational and calculating human capitalists:

> ... as an undifferentiated mass with the same kinds of capabilities, motivations and levels of support and encouragement, as if they were all equally ready and able to take the opportunity to upskill. The uneven distribution of relevant 'capitals' (eg social, economic, cultural, human) and differences in acquired learning identities are set aside. (Chapter One, this volume)

Fourth, the practical relevance of these differing visions is that whatever option, or combination of options, is chosen will drive policy from then on. The introduction to the second collection of overview articles on the work of the remaining projects will deal with the most significant implications of the Programme's research findings for policy.

Finally, as was mentioned earlier, the 10 models can also be used to evaluate official policy on lifelong learning and the English White Paper of 1999, *Learning to Succeed*, has been chosen for study. This aims, in the words of a government minister, to break down "arbitrary borders between the further education sector, workplace training and community-based provision" (Blackstone, 2000), by establishing a single national organisation, the Learning and Skills Council, to plan and fund all post-16 provision, apart from higher education. The exclusion of higher education, however, shows that the new Labour government is failing to treat lifelong learning as one coherent system (see Model 10 above), and the gap between academic and vocational learning may be widened as a result.

What model or models of a learning society lie behind the new Bill now before Parliament? The theory of human capital remains the sole explicit justification for change and previous arguments, about replacing past patterns of investment in plant and physical labour with investment in the intellect and creativity of people "in the information and knowledge based economy" (DfEE, 1999, p 12), are repeated as though they were the latest and most secure of research findings (Model 1, ie skills growth).

The principle that runs through all of the Government's social legislation is the determination to rebuild the welfare state around work, by which is meant paid employment: "The new welfare state should help and encourage people of working age to work where they are capable of doing so" (DSS, 1998, p 23). So, although personal development (Model 2) is mentioned in the White Paper, it plays a negligible role compared with the pivotal roles awarded to employability, flexibility and the need to ensure that job seekers "maintain a strong attachment to the labour market" (DfEE, 1999, p 62).

Too sharp a dichotomy, however, between social inclusion for those who obtain paid employment and social welfare for those who do not may act as a powerful source of injustice. That is the conclusion from an in-depth study in Scotland of the lives of 30 adults with learning difficulties by Sheila Riddell, Stephen Baron and Alastair Wilson, whose overview article will appear in the second volume. The marginalisation of such adults presents an ethical and economic challenge to any definition of a learning society in which the dominant ethos is employability, because "the person with learning difficulties could appear as a poor investment, being more expensive to train and potentially less able to adapt to changing work practices" (Riddell et al, 1999, p 7). People with learning difficulties, who form a significant minority of the population (numerically analogous to ethnic minorities), get caught in endless 'circuits of training' without ever reaching the goal of paid employment. Their fate may befall other groups in future because people with learning difficulties may be pioneers "of a nightmare version of the learning society: excluded groups confined to segregated settings undergoing continuous training as a form of warehousing" (Riddell et al, 1999, p 11).

The determination to tackle social exclusion at its roots within the education system and the battery of measures designed for this purpose are powerful evidence of a social learning dimension (Model 3) to government's thinking, particularly the new employment right for employees aged 16-17 to study or train for qualifications, Education Maintenance Allowances for 16-19 year olds from low-income families, and the proposals from the Social Exclusion Unit (1999) for a new support service for those young people not in education, employment or training.

Proposals are also made to mitigate some of the worst features of the learning market (Model 4) in post-16 provision by requiring more collaborative planning by FE colleges and school sixth forms. Interestingly the existence of the market which dominates the daily practice of such institutions is only fleetingly acknowledged, and coordination will be difficult to achieve if separate funding mechanisms stay in force.

The local Learning and Skills Councils and the local Learning Partnerships are charged with the responsibility of creating local learning societies (Model 5). If, however, we are to learn from the failure of the Training and Enterprise Councils (TECs), two changes need to take place. First, these new bodies will need sufficient funds and discretion to respond sensitively to local conditions and to help build the new system from the bottom up. Second, they will need to be more democratically representative and accountable than the TECs ever were. And yet the government proposes that "a Learning and Skills Council at national and local level will give employers unprecedented influence over the education system and promote a better match between demand and supply for skills" (DfEE, 1999, p 10). So much for placing "the learner at the heart of the new system", as is claimed in the Secretary of State's Foreword (DfEE, 1999, p 3).

The White Paper eschews any mention of lifelong learning as a form of social control (Model 6), but on the other hand the Council will publish annually a 'skills assessment' at both national and local levels (Model 7). There is no definition and no discussion of learning in the White Paper (Model 8), the future of unification of academic and vocational learning remains uncertain because of the reluctance to reform A levels (Model 9), but structural change (Model 10) is thought necessary. Unfortunately, this is largely restricted to an elimination of "duplication, confusion and bureaucracy in the current system" (DfEE, 1999, p 21). In sum, the strong instrumental and utilitarian streak in policies inherited from the Tories remains in pride of place, but at least that bleak inheritance is tempered by a genuine commitment to combat social exclusion. On the other hand, the potential of lifelong learning as a lever on structural change has yet to be recognised, the black box called learning remains unopened and business will continue to be politely *exhorted* to invest more in training its workers, while education will be *forced* via legislation and regulation to 'modernise'.

The concentration on government policy in the above has been deliberate because the distinctive role of the state in relation to lifelong learning is to develop a vision and a policy framework capable of turning that vision into reality. Unlike its predecessor, the current administration has published a broad and inspiring vision, accompanied by a barrage of initiatives, in the hope that some of them at least will hit their targets. But this scatter-gun approach prompts a number of questions because the sheer number of initiatives raises the chances of policies acting in mutually inconsistent and even contradictory ways. For example, on the one hand, the White Paper seeks to expand the learning market where providers are more responsive to the needs of learners and, on the other, the Learning and Skills Council will impose more planning and regulation on that market. Furthermore, if arguably the central problem is consistently low *demand* for lifelong learning by certain groups, then even the most sophisticated *supply*-side measures such as the University for Industry and Individual Learning Accounts may fail to alter participation rates.

A further conclusion is that, although the role of government is pivotal, it promises more than it can deliver. Policy texts have, for instance, invested lifelong learning with omnipotent qualities. As David Robertson has commented, the government has set itself these demanding benchmarks: "[lifelong learning] will improve educational standards, national competitiveness, wealth creation, personal well-being, social cohesion, citizenship and the quality of life" (1998, p 27). Such an ambitious concept of lifelong learning will require commitment and action from all the social partners, from active citizens, enlightened employers and energetic voluntary groups across civil society. In this view, lifelong learning is a collective, cultural and interactive process which:

> ... does not simply require new government measures, but rather a new approach to government. This requires the development of a broad range of new capabilities not only on the part of the wider population 'out there', but also of policy-makers and providers. It also requires a new concept of government that is rooted in a recognition of inter-dependence and inter-relationships between state (and its different arms), market and civil society. (Field, 2000)

When *The Learning Society Programme* was established, four main objectives were selected:
* to treat the concept of a learning society as an issue for critical exploration;
* to develop the theoretical understanding of the processes of learning, the concept of human capital formation and relationships between employment, training and education;
* to maintain a policy focus; and
* to learn from comparative study of the different education and training systems within the British Isles and beyond.

All of these objectives have been touched on briefly in this introduction, but they receive comprehensive treatment in the seven chapters which follow. The reader is, however, requested to wait before deciding to what extent these objectives have been met until the publication of the second volume of overview articles (Coffield, 2000: forthcoming), which will also contain some important lessons learned from the comparative studies, the most significant implications for policy of the programme's findings and some general conclusions[10].

Notes

[1] This project was co-funded by the ESRC and the Higher Education Quality Council in the first year; and by the ESRC, the Higher Education Funding Council and the Department for Education and Employment in the second. The research team consisted of Professor Harold Silver, Dr Andrew Hannan and Ms Sue English of the University of Plymouth and they describe their project in the second volume. The Director of the Programme would also like to thank the Department of Education, Northern Ireland for generously co-funding the Programme as a whole.

[2] The first publication in the series, entitled *Learning at work*, contains articles by Michael Eraut et al (on learning from other people at work; Davis Ashton (on learning in organisations); Peter Scott and Antje Cockrill (on training in the construction industry in Wales and Germany); Reiner Seibert (on Jobrotation), Kari Hadjivassiliou et al (on Continuous Vocational Training); and Stephen Baron et al (on what the learning society means for adults with learning difficulties).

[3] The second report, entitled *Why's the Beer always stronger up North? Studies of lifelong learning in Europe*, contains some cross-national observations on lifelong learning by Walter Heinz (Bremen); an article on adult guidance services in Europe by Teresa Rees and Will Bartlett; a chapter on different models of Continuous Vocational Training in the UK, France and Spain by Isabelle Darmon and colleagues; a comparison of credit-based systems of learning in London and Northern France by Pat Davies; a study of the links between initial and continuing education in Scotland, Northern Ireland and England by Tom Schuller and Andrew Burns; a comparison of policy strategies to reduce the divisions between academic and vocational learning in England and Scotland by David Raffe and colleagues; and, finally, reflections on devising and conducting cross-national studies in the social sciences by Antje Cockrill and colleagues.

[4] The third report, entitled *Speaking truth to power: Research and policy on lifelong learning*, contains two overview articles on the impact of research on policy (by Frank Coffield and Maurice Kogan); a chapter on the impact of the manager on learning in the workplace (by Michael Eraut, Jane Alderton, Gerald Cole and Peter Senker); a study of a post-compulsory education and training market in one urban locale in London (by Stephen Ball, Sheila Macrae and Meg Maguire);

an examination of the policy implications of changes in training of NHS staff (by Therese Dowswell, Bobbie Millar and Jenny Hewison); the first findings from a major new survey of the skills of a representative sample of British workers (by Alan Felstead, David Ashton, Brendan Burchell and Francis Green); and, finally, a paper on the provision of adult guidance services in England (by Will Bartlett and Teresa Rees).

[5] The fourth and final report argues for a fundamental reassessment of the significance of informal learning. Under the title of *The necessity of informal learning*, it consists of five articles as follows: a seminal, theoretical piece by Michael Eraut on non-formal learning, implicit learning and tacit knowledge in professional work; an essay on informal learning and social capital by John Field and Lynda Spence, drawing on their empirical research in Northern Ireland; a study of implicit knowledge in the training of people with learning difficulties by Stephen Baron, Alastair Wilson and Sheila Riddell; a report on the impact of accreditation on formalising learning by Pat Davies; and an historical and sociological analysis of necessary and unnecessary learning in the acquisition of knowledge and skills in and outside employment in South Wales in the 20th century by Ralph Fevre, Stephen Gorard and Gareth Rees.

[6] See the collection of eight articles which explored the concept of a learning society in the special edition of the *Journal of Education Policy*, vol 12, no 5, November–December, 1997.

[7] These brief summaries from *The Learning Society Programme* are available in two forms. A set of summaries in hard copy is available, free of charge while stocks last, from Frank Coffield, Department of Education, University of Newcastle, St Thomas' Street, Newcastle upon Tyne, NE1 7RU. The same summaries are also available from the programme's website, whose address is http://www.ncl.ac.uk/learning.society/. The website provides more detailed information on publications by individual projects as well as by the programme as a whole.

[8] Readers may wish to consult a more extended version of these two opposing viewpoints. In April, 1999, the Campaign for Learning organised a debate at the Royal Society of Arts in London between Sir Christopher Ball and Frank Coffield on the topic 'Visions of a Learning Society: individual responsibility versus social structure'. The text of the debate is available in the *RSA Journal*, vol 4, no 4, 1999, pp 83-90.

[9] The first, directed by Phil Cooke, is described in Chapter Six of this book and the other, directed by Gareth Rees, in the second volume.

[10] For their constructive comments on an earlier draft of this introduction I would like to thank Stephen Ball, John Bynner, Bruce Carrington, Pat Davies, Kathryn Ecclestone, Tony Edwards, John Field, David Raffe and Geoff Whitty.

References

Ball, S., Macrae, S. and Maguire, M. (1999a) 'Young lives at risk in the "Futures" market: some policy concerns from ongoing research', in F. Coffield (ed) *Speaking truth to power: Research and policy on lifelong learning*, Bristol: The Policy Press, pp 30–45.

Ball, S.J., Maguire, M. and Macrae, S. (1999b) 'Whose learning society? The post-16 education and training market in one urban locale', ESRC conference paper, 6 July.

Barnett, R. (1994) *The limits of competence: Knowledge, higher education and society*, Buckingham: Open University Press.

Beinart, S. and Smith, P. (1998) *National adult learning survey, 1997*, London: DfEE.

Bernstein, B. (1996) *Pedagogy, symbolic control and identity*, London: Taylor and Francis.

Blackstone, T. (2000) Letter in *Guardian Higher*, 1 February.

Blunkett, D. (2000) 'Influence or irrelevance: can social science improve government?', Secretary of State's ESRC Lecture, 2 February, London: DfEE.

Brown, A. and Keep, E. (2000: forthcoming) *Review of vocational education and training research in the UK*, Luxembourg: European Commission.

Bynner, J. and Parsons, S. (1997) *It doesn't get any better: The impact of poor basic skills on the lives of 37 year olds*, London: Basic Skills Agency.

CEC (Commission of the European Communities) (1997) *Towards a Europe of knowledge*, Luxembourg: CEC.

Claxton, G. (1999) *Wise up: The challenge of lifelong learning*, London: Bloomsbury.

Cochinaux, P. and de Woot, P. (1995) *Moving towards a learning society*, Brussels: ERT/CRE.

Coffield, F. (1994) *Research specification for the Learning Society Programme*, Swindon: ESRC.

Coffield, F. (1998) 'A fresh approach to learning for the learning age: the contribution of research', *Higher Education Digest*, no 31, pp 4-6.

Coffield, F. (1999), 'Breaking the consensus: lifelong learning as social control', *British Educational Research Journal*, vol 25, no 4, pp 479-99.

Coffield, F. (2000) 'Lifelong learning as a lever on structural change? Evaluation of the White Paper: *Learning to Succeed: A new framework for post-16 learning*', *Journal of Education Policy*, vol 15, no 2, pp 237-46.

Coffield, F. (2000: forthcoming) *Differing versions of a Learning Society: Research Findings*, vol II, Bristol: The Policy Press.

Delors, J. (1996) *Learning: The treasure within*, Paris: UNESCO.

DfEE (Department for Education and Employment) (1998) *The learning age: A renaissance for a new Britain*, Cm 3790, London: The Stationery Office.

DfEE (1999) *Learning to Succeed: A new framework for post-16 learning*, London: The Stationery Office.

DSS (Department of Social Security) (1998) *A new contract for welfare: New ambitions for our country*, Cm 3805, London: The Stationery Office.

Ecclestone, K. (1999) 'Care or control? Defining learners' needs for lifelong learning', *British Journal of Educational Studies*, vol 47, no 4, pp 332-47.

Edwards, R. (1997) *Changing places? Flexibility, lifelong learning and a learning society*, London: Routledge.

Eraut, M. (1997) 'Perspectives on defining "The Learning Society"', *Journal of Education Policy*, vol 12, no 6, November-December, pp 551-8.

European Round Table of Industrialists (1995) *Education for Europlans: Towards the learning society*, Brussels, ERT.

Fevre, R. (1997) *Some sociological alternatives to human capital theory and their implications for research on post-compulsory education and training*, Working Paper 3, Cardiff: School of Education, University of Cardiff.

Field, J. (1999) 'Participation under the magnifying glass', *Adults Learning*, November, pp 10-13.

Field, J. (2000) 'Governing the ungovernable: explaining why lifelong learning policies promise so much and deliver so little', *Educational Management and Administration*, vol 28, no 3.

Field, J. and Schuller, T. (1999) *End of award report*, Swindon: ESRC.

Forrester, V. (1999) *The economic horror*, Cambridge: Polity Press.

Fryer, R.H. (1999) *Creating learning cultures: Next steps in achieving the learning age*, Second Report of the National Advisory Group for Continuing Education and Lifelong Learning, Sheffield: Moorfoot, DfEE.

Fuller, A. and Unwin, L. (1999) 'Credentialism, national targets and the learning society: perspectives on educational attainment in the UK steel industry', *Journal of Education Policy*, vol 14, no 6, pp 605-17.

Green, A., Wolf, A. and Leney, T. (1999) *Convergence and divergence in European education and training systems*, London: Institute of Education.

Hodgson, A. and Spours, K. (1997) *Dearing and beyond: 14-19 qualifications, frameworks and systems*, London: Kogan Page.

Holford, J., Griffin, C. and Jarvis, P. (eds) *International perspectives on lifelong learning*, London: Kogan Page.

Ignatieff, M. (1998) *Isaiah Berlin: A life*, London: Chatto and Windus.

Jarvis, P. (1999) 'Paradoxes of the learning society' in J. Holford, C. Griffin and P. Jarvis (eds), *Lifelong learning: Reality, rhetoric and public policy*,

Jones, S. (1996) *Developing a learning culture*, London: McGraw-Hill.

Ministry of Education, Finland (1997) *The joy of learning: A national strategy for lifelong learning*, Helsinki: Ministry of Education.

Moser, C. (1999) *A fresh start: Improving literacy and numeracy*, London: DfEE.

National Committee of Enquiry into Higher Education (1997) *Higher education in the learning society*, London: HMSO (The Dearing Report).

OECD (1996) *Lifelong learning for all*, Paris: OECD.

Payne, J. (2000) 'Making an investment', *Adults Learning*, vol 11, no 5, January, pp 19-22.

Raggatt, P., Edwards, R. and Small, N. (1996) *The learning society: Challenges and trends*, London: Routledge for Open University.

Ranson, S. (1998) 'Towards the learning society', in S. Ranson (ed) *Inside the learning society*, London: Cassell, p 91–108

Ranson, S. (1998) (ed) *Inside the learning society*, London: Cassell.

Ranson, S. and Stewart, J. (1998) 'The learning democracy', in S. Ranson (ed) *Inside the learning society*, London: Cassell, pp 253-70.

Rees, G., Fevre, R. and Furlong, J. (1999) *Participation in post-compulsory education and training: A regional study*, Swindon: ESRC End of Award Report.

Riddell, S., Baron, S. and Wilson, A. (1999) *End of award report*, Swindon: ESRC.

Robertson, D. (1998) 'The piggy-bank goes to market', *Parliamentary Brief*, vol 5, no 5, May, pp 27-9.

Robinson, P. (1999) 'The drivers for change in post–16 learning', London: IPPR/FEDA Seminar, 14 December.

Schuller, T. and Bamford, C. (2000) 'A social capital approach to the analysis of continuing education: evidence from the UK Learning Society research programme', *Oxford Review of Education*, vol 26, no 1, pp 5-19.

Sennett, R. (1998) *The corrosion of character: The personal consequences of work in the new capitalism*, New York, NY: W.W. Norton.

Social Exclusion Unit (1999) *Bridging the gap: New opportunities for 16-18 year olds not in education, employment or training*, Cm 4405, London, The Stationery Office.

Stahl, T., Nyham, B. and D'Aloja, P. (1993) *The learning organisation: A vision for human resource development*, Luxembourg: Commission of the European Communities.

Stern, E., Hadjivassiliou, K. and Darmon, I. (1999) *Innovations in continuing vocational training: A comparative perspective*, Swindon: ESRC End of Award Report.

Towers, J. (1996) 'European Foreword', in N. Longworth and W.K. Davies, *Lifelong learning*, London: Kogan Page.

Young, M.F.D. (1998) *The curriculum of the future,* London: Falmer Press.

ONE

'Worlds apart' – Education markets in the post-16 sector of one urban locale 1995-98

Stephen J. Ball, Meg Maguire and Sheila Macrae

Background

The background to our study is complex and multifaceted. Three contexts of change which frame the setting examined need to be noted here. They are highly interrelated:
• economic and labour market changes;
• policy responses;
• the reform of post-compulsory education and training.

The most general aspect of all this relates to the rapid change in the UK's internal labour market and competitive position within the world economy during the 1970s and 1980s. That is, the massive decline in manufacturing capacity and traditional working-class employment opportunities and the more recent expansion of a very different kind of leisure and service industry employment. In particular the transformation of post-compulsory education and training over the past 20 years is tightly tied to increases in youth unemployment on the one hand, and to the rhetorics and politics of the 'skills revolution' on the other. In 1960 the rate of unemployment among the under-25s was 2.4%; by 1981 it had reached 21.4%; in 1993 it stood at 17.5% (Coles, 1995). But these latter figures exclude those on training or employment schemes. In our research locale, jobs for 16-year-old school leavers are currently few and far between and mostly low-paid retail or service positions (see Skilbeck et al, 1994). "If you haven't got an education, it isn't very good because there aren't many jobs around. So you need to stay in education" (James, Year 11 student). By the time they were 17, 11% of our research cohort were unemployed (the employment status of another three, 5%, was unknown to us), compared with 21.3% nationally (in 1995) and 14% were in employment (no national figures); 51% were in full-time education, compared with 59.3% nationally.

This local lack of labour market opportunities at the age of 16 is crucially important in understanding the 'choices' of young people in our research locale. For some the limited employment prospects at 16 is a definite spur to 'get qualifications' (as James indicates). For others, as we shall see, a used-up or impoverished learning identity drives them to seek work and approximately half of this group were unemployed at any time. Decision making at 16 is, in part at least, a response to a social context of uncertainties. Many working-class young people in particular find themselves in a *liminal state*; "one without a defined status or future in the world of work" (Bettis, 1996, p 106). And this reflects, and is produced by, the liminal state of the urban economy – a postmodern urban complexity: "the fragmentation, loss of community, and deindustrialisation of cities, along with the postindustrial plethora of images, focus on consumption, and changes in types of employment" (Bettis, 1996, p 107). However, as Skilbeck et al (1994) indicate, there is no simple relationship between regional employment opportunities and staying-on in education. The political and educational emphases on credentialising have a powerful impact on the thinking of many of our young people.

While it is important to note the lack of employment opportunities for 16-year-olds in our research locale in South West London, it also has to be recognised that the city as a whole offers other possibilities. Apart from the various part-time and temporary jobs in the huge and growing service and leisure economy, there are opportunities for young people to experience and experiment with other identities and life-styles. There are also peripheral or informal economies operating: for example, D J-ing[1], which attracted several young men in our study (three derived some income from this work) and childcare, which involved several of our young women. For some, the vivid complexities of city life made it possible to think about combining work with life-style and personal identity in a single project. Again, however, there are systematic differences within the group in relation to such opportunities, particularly in relation to differences in 'spatial horizons' of action. Those locals who, for various reasons, were limited to the immediate locality in their search for employment, were much more likely to remain unemployed.

Brown and Lauder (1996) suggest two ideal types of political response to the problems of unemployment, labour market skills needs and international competitiveness: first, neo-Fordism, which, "can be characterised in terms of creating greater market flexibility through a reduction in social overheads and the power of trade unions, the privatisation of public utilities and the welfare state, as well as the celebration of competitive individualism" (p 5); and second, post-Fordism, which can, "be defined in terms of the development of the state as a 'strategic trader' shaping the direction of the national economy through investment in key economic sectors and in the development of human capital" (p 5). In practice in the UK, the policy responses in the field of post-compulsory education and training have combined aspects of both these with the Conservatives giving primary emphasis to the former and Labour slightly more weight to the latter. In the policy rhetorics which interpolate these responses the fate and responsibility of individuals are intricately interwoven with national well-being: "Learning is the key to prosperity – for each of us as individuals, as well as for the nation as a whole" (Forward to *The Learning Age*, DfEE, 1998).

This policy dualism is well represented in contemporary education policies which tie together individual consumer choice in education markets with rhetorics and policies aimed at furthering national economic interests. Carter and O'Neill (1995) summarise evidence on the state of education policy making in their two-volume collection on international perspectives on educational reform by identifying what they call the 'new orthodoxy' – "a shift is taking place", they say, "in the relationship between politics, government and education in complex Westernised post-industrialised countries at least" (p 9). They cite five main elements to this new orthodoxy:

• improving national economics by tightening the connection between schooling, employment, productivity and trade;
• enhancing student outcomes in employment-related skills and competencies;
• attaining more direct control over curriculum content and assessment;
• reducing the costs to government of education;
• increasing community input to education by more direct involvement in school decision making and pressure of market choice.

These features of the 'new orthodoxy' have a specific relevance to UK post-compulsory education and training. Indeed, Avis et al (1996) use similar terminology, the 'new consensus', to refer to the sublimation of 'learning policy' within economic policy via concepts like the 'learning society'. The 'learning society' is a potent condensate for a range of policies which bring together market individualism, where individuals take an "increasing responsibility for their own adaptability and reskilling throughout their working lives" (DfEE, 1995, p 76), with a target and standards driven agenda of 'national interest'. A rhetoric of individualised lifelong learning is in circulation which, it is alleged, will shore up the skills shortage and "gain the country a competitive edge in fast changing global markets" (Ainley, 1994, p 21). The consequence for many 16-year-olds is a mix of 'carrot and stick' tactics directed towards 'encouraging' them to participate in post-compulsory education and training through the withdrawal of benefits in a context of continuing high levels of youth unemployment (Maguire, 1995). Also Labour government policy texts give a particular stress to the individual's responsibility to 'learn' (see Macrae et al, 1998).

The post-compulsory sector, even more clearly perhaps than the school sector, is now thoroughly embedded within the dynamics of a quasi-market and infused with the values of commerce and business. Nonetheless, "The FE [Further Education] market is highly contrived and constrained, as are most other markets" (Foskett and Hesketh, 1996, p 2). The 1992 Further and Higher Education Act delivered to the government, via the funding arrangements of the Further Education Funding Council (FEFC), indirect but decisive control of the growth and cost of the FE sector, through the mechanism of 'convergence' of funding. The FEFC regime required of incorporated institutions that they expand their student numbers by 28% (from 1992/93 to 1996/97) while reducing the level of per capita funding to achieve an annual 'efficiency gain'. In effect institutions must run faster in order to stand still. "An active expansionist market has been created" (Foskett and Hesketh, 1996, p 2); but there is an over provision of supply in many localities. By 1995 most incorporated institutions had failed to reach the expansion targets. Some estimates (see, for example, FEFC, 1998) suggest that, unless the funding regime is altered, up to 200 Colleges might close or merge. The 1997 Association for Colleges Conference heard that 40% of colleges were in financial deficit and 20% were in serious financial difficulty.

As is the case with other public sector markets, the post-compulsory education and training market is diverse, localised and, therefore, differentially intense. It is also highly segmented. Nationally there are many very different 'lived' markets. Nonetheless, Foskett and Hesketh

(1996, pp 48-9) identify two broad types of market place: contiguous *or overlapping*, and parallel *or distinct* markets. We are concerned here with an example of the former.

These, then, were the major considerations which provided the background to the study.

Our project has explored the above issues in 'close up' as they were being played out in a single urban setting. We have tried to recognise and retain the distinctiveness of place (Brice-Heath and McLaughlin, 1993; Gewirtz et al, 1995) in our work, as well as attending to the ways in which cities provide concentrated expressions of social and material forces (Pahl, 1970). Pearce and Hillman (1998) make the point that: "... local studies present a richer and potentially more valuable picture of non-participation in education, training and work than can be supplied by national data sources" (p 34). The complex and contradictory nature of the 'city economy' indicated above is one example of the importance of 'the local' in making sense of 'the learning society'.

Our local market extends over an inner-city/suburban setting based around the Northwark area of London (see Gewirtz et al, 1995) and is defined in terms of the expressed interests and choices of a cohort of Year 11 students from one comprehensive school – Northwark Park[2] – and one Pupil Referral Unit (PRU) (see below). This local, lived market encompasses several different, small local education authorities (LEAs) that organise their schools' provision in different ways. The main players in this market are two 11-18 secondary schools, five FE colleges, a tertiary college, a denominational sixth form college and two Training and Enterprise Councils (TECs). Three other FE colleges, another sixth form college, and an 11-18 denominational school impinge upon the margins of this market (see Appendix to this chapter). We have engaged with the main groups of actors in this market – providers, that is, those offering education, training or employment; intermediaries, those offering advice or support, including teachers, careers officers and parents; and consumers or choosers, the young people themselves and their families.

Aims

The central aim was to investigate the ways in which one local, post-compulsory education and training market operates. In particular, we set out to explore:

• the dynamics of post-16 education and training markets in the urban context;

- choice making (by parents and young people) within post–16 provision and the role played by educational intermediaries in this process;
- the role played by differences in material, cultural and social capital in the processes and possibilities of choice, particularly as these relate to 'race', class, and gender;
- the nature of what we refer to as the informal learning society: that is, the experiences and prospects of those young people post–16, who fall outside education, training and paid employment;
- the market behaviour of the main providers in the post–16 education and training phase.

Our interviews with young people, their parents, local providers of education and training and those providing support through the post–16 transition, have provided the basis for a rich and theoretically informed analysis of choice making. As in other studies, the detailed coding of a large number and wide variety of interviews has highlighted the dynamic role of class, 'race' and gender as elements which impact on choice making and choice getting (Cross and Wrench, 1991; Furlong, 1992; Roberts, 1993). Additionally, what became increasingly evident in the course of the study is the sometimes less acknowledged influence of life–style patterns, culture and social relationships in young people's interest in, and willingness to engage in, further education or training and the impact of specific local factors on patterns of choice and types of transition[3].

More specifically, we have addressed our objectives as follows:

(i) and (v) The dynamics of post–16 education and training markets in the urban context and the market behaviour of the main providers

Based on data obtained from a total of 110 students from Northwark Park (an inner-city, co-educational comprehensive school) and students from the local PRU, we mapped-out the full range of local providers. We interviewed various key personnel in these institutions. We attended careers fairs and open days/evenings organised by the local TEC, schools and colleges. We collected and analysed available documents (brochures and prospectuses). All this powerfully illustrated the insertion of market behaviours and tactics in one urban setting (Ball et al, 1997; Macrae et al, 1997a).

(ii) Choice making (parents and young people) within post-16 provision and the role played by educational intermediaries in this process

A questionnaire was administered to 110 young people (see below). We subsequently conducted in-depth interviews with 59 of these young people, most of them on three occasions: a total of 144 interviews (in the first phase of the study). These interviews were conducted in a wide range of settings, at the convenience of the young people involved, for example, at school, in their homes, cafes, at King's College, bus stops and so on. We interviewed a small sample of parents (10) and educational intermediaries (16). We examined key publications and software supporting choice at this stage (eg Choices at 16, Occupations, Kudos).

(iii) The role played by differences in material, cultural and social capital in the processes and possibilities of choice as these relate to 'race', class, and gender and (iv) in particular the situation of those in the informal learning society

Our sample (see below) was constructed in order to open up to investigation issues of difference, reflecting the ethnic and socioeconomic diversity of the locality. The urban setting provided particular opportunities to address this objective (Macrae et al, 1996a; Macrae, 1997; Ball, 1998b). These issues have been explored in our repeat interviews with the young people and, in some cases, with their parents.

We would want to signal some difficulties tackled in order to meet our objectives. In particular, we would highlight the issue of maintaining contact. As the young people moved from school/PRU, it was apparent that maintaining contact with some was going to require a great deal of effort. Several became homeless or moved house; others were placed in temporary accommodation after the births of their babies; others moved into care or moved between foster homes. Their interests were not with the project. Thus we developed a range of tactics and strategies: telephone contact, postcards, letters, 'door-stepping' and talking to neighbours and friends, persistent and repeated appointment setting in order to maintain a successful research relationship and meet our objectives. In the second phase of the study we have been able to employ an 'outreach' research assistant to help us 'find' some of our 'lost' young people.

Methods

Methods and sample

By starting with an inner-city comprehensive school with a wide and diverse intake (the school had participated in an earlier ESRC-funded study; see Gewirtz et al, 1995), we sought to capitalise on prior knowledge of the setting and of some participants to map out our research concerns. We included students from the local PRU to increase sample diversity. These had been excluded from or had otherwise opted out of mainstream education but were still part (rhetorically at least) of the 'learning society'. A great deal of recent policy and research has focused exclusively on the 70-80% of post-16-year-olds who are active participants in education, training and employment. Our student samples were constructed as follows. Initially, a full cohort of 81 students from Northwark Park School and 29 students from the local PRU completed a questionnaire which elicited data about their backgrounds, status and proposed post-16 destinations. From this we constructed a sub-sample which included representations of difference, for example, destination, course, 'race', class and gender.

Several significant issues arise from the constitution of the sample. First, issues of class are not always straightforward. For example, while our refugee students[4] should be regarded positionally as working-class, their backgrounds are mainly professional middle-class and their cultural capital often reflects this. For other young people their class location is difficult to determine; material support and advantage may be present but, as one explained: "my mum says I'm economically middle-class but that I have lots of working-class values". There was a lack of representation of middle-class males in the school and the PRU which is reflected in the sample. In an attempt to redress this, we did, with the help of a key informant, add two middle-class, Northwark Park males to the cohort.

In the case of 'race', the sample contains many of the 'races'/ethnicities present in the school/PRU and again the categorisation of young people in these terms was sometimes difficult. (We asked them to identify themselves for purposes of categorisation.) For example, two are British-Chinese but their families originate from different geographical regions; there are both African-Caribbean and Indo-Caribbean young people represented. There were also dilemmas around questions of dual heritage and identity (Solomos and Back, 1994). In some cases the young people's own sense of ethnicity changed during the course of the study.

Nonetheless, it is this social and cultural variety that typifies the urban locale and allows us to make claims which are more nuanced and reflexive, moving beyond limiting essentialisms; although, on the other hand, the variety and diversity of the sample is a constraint upon, and a constant reminder of, the dangers of generalising about 'youth'.

Our methods have been primarily qualitative and ethnographic in style, relying mainly on loosely-structured ethnographic interviews, supplemented by observation and documentary analysis. The interviews were used to elicit detailed narratives from the young people, dealing with key events in their education or employment, and their social relationships, aspirations and family lives.

Data and analysis

Our analysis employed Straussian (Strauss, 1987) coding techniques. At different times we engaged in open, selective and axial coding, both individually and in joint coding sessions. We did a number of frequency counts and used some diagramming techniques suggested by Strauss. In analysing interviews with young people we were able to compare change over time across three interviews. We also constructed a number of individual profiles. In some cases we were able to set interviews with young people against interviews with their parents. In the case of providers we were able to set interviews with 'recruiters' against those with our 'choosers'. We also initiated a semiological analysis of providers' brochures (Maguire et al, 1999) in conjunction with our French collaborators. Comparative work on market ethics in France and England was also undertaken (Ball and Van Zanten, 1998).

Research issues

We indicated above the challenge of maintaining contact with some of the cohort. Research which attempts to follow a diverse cohort of young people beyond any formal setting clearly runs the risk of sustaining some sample attenuation. We had anticipated this dilemma and had over-recruited to accommodate this situation. However, with only four of our initial sample we have been unable to maintain ongoing contact.

It proved helpful to use a range of interviewers for some of the work. We were able to draw on the support of two final year undergraduates, both of minority ethnic heritage, to help with interviews and data analysis.

This was also valuable in relation to issues of language, construction of research instruments and data coding.

Early on it became apparent that some of our male students (generally the 'underachievers') were apprehensive, sometimes monosyllabic in interview settings and generally less forthcoming than their female peers. This difference was less evident in the later interviews.

It may have achieved the status of a truism but it is probably worth restating here that we do not simply see these interviews as voicing or expressing a singular essential identity. Rather we take it that the self is discursively and interactively constituted. These narratives are self-constructions which are not merely representational, but also conventionally and unconventionally performative. We might see the interviews working – for some young people – as 'technologies of the self', offering the possibility "of no longer being, doing or thinking what we are, do or think" (Rabinow, 1987, p 46). Furthermore, we remain aware that, to paraphrase Foucault, these interviews may be "a space into which the speaking subject constantly disappears" (Foucault, 1986, p 102). Even in the simplest sense these young people live 'other' lives, at other times, which are only partly accounted for in these texts (see Macrae and Maguire, 1999). We have access to only part of who they are, might be, or might become. Zinneker (1990, p 25) suggests that: "the threefold structural background for extended youth comprises education, leisure and flexible underemployment. In the future, young people will be constructing their social identities and establishing a stable way of life in the midst of simultaneous participation in all three fields" (p 25). Du Bois-Reymond (1998) makes a similar point, stressing the way in which the sequence of the status passage to adulthood is changing and how: "in this way, youth biography acquires new qualities of experience and allows subjects to feel contingency and openness" (p 66).

Findings

We report our findings under five major headings corresponding to our main objectives. And, while there is no space here for any systematic presentation of research data, we have included the faint whispers of some voices from our field in the text.

The dynamics of post-16 education and training markets in the urban context

It quickly became apparent that the local education and training market which spreads out from our school and PRU is quite tightly demarcated. Most students choose to stay within the local area; a few travel farther afield to follow special interest courses or move out because their families relocate or are seeking a fresh start away from 'bad influences'. While some 'high fliers' are part of what we describe as the 'westward drift', choosing to go to sixth form or tertiary colleges in the Western, leafy, 'whiter' suburbs of the city, the power of the 'local' in the young people's spatial representations and material spatial practices, is very evident. The use and conceptualisation of space in our study also appears to be related to class. Middle-class young people, certainly as far as choice is concerned, tended to be more knowledgeable, confident and prepared to consider institutions farther afield than their working-class peers. But space is also structured through the networks of interest communities – "localities can give a sense of identity to parts of the landscape. They can help people to build a feeling of belonging and security – people know where they are [and], who they are" (Smith, 1994, p 11). Our study enabled us to explore the role and power of spatial factors in local lived markets (Glatter et al, 1996). Earlier work (eg Garner et al, 1988) on the impact of spatial inequality in inner cities has tended to describe the lack of employment opportunities in the city as a whole. While it is possible to talk in generalised ways about the city and employment patterns, there is a need to focus on the specificity of place and the role of locality *within* the city.

From our interviews with many local providers and intermediaries (those providing formal support and advice), it is clear that they consider only a small number of local institutions as 'real' competition. This is despite the fact that good transport routes could potentially open up the whole city as part of the post-16 education and training market. Within the locality there is clear evidence of niche-marketing for different social groups in the area (colleges which target special needs or black students). For example, Mainwaring College offers a range of courses in music production aimed particularly at the African-Caribbean students in its locality; Bracebridge gives particular attention to special needs provision.

Choice making (by parents and young people) within post-16 provision and the role played by educational intermediaries in this process

This second objective has in many ways been at the heart of the investigation. Here we report our results under three sub-headings: choice, parents and educational intermediaries.

Choice

Briefly, in the post-16 education and training market, students can choose to stay on at school (if the school is 11-18), transfer to a sixth form, tertiary or FE college, undertake various forms of vocational training or look for employment or, indeed, retreat into the home and pursue a 'domestic career'. However, not all these options are available to all young people. Their choice as such is constrained in two ways. Some routes will be less/more available in relation to their academic profile at GCSE level. At the same time, although providers will aim to recruit above their target numbers (to increase the likelihood of achieving their quota), popular and successful institutions will actually be in the position of doing the choosing. As in other education markets, some students are highly valued and strongly competed for by providers, others are less desirable and find their choices constrained. There is an 'economy of student worth'. This is not simply a recent phenomenon but may be becoming more stark: "The orientations of schools, colleges and employers are still fundamentally selective rather than facilitative" (Banks et al, 1992, p 188). Or, as Ainley puts it, the A level route continues to dominate and drive the post-16 system with its "schooling for higher education" (1994, p 6). Thus the rhetoric of choice sits uneasily alongside the practice of choice making, and more importantly choice getting in the post-16 education and training market for reasons which are explored below. Our research underlines the point made by Bates and Riseborough (1993) in a previous ESRC programme that "the social organisation of each route is premised upon class-gendered student or trainee types and related assumptions concerning other material and cultural resources" (p 11). "The market provides a mechanism for the reinvention and legitimation of hierarchy and differentiation via the ideology of diversity, competition and choice" (Ball, 1993, p 8).

One way of making sense of decision making at this point, from the perspective of the young people, is in relation to the role of 'imagined futures'. For some their imagined futures are relatively clear, relatively stable and relatively possible. For a second group their imagined future is vague, relatively unstable and beset with uncertainties. A third group has at this stage no imagined future which can provide a focus or locus for decision making. They may display a sense of aimlessness, or see their life in terms of 'getting by' and coping on a day-to-day basis, or they are overtaken or dominated by events beyond their control, for example illness, pregnancy, family breakdown, personal crises. In each case an ideal-type 'learner identity' (Rees et al, 1997, p 11) and attendant "view of the process of learning" may be discerned. (The work of Rees et al forms another project within *The Learning Society Programme* and an overview of their research will appear in volume II – see Coffield, 2000: forthcoming.)

The first group is made up mostly of young people who 'see themselves' taking and completing A levels, going to university and embarking on a career. The trajectory at each stage seems to reflect and fulfil their interests. It is a natural sequence that is viewed both as satisfying and rewarding in its own right and as a sensible investment of time and energy that will provide advantages at the point of entry into the labour market. Their centre of gravity and sense of self is rooted in education. The learning opportunities on offer have been solidly absorbed into their "social understanding and normative structures" (Rees et al, 1997 p 489). These young people, especially the young women, are usually able to speak reflexively about themselves as learners, about the possibilities they envisage for themselves and about the problems they might confront. Learning is talked about in positive and constructive terms. The choices made are socially reproductive or a form of reconversion strategy for the family. These people aspire to a gender specific, normal biography. Their families are typically supportive and directive in a variety of ways and also often able to facilitate aspects of the envisaged trajectory. The 'educational inheritance' of the family is in 'the right currency' and the young people are following well worn or eagerly sought routes.

As Quicke (1993) notes of his sample of A level students "for nearly all these students, parents still constituted significant others in their lives ... they were principal agents in maintaining the students' sense of self and identity in the world" (p 111). "They just want the best, because mum and dad, ever since we were little, have sort of thought we would both go to university. And then you start thinking you'll do your GCSEs and then your A levels and then go to university and then you'll get a job and that's how it's always been in my home" (Kirsty, Year 11 student). Nonetheless, as the ongoing narratives of these lives demonstrate, it would be a mistake to over-emphasise the fixity of even these apparently 'over-determined' middle-class lives. There is always the possibility of contingency and reversibility (eg poor A level grades, the opportunity to travel, illness). As Du Bois-Reymond puts it: "The 'project' therefore has to be constantly adapted to changing circumstances" (1998, p 63).

The other young people with particularly vivid imagined futures are those with strong and clear vocational commitments. There are several in our sample with interests ranging from horses, to acting and dancing and the RAF. There is a different kind of continuity in the trajectories of this group. Typically, they are already well embedded in their vocational subculture through part-time work, training, clubs, extracurricular activities and so on. The "emotional as well as intellectual dimensions" (Rees et al, 1997, p 493) of their learning identity are usually very apparent. The relationship between vocational choice, sense of self and learner identity seems by far the closest among these young people, very much part of a "personal project, related to an elaboration of an individual's identity" (Furlong, 1992, p 1); the projection of self into future scenarios. Here the young people are typically far more knowledgeable about their vocation and its fulfilment than their parents and are highly proactive in searching out information about their imagined future. But, here again, determination has to be weighed against contingency.

The next group has a future orientation but it is uncertain and tentative. Their familial resources do not provide a clear sense of 'what might be', and what things could be like or the links between the here and now and the possible futures. They are moving beyond the "things to do or not to do" (Bourdieu, 1990, p 53), defined by their habitus. They are embarking on a route of 'unrealised ends'. Cultural capital is stretched beyond its limits. Here we see habitus as the "art of inventing" (Bourdieu, 1990, p 55), as improvisation, producing new practices, but also, as a result, creating uncertainties. Transposition is displaced by vagueness and durability by contingency – particularly for young men for whom there is no 'men's work'. The families here are typically encouraging, even pressurising, without necessarily being able to offer tangible support or facilitation. The learning identity displayed by such young people is certainly rooted in some degree of academic success but is hardly robust. Learning is a challenge and a chore – a necessity for achieving some kind of future. The relationships between learning and the self are utilitarian rather than affirmatory. This is what Evans and Heinz call, "passive individualisation in which goals are weakly defined and strategies to achieve them uncertain" (1994, p xiv). Such young people also display what Evans and Heinz call 'step-by-step' behaviour. They suggest, in their comparative study of the UK and Germany, that "for those with occupational goals in England, the ways of achieving them were often less transparent and, therefore, step by step behaviour was often the dominant regime" (p xv). Most students, including many of those on the A level/university and special interest routes, remained vague about the relationships between qualifications and job market opportunities.

This last group of young people are in one way or another locked into the here and now. The future is short term, it is uninhabited, or it may just be more of the present or a matter of wait and see, of what turns up, of vague maybes or unlikely flights of fancy. "I just want to try and find out what I am going to do for the rest of my life and I'm taking each day as it comes" (Jolene, Year 11 student). Choices for such young people are heavily constrained by economic circumstances – the very sparse youth labour market – and inhibited by learner identities which may be at best estranged, or at worst damaged. Leaving school may be the only immediate goal in play although for some there may be the possibility of a fresh start of some kind. Often the immediate future is, to a significant degree, negatively constructed but otherwise consists of an 'ordinary life'. These young people certainly know what they do not want. "Most people, you know, they have been in school for so many years they just want to get on with their lives now. They've had enough of sitting in classrooms, they're bored, they just want to get a job and some money ... they want a fresh start, a job, a new life, not more writing and learning things, that nobody cares about" (Wayne, Year 11 student).

For a few young people the gap between the here and now and some kind of future is filled by fantasies. Fantasy works as an unstable stage or as a tactic in response to the pressures of choice. And indeed there is clearly sometimes a fine distinction between fantasy and ambition. But the point about fantasies is that they are 'out of place'. They can be seen as "escape attempts" (Bettis, 1996, p 115). They are logically and practically unconnected with the here and now realities of a young person's positionings and opportunities; although not all fantasies are unrealisable. Most are transient, clutches-at-straws, substitutes for high uncertainty or bleak alternatives. For some, everything and nothing is possible. It is not that all of our young people do not fantasise at times; it is that for some, fantasies predominate or serve as an alternative to apathy or despair.

For those young people who do engage with education or training post-16 it is evident that 'race' and social class are part of their complex topography of choice. "A college like Riverway, it sounds very upper class and I am thinking to myself, well, how many black people go there, and so I look around. I look in the pages to see whether there are black people in there" (Amma, Year 11 student). 'Race' and class are embedded for most, but not all, in their personal social geographies, social stereotypes and general fearfulness or confidence about the future. For both black and white students, their spatial practices within the education market are imbued with racial meanings and class meanings. The education market in this locality provides the possibility of 'escape' for some, while leaving untouched, and indeed reinforcing, the classed and racialised categorisation of space and spatial separation, and it erects barriers for others. Also 'race' in particular means different things to different students in their landscape of choice. Even so, the particular symbolic ordering – that is, racialisation – of space provides a particular general framework of experience for these young people. "Spatial practices derive their efficacy in social life only through the structure of social relations within which they come into play.... They take on their meanings under specific social relations of class, gender, community, ethnicity, or 'race' and get 'used up' or 'worked over' in the course of social action" (Harvey, 1989, p 223). Nonetheless, such practices vary between individuals as well. What de Certeau (1984) calls the 'space of enunciation', literally 'footsteps in the city', are a collection of 'innumerable singularities' which 'weave places together' and keep other places apart. For some of the young people (the locals) in our study, their footsteps are set within tightly defined spatial horizons and imaginary spaces; others (the cosmopolitans) range more widely in both respects. The choices of the Northwark Park students for further education and training are located within these individual and 'social spaces of enunciation' (de Certeau, 1984).

Parents

Initially we had expected that the role of parents would be less influential than was actually the case. Drawing on recent studies of adolescent identity formation (Head, 1997), we had imagined that most of our young people would be making their own choices and decisions about post-compulsory destinations. This was not so. From detailed coding and frequency counts of initial interviews, the active role and influence of parents (and significant others) was evident. As in other research, the practical involvement of mothers in the choice process emerged as particularly significant. The majority of our students, regardless of sex, class or 'race', relied heavily on their (sometimes extended) families for support and advice. In some cases, it was local family–friendship networks which led to employment or the pursuit of particular courses.

From our small sample of interviews with parents it was evident that they had been proactive on behalf of their teenage children: obtaining brochures, accompanying them to open evenings, ringing local colleges and so on. It was evident in middle-class homes that, while the young people were active and vocal in discussing their post-school destinations, work done in the family over time had laid down class-appropriate values/ choices. All of the parents we interviewed expressed some degree of fearfulness for their children but they were not always able to translate this into really useful support: "in the prefigurative (late modern) culture there is less of what the future holds for offspring, and the life experiences of parents are of less use to offspring" (Cote, 1996, p 419). Nonetheless, very often parents are seeking to interpret the world for their children and attempting to instil an attitude or disposition. These "categories of perception and assessment" and the possibilities and impossibilities which structure them are "inscribed in objective conditions" (Bourdieu, 1990, p 57). This is part of the construction of what Bourdieu calls "a matrix of perceptions". "I do think it is harder for young black people. I think they've got to be really good and that ... I think qualifications are the thing nowadays. If you've got a bit of paper, I don't think it matters what colour you are. That's what I tell Earl..." (Mrs P).

Educational intermediaries

From our extensive interviews with students and with the formal intermediaries it was evident that there was a significant mismatch between the rhetoric of support and advice represented in official and institutional documents and practice as experienced by the client group. Many schools have cut their pastoral work and careers guidance in the final year of schooling in order to focus on GCSE grades and to achieve a reduction in 'non-essential' expenditures. Thus, there has been an increased reliance on external agencies and specialist careers advisors. In our locale, the careers service underwent a process of privatisation as our study began. The service contract requires that the careers officers ensure all school leavers are interviewed and Action Plans completed. These become the 'evidence' of task completion in the newly privatised service. Many young people expressed unease about, and dissatisfaction with, the support they received. The majority reported that the interviews were of little or no use and very few found the advice or information provided to be relevant to their needs. "I've seen a careers officer once in secondary school; they just really 'draw an outline of what you want to do' and you can go to a library and get a book like that instead of making that appointment. They don't make that much difference" (Delisha, Year 11 student). The timing of the interviews, clashing with GCSE coursework and revision, was also a problem but some young people did find that they served as a reminder of the need to start thinking seriously about post-16 possibilities. (The problem of support is not confined to school students, however. The work of Bartlett and Rees, in Chapter Four, demonstrates the patchy nature of guidance for adults.)

The students from the PRU were much better served. They were interviewed by the Careers Officer at the PRU and follow-up interviews were arranged at the Careers Office. Furthermore, their parents were actively encouraged to attend these interviews and several did attend. Generally these young people received longer, more regular and consistent ongoing support than those in school. However, it could be that, because they are positioned as 'clients' or 'subjects of concern' for tutors/social services rather than as autonomous young people, some are 'shoe-horned' into inappropriate routes through what Corbett calls "the oppression of apparent kindness" (1990, p 3). Nevertheless, these young people were fairly positive about the support they received, however stereotyped it was.

In many ways these three themes (choice, parents and intermediaries) are interrelated and interdependent. One particular finding is illustrative of this connectedness. It was evident from our data that informal networks (what we have termed the local 'grapevine'), informed the choices of young people and their parents and supported their post-16 transitions. First hand, experiential knowledge of courses and providers was highly valued by young people, while documentary knowledge (brochures etc) was regarded sceptically. Positive or negative recommendations by significant others were often decisive in selecting or rejecting particular institutions. Typically students could not substantiate much of the 'information' about 'good' or 'bad' colleges, but it was frequently given priority over information in college brochures. Some students were prepared to consider (or reject) colleges on vague advice from friends. There is a very strong polarisation in the data between 'cold', abstract, impersonal information (brochures etc) and 'hot', 'hands on', experiential, direct knowledge (the grapevine) (Macrae et al, 1996b).

Most of the providers, while spending considerable sums on advertising and promotion, were well aware that reputation and recommendation were the major influences in most choosers' decisions.

> "We are doing some market research on this, asking students how they heard of us and interestingly enough it is very rarely through press advertising, it is nearly always through friends, cousins, word of mouth. [However] ... I don't think we can afford not to advertise or not to have press releases because they just keep a high profile really in terms of what we are doing." (Vice-principal, St Faith's Sixth Form College)

The role played by differences in material, cultural and social capital in the processes and possibilities of choice, particularly as these relate to 'race', class and gender

Our findings indicate that all our providers are driven by reasons of expediency, by the need to recruit in general terms, and the need to recruit 'good' students who will maintain, if not enhance, the institution's reputation and market position. However, some providers have to manage and cope with 'less desirable' school leavers. This leaves employment-related trainers (the local TEC) in the position of having to cope, as they see it, with the 'left-overs'. However, this creaming-off process is not only managed through constructs of ability or aptitude. Social class and 'race' become filters through which desirability/undesirability is constructed while concomitantly deprivation, special needs and 'race' become categories for niche-marketing or course-filling, as indicated already. As is the case with 'the economies of student worth' in other educational markets, girls and young women are highly desirable as students (Ball and Gewirtz, 1997). As one provider remarked: "If you get the impression it is a college that looks as if it has lots of females and treats them well, you will get lots of women – and that will always attract the males anyway."

What we would want to underline is that while the post-16 sector now caters for many more people, including a broader, more diverse clientele, it remains strongly segmented by the status of routes and the status of students. And for those first generation post-16 students typically their concerns are focused on the need for qualifications, on achieving the requirements for a later and different entry point into the labour market, not a totally reconstructed sense of possibilities and aspirations – instrumentalism is the primary motivation. In the field of social relations explored here we can begin to see something of both the way things change and the way they stay the same – the way that "change does occur, though never willy-nilly" (Harker, 1984, p 122). The expansions of further and higher education, and the economic upheavals and changes in the distribution and nature of work which they reflect do change class relations and the reproduction of social class in significant ways but not absolutely. The links between class, education and work are significantly reworked – as they were at other moments of rapid economic restructuring – but not dissolved. They are reassembled differently, perhaps more loosely, but it would be a mistake to see social class as somehow now irrelevant or contingent. What we are seeing *is* a break down of *some* of the stark and obvious class divisions of the past in post-16 education and employment, but nonetheless some of these divisions obstinately remain and there is the emergence of a more fuzzy, more complex hierarchy with new markers of differentiation. This is evident if we look at the achievements and origins and destinations (at June 1998, see Ball et al, 2000 for later data) of our cohort in relation to social class.

The number of GCSE A*-C grade passes per student were 1.4 for the working-class group and 4.9 for the middle-class group. As Pearce and Hillman (1998) note: "Attainment at 16 is the strongest predictor of both future participation in education and labour market prospects" (p 35). We can note that five (10%) of the working-class young people in our sample started doing A levels, two of those subsequently dropped out and another is doing only one A level. Against this, seven (46.6%) of the 15 middle-class group were doing A levels, all of whom completed their courses. The A level route is still dominated here by the offspring of the middle class. Significantly, eight of the working-class group with three or more GCSE A*-C passes, are not doing A level courses – self-exclusion perhaps? Six of the working-class group are unemployed, none of the middle-class. Only two (13%) of the middle-class group are not on courses of some kind, compared with 16 (32%) of the working-class group. (See Pearce and Hillman, 1998, for similarities with other local studies.)

It is difficult to escape from the point that within the risk culture: "Neither risks nor opportunities are evenly distributed. Long-standing forms of class and gender inequalities are being reproduced in new ways" (Jones and Wallace, 1990, p 153). The lives and experiences of young people continue to be "substructured by relations of race, ethnicity, class and gender" (Essed, 1991, p 49)[5]. Thus, while trying to escape from what Wexler (1992) calls the "overcoded interest" in class, and to develop a more "textured understanding of class differences", it is also very evident from our analysis of this particular set of 'youth transitions' that "becoming somebody', the identity project, and class difference, taken together, is what best makes sense of the social life of [our young people]" (Wexler, 1992, p 128).

The nature of the informal learning society: the experiences and prospects of those young people post-16 who fall outside education, training and paid employment

As explained above, our sample was constructed to ensure a wide representation of inner-city young people. We included those on the register of the local PRU; those who had already found mainstream schooling inappropriate to their needs and social situations; others who had opted out entirely; several refugees, young parents, as well as some in the care of social services. As outlined earlier we were concerned that, while the rhetoric of *The Learning Society* is inclusive in its aims and intentions, some young people would fall outside the range and scope of what was provided (Macrae et al, 1997b). Our findings have supported this concern. The policy texts of *The Learning Age* almost exclusively portray learners as an undifferentiated mass with the same kinds of capabilities, motivations and levels of support and encouragement, as if they were all equally ready and able to take the opportunity to upskill (Macrae et al, 1998). The uneven distribution of relevant 'capitals' (eg social, economic, cultural, emotional) and differences in acquired learning identities are set aside. And yet, in reality, as Apple notes:

> We do not confront abstract 'learners'.... Instead, we see specific classed, raced and gendered subjects, people whose biographies are intimately linked to the economic, political and ideological trajectories of their families, and communities, to the political economies of their neighbourhoods. (Apple, 1986, p 5)

From an analysis of the data we have identified a loose typology of five, broad categories of propensity towards and opportunity for participation in post-16 education and training. Briefly, these categories are: choosers otherwise, choice-avoiders, unstable choosers, pre-emptive choosers and active choosers (see Macrae et al, 1997b). Essentially, our findings indicate that for some young people, obtaining qualifications and staying in the formal learning process do not match their needs, interests or current identities. They have had enough of education and simply want a job. Some young people in these categories enrol on courses which are little more than 'warehouses': somewhere to be until something better comes along. As we have written elsewhere, "self worth, personal satisfaction, identity and personal development seem to have no place in the education and training agenda of the competitive state. Many of those who experience the learning society are left with empty calculation and little real hope" (Macrae et al, 1997b, p 22).

The market behaviour of the main providers in the post-16 education and training phase

As more and more school leavers postpone their entry to the labour market, the post-16 sector has had to respond to a new and non-traditional client group. Currently, post-16 provision is attempting to cater for a broader swathe of young school leavers including those with learning difficulties and the disaffected. As a consequence of the drive to expand their recruitment many institutions are forced to enrol less desirable students with little or no previous experience of educational success, while others are able to cream off the high fliers, as discussed at various points in this report. This then becomes what we have described as a market beset by "cut throat competition" where "dog eats dog over students" (MacLeod, 1997, p 13). Mis-information is commonplace and providers allocate considerable resources to impression management activities and marketing exercises. The new 'ethical' framework created by the 'commercial civilisation' of the FE market is also affecting the practice of managers and recruiters (Ball, 1998a).

Our findings suggest that the old cooperation which once existed between providers in our locale has disintegrated, to be replaced by hostility. In the words of one respondent: "... because of all this competition, institutions are isolated in a way that wasn't the case in the days for example of the ILEA [Inner London Education Authority], where there was a lot of networking, there was a lot of cooperation. Now there seems to be a sort of suspicion" (FE college student counsellor). Particular tensions arise when 11-18 schools are competing for student retention and recruitment with FE and sixth form colleges.

Below we have highlighted the main effects of the market form on the post-16 institutions in our particular study.

- The two systems are increasingly in direct competition for a wide range of post-16 provision. Colleges are keen to attract academic sixth formers away from schools and schools are keen to retain and attract *some* vocational students and run GNVQ courses. In addition, more schools are applying to open sixth forms, in response to the incentives and disciplines of the 11-16 market. This is heightening competition in an already crowded market.

- College providers feel themselves to be financially and strategically disadvantaged by the differences in the funding regimes between themselves and schools.

- The nature of the relationship between schools and colleges can be very different in 11-16, compared with 11-18, systems. By definition the latter are more competitive and contentious than the former. The former is much more likely to be characterised by positive relationships and an open flow of information about opportunities; school teachers and Year 11 students are likely to be relatively better informed about post-16 alternatives. The latter is more likely to be marked by suspicion and poor information flow, teachers and Year 11 students are likely to be poorly informed or misinformed about post-16 alternatives. This was particularly the case at Northwark Park school where students reported great difficulty in obtaining information on post-16 courses in any institution other than the school itself.

- There is an increasing degree of cross-over of ethos and practice between the two systems, with colleges in particular giving greater emphasis to their pastoral and tutorial support for students (although new contracts and increasing student numbers work against the effectivity of this) and schools giving greater emphasis to their 'adult' environment and curriculum mix.

It is important to append to these points that the 16-19 market is not the sole or sometimes even the primary recruitment concern of our FE providers. Indeed, the 16-19 sector is already seen by several of our providers as fairly much 'worked out' with little room for further expansion, except by attracting students away from direct competitors. Other age groups are now of increasing importance. But the caveat to the caveat is that the changing funding regime of FE means that for most providers any and (almost) all potential consumers are important in their efforts to maintain or enhance income. No possibilities for recruitment are overlooked. Courses are arranged quickly in response to almost any opportunity for recruitment, regardless of whether or not these would enhance opportunities for employment. Overseas students are a relatively new and lucrative area of expansion.

Overall, the market presented here can be characterised in a variety of ways. It might well be thought of, as one respondent described it, as a "cut-throat" market or, put another way, from the point of view of the providers, "it's grow or die". This 'cut-throat' quality, which is generated in part by the proximity of multiple providers, in part by the entry of new players and in good measure by the FE funding regime itself, is evidenced in a variety of ways in the market behaviour of, and relationships between, providers. Markets reward shrewdness rather than principle and privilege the values of competition over professional values (Ball et al, 1994; Gewirtz et al, 1993). Education markets, like other markets, are driven by self-interest – "the college cannot afford to take a moral stance", as one respondent put it. The self-interest of consumers who choose is set alongside that of producers aiming to thrive, or at least survive (Gewirtz et al, 1995). The 'cut-throat' quality and values of competition increasingly in play in this market make possible and encourage a variety of dubious actions and tactics.

What learning?

The choices made by the young people in our study, with the exception perhaps of those going on to A levels and higher education, bear little resemblance to the calculative, individualistic, consumer rationalism which predominates in official texts. Our analysis of these choices identifies patterns and points of significance similar in many respects to those outlined by Hodkinson et al (1996). As they put it: "Young people make career decisions within their horizons for action, which incorporate externally located opportunities in the labour market as well as the dispositions of habitus" (p 149). Those horizons are social/perceptual but also spatial and temporal. For some young people all three aspects are narrowly set. They are locked into a set of limited possibilities which are local and short term. Their knowledge about and confidence in the education, training and labour market are framed by what is familiar and necessary and often beset by multiple contingencies. Their personal narratives are tentative and often fragmented, punctuated with 'not yets', but are typically aimed at the achievement of a 'normal biography', an 'ordinary life'.

Others envisage long-term career development, move with confidence around the city and experiment with different sorts of lives and identities. Their narratives stress possibility and opportunity. There is nothing in their previous education or experience in the training market to suggest that they might not achieve a 'glossy' life or high ambition. Our sample of young people is stretched across this continuum although there are distinct clusters at either end. The labour market opportunities at the extremes are very different. Clearly, though, some young people change position on this continuum over time as they encounter set backs or (less often in our sample) break away. These are what Hodkinson et al (1996) call 'turning points'. It is important to bear in mind also that these are unfinished stories and that many of the young people are continuing to struggle to find themselves and to make a life for themselves often in difficult circumstances. For almost all, the family remains a major point of reference, either as a source of support or, for a few, an inhibiting factor. At the time of writing (November 1999), the cohort is 19-20 years old and only four or five are socially or financially independent of their family.

One thing that is very evident, and a point we have made several times previously (see Ball et al, 1999), is that the different 'learning identities', 'horizons of action' and market positions that make up these young people are both rooted in particular socio-cultural systems of behaviour and perception and constituted (or reconstituted) in the 'triumphs and tears' of compulsory schooling. These stories had begun to take shape long before the young people approached school-leaving age.

As far as the post-16 market itself is concerned, we have described a set of 'cut-throat', commercial relationships. The institutional providers are driven by the discipline and exigencies of the FEFC funding regime and the government's complex curricular and assessment structure. The logics and ethics of this market value and handle young people according to a hierarchical 'economy of student worth', invested with class, 'race' and gender inequalities.

The policies, rhetorics and practices of the post-16 market seem unrelated to, unrecognising of, the lives, interests and concerns of many of the young people with whom we work. With a few points of exception, the market system is neither supportive of nor empowering for them. Neither the 'hidden hand' of market order nor the vague exhortations of policy texts, the main constituents of *The Learning Society*, appear to understand or appreciate the risks, fears or desires of youth. Neither the rational economism of this learning society nor the vague, abstract, desocialised figures conjured up in policy texts bear much resemblance to the complex, struggling, diverse and uncertain young people in our study and the lives they are leading. They are, in a very real sense, 'worlds apart'.

Notes

[1] D J-ing is a term used to describe the work of disc jockeys.

[2] Northwark Park is a pseudonym, in common with other institutions named here.

[3] These are some of the issues explored further in our ESRC study: 'Choice, Pathways and Transitions: 16-19 Education, Training and (Un)employment in One Urban Locale', R000237261.

[4] In our cohort we had four refugees: two females from Ethiopia, one male from Somalia and one female from Peru.

[5] The sub-structures of 'race' and gender are examined and discussed in other project papers (see for example, Ball et al, 1998).

References

Ainley, P. (1994) *Degrees of difference: Higher education in the 1990s*, London: Lawrence and Wishart.

Apple, M. (1986) *Teachers and texts: A political economy of class and gender relations in education*, New York, NY: Routledge.

Avis, J. (1993) 'Post-fordism, curriculum modernisers and radical practice: the case of vocational education and training in England', *Journal of Vocational Education and Training*, vol 45, no 1, pp 3-11.

Avis, J., Bloomer, M., Esland, G., Gleeson, D. and Hodkinson, P. (1996) *Knowledge and nationhood: Education politics and work*, London: Cassell.

Ball, S.J. (1993) 'Education markets, choice and social class: the market as a class strategy in the UK and the USA', *British Journal of Sociology of Education*, vol 14, no 1, pp 3-21.

Ball, S.J. (1998a) 'Ethics, self-interest and the market form in education', *Markets, managers and public service?*, Occasional Paper No 1, London: Centre for Public Policy Research, King's College London.

Ball, S.J. (1998b) 'It's becoming a habitus: identities, youth transitions and socio-economic change', Paper presented at BERA Annual Conference, Queens University, Belfast, 27-30 August.

Ball, S.J. and Gewirtz, S. (1997) 'Girls and the education market', *Gender and Education*, vol 9, no 2, pp 207-22.

Ball, S.J. and Van Zanten, A. (1998) 'Logiques de marche ethiques contextualiseés dans les systèmes scolaires française et britannique', *Education et Societies*, vol 1, no 1, pp 47-71.

Ball, S.J., Bowe, R. and Gewirtz, S. (1994) 'Competitive schooling: values, ethics and cultural engineering', *Journal of Curriculum and Supervision*, vol 9, no 4, pp 350-67.

Ball, S.J., Macrae, S. and Maguire, M. (1997) *The post-16 education market: Ethics, interests and survival*, London: School of Education, King's College London.

Ball, S.J., Macrae, S. and Maguire, M. (1998) 'Race, space and the further education marketplace', *Race, Ethnicity and Education*, vol 1, no 2, pp 171-89.

Ball, S.J., Macrae, S. and Maguire, M. (1999) 'Young lives, diverse choices and imagined futures in education and training market', *International Journal of Inclusive Education*, vol 3, no 3, pp 195-224.

Ball, S.J., Maguire, M. and Macrae, S. (1999) 'Young lives at risk in the "futures" market: some policy concerns from on-going research', in F. Coffield (ed) *Speaking truth to power: Research and policy in lifelong learning*, Bristol: The Policy Press.

Ball, S.J., Maguire, M. and Macrae, S. (2000) *Choice, pathways and transitions: New youth, new economies in the global city*, London: Routledge Falmer.

Banks, M., Bates, I., Breakwell, G., Bynner, J., Elmer, N., Jamieson, L. and Roberts, K. (1992) *Careers and identities: Adolescent attitudes to employment, training and, their home life, leisure and politics*, Milton Keynes: Open University Press.

Bates, I. and Riseborough, G. (1993) 'Deepening divisions, fading solutions', in I. Bates and G. Riseborough (eds) *Youth and inequality*, Buckingham: Open University Press.

Bettis, P.J. (1996) 'Urban students, liminality, and the postindustrial context', *Sociology of Education*, vol 69, pp 105-25.

Bourdieu, P. (1990) *The logic of practice*, Cambridge: Polity Press.

Brice-Heath, S. and McLaughlin, M.W. (eds) (1993) *Identity and inner-city youth: Beyond ethnicity and gender*, New York, NY and London: Teachers College Press, Columbia University.

Brown, P. and Lauder, H. (eds) (1992) *Education for economic survival*, London: Routledge.

Brown, P. and Lauder, H. (1996) 'Education, globalism and economic development', *Journal of Education Policy*, vol 11, no 1, pp 1-25.

Carter, D.S.G. and O'Neill, M.H. (1995*) International perspectives on educational reform and policy implementation*, Brighton: Falmer Press.

Coffield, F. (ed) (2000: forthcoming) *Differing visions of a learning society: Research findings*, Volume II, Bristol: The Policy Press.

Coles, B. (1995) *Youth and social policy*, London: UCL Press.

Corbett, J. (ed) (1990*) Uneasy transitions: Disaffection in post-compulsory education and training*, London, New York, NY: Falmer Press.

Cote, J.E. (1996) 'Sociological perspectives on identity formation: the culture identity link and identity capital', *Journal of Adolescence*, vol 19, pp 417-28.

Cross, M. and Wrench, J. (1991) 'Racial inequality on YTS: careers service or disservice', *British Journal of Education and Work*, vol 4, no 3, pp 5-23.

de Certeau, M. (1984) *The practice of everyday life*, Berkeley, CA: Univeristy of California Press.

DfEE (Department for Education and Employment) (1995) *Forging ahead*, London: HMSO.

DfEE (1998) *The Learning Age*, London: The Stationery Office.

Du Bois-Reymond, M. (1998) '"I don't want to commit myself yet": young people's life concepts', *Journal of Youth Studies*, vol 1, no 1, pp 63-79.

Essed, P. (1991) *Understanding everyday racism*, London: Sage Publications.

Evans, K. and Heinz, W.R. (1994) *Becoming adults in England and Germany*, London: Anglo-German Foundation.

FEFC (Further Education Funding Council) (1998) *Mergers, transfers and incorporations*, Circular 98/36, 16 October, Coventry: FEFC.

Foskett, N.H. and Hesketh, A.J. (1996) *Student decision-making and the post-16 market place*, Report of the Post-16 Markets Project, Southampton: Centre for Research in Education Marketing.

Foucault, M. (1986) *Death and the labyrinth: The world of Raymond Roussel*, New York, NY: Doubleday.

Furlong, A. (1992) *Growing up in a classless society? School to work transition*, Edinburgh: Edinburgh University Press.

Garner, C., Main, B.G.M. and Raffe, D. (1988) 'A tale of four cities: social and spatial inequalities in the youth labour market', in D. Raffe (ed) *Education and the youth labour market*, London, New York, NY: Falmer Press.

Gewirtz, S., Ball, S.J. and Bowe, R. (1993) 'Values and ethics in the marketplace: the case of Northwark Park', *International Journal of Studies in Education*, vol 3, no 2, pp 233-53.

Gewirtz, S., Ball, S.J. and Bowe, R. (1995) *Markets, choice and equity in education*, Buckingham: Open University Press.

Glatter, R., Bagley, C. and Woods, P. (1996) 'Modelling local markets in schooling', Paper prepared for *Markets in Education: Policy, process and practice: A symposium*, University of Southampton, 4-5 July.

Harker, R. (1984) 'On reproduction, habitus and education', *British Journal of Sociology of Education*, vol 5, no 2, pp 119-27.

Harvey, D. (1989) *The condition of postmodernity*, Oxford: Blackwell.

Head, J. (1997) *Working with adolescents: Constructing identity*, London: Falmer Press

Hodkinson, P., Sparkes, A.C. and Hodkinson, H. (1996) *Triumphs and tears: Young people, markets and the transition from school to work*, London: David Fulton.

Jones, G.C. and Wallace, C. (1990) 'Beyond individualization: what sort of social change?', in L. Chisholm, P. Buchner, H.H. Kruger and P. Brown (eds) *Childhood, youth and social change: A comparative perspective*, London: Falmer Press.

MacLeod, D. (1997) 'Dog eats dog over students', *Guardian Education Supplement*, 28 October, p 13.

Macrae, S. (1997) 'Parents: active participants or puzzled bystanders in the choice of post-16 education and training?', ESRC Project Paper, London: King's College London.

Macrae, S. and Maguire, M. (1999) 'All change, no change: gendered regimes in the post-16 market', in S. Riddell and J. Salisbury (eds) *Gender equality policies and educational reforms in the United Kingdom*, London: Routledge.

Macrae, S., Maguire, M. and Ball, S.J. (1996a) 'Opportunity knocks "choice" in the post-16 education and training market', *Markets in Education: Policy, Process and Practice*, University of Southampton: Centre for Educational Marketing.

Macrae, S., Maguire, M. and Ball, S.J. (1996b) 'The role of grapevine knowledge in student decision-making', Paper presented at *Choice and Markets*, ESRC Learning Society Conference, University of Bristol, 17–18 September.

Macrae, S., Maguire, M. and Ball, S.J. (1997a) 'Competition, choice and hierarchy in a post-16 education and training market', in S. Tomlinson (ed) *Education 14-19: Critical perspectives*, London: Athlone Press.

Macrae, S., Maguire, M. and Ball, S.J. (1997b) 'Whose "learning society"? A tentative deconstruction', *Journal of Education Policy*, vol 12, no 6, pp 499-509.

Macrae, S., Ball, S.J., Maguire, M. and Charles, V. (1998) 'The Learning Age: another dead end or the road to success?', ECER Annual Conference, University of Ljubljana, Slovenia, 17-20 September.

Maguire. M. (1995) 'The youth labour market in the 1990s', Paper presented at *Young People and The Labour Market* Conference, Institute of Employment Research, University of Warwick, 14 February.

Maguire, M., Ball, S.J. and Macrae, S. (1999) 'Promotion, persuasion and class-taste: marketing (in) the UK post-compulsory sector', *British Journal of Sociology of Education*, vol 20, no 3, pp 291-308.

Pahl, R. (1970) *Patterns of urban life*, Harlow: Longman.

Pearce, N. and Hillman, J. (1998) *Wasted youth: Raising achievement and tackling social exclusion*, London: Institute for Public Policy Research.

Quicke, J. (1993) 'A yuppie generation', in I. Bates and G. Riseborough (eds) *Youth and inequality*, Buckingham, Open University Press.

Rabinow, P. (ed) (1987) *The Foucault reader*, Harmondsworth: Penguin.

Rees, G., Fevre, R., Furlong, J. and Gorard, S. (1997) 'History, place and the learning society: towards a sociology of lifetime learning', *Journal of Education Policy*, vol 12, no 6, pp 485-98.

Roberts, K. (1993) 'Career trajectories and the mirage of increased social mobility', in I. Bates and G. Riseborough (eds) *Youth and inequality*, Buckingham: Open University Press.

Skilbeck, M., Connell, H., Lowe, N. and Tait, K. (1994) *The vocational quest: New directions in education and training*, London: Routledge.

Smith, M.K. (1994) *Local education: Community, conversation, praxis*, Buckingham: Open University.

Solomos, J. and Back, L. (1994) 'Conceptualising racisms: social theory, politics and research', *Sociology*, vol 28, no 1, pp 143-63.

Strauss, A.L. (1987) *Qualitative data analysis for social scientists*, New York, NY: Cambridge University Press.

Wexler, P. (1992) *Becoming somebody: Toward a social psychology of school*, London: Falmer Press.

Zinneker, J. (1990) 'What does the future hold? Youth and sociocultural change in the FRG', in L. Chisholm, P. Buchner, H.H. Kruger and P. Brown (eds) *Childhood, youth and social change: A comparative perspective*, London: Falmer Press.

Appendix: Location of main providers of post-16 education and training

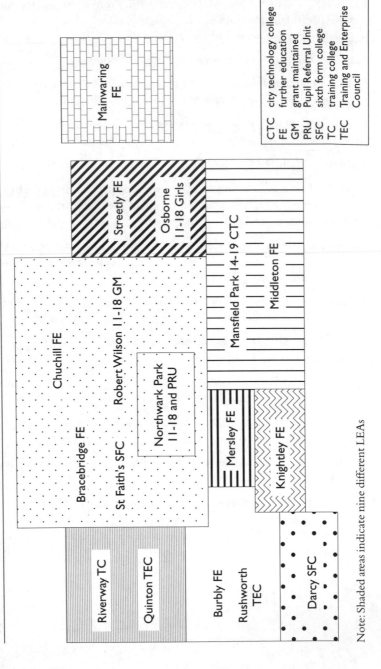

Note: Shaded areas indicate nine different LEAs

CTC	city technology college
FE	further education
GM	grant maintained
PRU	Pupil Referral Unit
SFC	sixth form college
TC	training college
TEC	Training and Enterprise Council

Mainwaring FE

Streetly FE

Osborne 11-18 Girls

Mansfield Park 14-19 CTC

Middleton FE

Chuchill FE

Robert Wilson 11-18 GM

Bracebridge FE

St Faith's SFC

Northwark Park 11-18 and PRU

Mersley FE

Knightley FE

Riverway TC

Quinton TEC

Burbly FE

Rushworth TEC

Darcy SFC

TWO

Unifying academic and vocational learning in England, Wales and Scotland[1]

Ken Spours, Michael Young, Cathy Howieson and David Raffe[2]

Introduction

Many different concepts of the learning society are employed in current debates (see chapters by Coffield, and Bartlett and Rees in this volume), but none is readily compatible with the continued division between academic and vocational learning. Notions of the learning society as a basis for economic competitiveness anticipate a need for new kinds of skills and knowledge which transcend this division. Visions of the learning society as a means to social equality or personal fulfilment reject the inequalities arising from divisions between tracks and the limits placed on the goals of learning by categorising it as academic or vocational. The view of lifelong learning and the learning society expressed in government rhetoric emphasises the need to break down barriers, including the barriers to access and progression arising from divisions between academic and vocational learning. To achieve a learning society, therefore, it is necessary to 'unify' academic and vocational learning: that is, to bring them together into a closer and more coherent relationship or to combine them within a unified system.

Most European countries are pursuing policies to unify post-compulsory education and training. In Britain, unification has been advocated by independent policy bodies such as the National and Scottish Commissions on Education (NCE, 1993; SCE, 1996), by industrialists (CBI, 1998), by educational providers (AfC et al, 1994), by teachers (David and Jenkins, 1996; Jenkins et al, 1997) and by some of us and our co-authors in *A British 'Baccalauréat'* (Finegold et al, 1990). However, there are different concepts and models of unification, and different unifying strategies within Europe and within Britain (Lasonen, 1996; Lasonen and Young, 1998). The government's policy in England has developed through the Dearing (1996) *Review of Qualifications for 16-19 Year Olds*, the *Qualifying for Success* consultation (DfEE, 1997) and the White Paper *Learning to Succeed* (DfEE, 1999). It reflects what we shall call a linkages strategy, which maintains the three post-16 tracks but tries to encourage links among them and emphasises their formal equivalence. Government policy in Wales goes beyond the English strategy by giving more emphasis to the role of a single credit-based qualifications framework for promoting lifelong learning (Welsh Office, 1998; ETAG, 1999). In Scotland government policy stands in contrast to that in England and Wales by adopting a unified system: instead of linking the tracks the *Higher Still* reform is replacing them with a unified system of post-16 education (Scottish Office, 1994).

In this chapter we summarise the main conclusions of the Unified Learning Project (ULP), a two-year study of developments in post-compulsory education and training as they relate to the unification of academic and vocational learning. The ULP focused on a 'home international' comparison of England, Wales and Scotland (Raffe et al, 1999a), but it was complemented by a study of strategies to promote parity of esteem between vocational and general learning in post-16 education in eight European countries (Lasonen and Young, 1998; Raffe et al, 1999b). We begin by outlining the main analytical tool developed during the project, a conceptual framework for mapping and analysing different concepts and strategies of unification. We then describe the different approaches to unification in England, Wales and Scotland, in the context of developments elsewhere in Europe, and suggest that countries are responding differently to similar global changes. We discuss a number of specific themes and issues raised by these developments and analyse the implications of unification for the policy process and for models of educational change. Finally, we review the prospects for unifying academic and vocational learning in Great Britain and consider whether the three systems of post-compulsory education and training are converging or diverging.

A conceptual framework

Our conceptual framework for analysing the unification of academic and vocational learning in post-compulsory education and training systems has three main elements. The first element is the distinction among three types of systems: a *tracked* system, with separate and distinctive tracks; a *linked* system, with features linking the tracks or common properties which underline their similarity or equivalence; and a *unified* system, which does not use tracks to organise provision and accommodates a diversity of provision within a unified set of arrangements. These three types can be seen as points along a continuum of unification, with tracked systems at one end, unified systems at the other end, and various forms of linked systems in between.

Each national system is likely to be a mixture of the three types: its position on the continuum between tracked and unified systems may vary across different dimensions of system change. These dimensions are the second element of our conceptual framework. Figure 1 lists eleven such dimensions, grouped for convenience into four areas. For each dimension, Figure 1 summarises the characteristic features of tracked, linked and unified systems respectively. The dimensions in the figure are those which proved relevant in our comparisons between Scottish and English developments in the late 1990s. Other dimensions of system change may be useful for analysing other periods or other systems. For example, funding is treated as part of the government and regulation dimension in Figure 1, but in the light of its growing policy role it may deserve in future to be considered as a dimension in its own right. Furthermore, at least two important dimensions of system variation cannot be easily represented in terms of our three types of system. These are the 'scope' of a system (for example whether it includes all learners over 16 or only those up to the age of 18 or 19) and the number of tracks in a system.

The third element of our conceptual framework is the distinction between open and grouped systems. In an open unified system, like the one being introduced in Scotland, there is weak prescription of the content, volume, level, mode and duration of study; the emphasis is on choice and flexible entry and exit points. A grouped system is based on common learning requirements or entitlements for all students, with stronger prescription of the content, volume and level of study. Examples include Baccalaureate models of a unified system or the programme model recently introduced in Sweden[3]. The distinction between open and grouped systems can be applied not only to unified systems (Young et al, 1997),

Figure 1: A matrix of unification: types of system and their dimensions

	Tracked system	Linked system	Unified system
Content and process			
Purpose and ethos	Distinctive purposes and ethos associated with each track	Purposes and ethos overlap across tracks	Multiple purposes and pluralist ethos
Curriculum	Different content (subjects, areas of study)	Some common elements across tracks	Curriculum reflects student needs and integrates academic and vocational learning
Teaching/learning processes	Different learning processes in different tracks	Different learning processes but some common features	Variation based on student needs and not tied to specific programmes
Assessment	Different assessment methodologies and grading systems	Different methodologies but with level and grade equivalences	Common framework of methodologies including a common grading system
System architecture			
Certification	Different certification for each track	Certification frameworks link tracks, eg overarching diplomas, equivalences	A single system of certification
Course structure and pathways	Different course structures and insulated progression pathways	Course structures allow transfer and combinations	Flexible entry points, credit accumulation, and single progression ladder
Progression to higher education	Not possible from some tracks	Conditions of progression vary across tracks	All programmes may lead to higher education
Delivery			
Local institutions	Different institutions for different tracks	Variable/overlapping relation of track to institution	One type of institution, or choice of institution not constrained by type of programme
Modes of participation	Tracks based on separate modes (academic/full-time), vocational/part-time)	Tracks partly based on mode	Single system covers different modes
Staff	Different staff for each track, with non-transferable qualifications	Variable/some overlap of staff	Socialisation, qualifications and conditions are consistent for all staff
Government and regulation	Different structures for different tracks	Mixed/variable organisational structure	Single administrative and regulatory system

Source: Raffe et al (1998b)

but to tracked or linked systems as well (Howieson et al, 1998a). England is located between open and grouped system types. It has a relatively open general track consisting of elective A levels, but it has grouped vocational qualifications such as General National Vocational Qualifications (GNVQs). The extent to which a system is open or grouped is typically related to the role of the national state in the development and governance of that system.

As described above, our framework allows us to analyse different types of system. It may also be used to analyse different policy strategies – respectively track-based, linkages and unified system strategies – each of which seeks to move towards one of the three types of systems or to consolidate the features of the system that already exist. In the next section we apply our framework to the systems of post-compulsory education and training in England, Wales and Scotland, to debates about unification within each country, and to their strategies for unification. We also refer, although more briefly, to other countries in Europe.

The current policy context

In England, Wales and Scotland policy and debates have been substantially qualifications-led, but the systems of qualifications are different (Howieson et al, 1997). There are three main types of qualifications for 16-19-year-olds in England and Wales – A levels, broad vocational qualifications (such as GNVQs and the National Certificates and Diplomas awarded by the Business and Technology Educational Council, now part of EDEXCEL) and occupational qualifications (National Vocational Qualifications [NVQs] and other occupational qualifications). These three types loosely correspond to Highers, National Certificates (NC) and Scottish Vocational Qualifications (SVQs), the main pre-1999 qualifications in Scotland. However, even before the *Higher Still* reforms these Scottish qualifications were more modular and more flexible, and they did not form distinct tracks to the same extent as the three types of qualifications in England. Scottish curricula tend to be broader, and there is a different division of functions among institutions: most 16 year olds who continue in full-time study do so at school. In many areas of England there is strong competition among institutions; relationships among Scottish institutions tend to be more collaborative and less competitive at the post-16 stage. In England and Wales independent bodies compete to award qualifications, subject to central regulation, while in Scotland a single government-controlled body is responsible for the design and award of most qualifications.

Several of the policy agendas which have driven change since the 1970s have been common to England, Wales and Scotland. These include the need to respond to youth unemployment in the early 1980s, the Conservative government's promotion of markets and its attack on 'producer dominance' later in the 1980s, the competitiveness agenda of the 1990s and, most recently, the need to promote employability and to combat social exclusion. Scotland has been somewhat more insulated from the fluctuations in political fashions; the 'Thatcherite' policy agenda of the 1980s had less impact north of the Border. The educational policy culture of Scotland is more consensual, the policy community is smaller and policy networks are more interconnected. Educational change in Scotland has been more incremental, more consultative but also more centrally led. During the 1980s and early 1990s educational change in England tended to be ideologically led, with stronger experimentation in areas such as institutional marketisation. Within this climate there developed stronger traditions of radical critique and local innovation. The leadership provided by educational professionals, especially the Inspectorate, has been stronger in Scotland, where it filled the political vacuum which existed before the Scottish Parliament. Training policy was only devolved to Scotland in 1994; Scottish policy has been more 'education-led' and Scottish debates about education have been largely separate from British debates about training.

In Wales the development of a distinct educational policy is a more recent process, which is still evolving. New 'quangos', established in the 1990s, assumed powers formerly exercised by bodies covering all of Britain or England and Wales. Wales shares the same courses, qualifications and basic institutional structure as England, but certain other features – its political culture, its policy networks, the more muted emphasis on institutional competition and greater uniformity among institutions – more closely resemble Scotland.

Debates and policy developments in England

We identify five phases of policy development and debates concerning post-compulsory education and training in England since the late 1970s. The first four phases are described in more detail by Howieson et al (1997). They covered, respectively: the responses to youth unemployment in the late 1970s and early 1980s, the development of pre-vocational qualifications and the 'new vocationalism' in the mid-1980s, the attempt in the late 1980s to develop a two-track qualifications system based on the reform of academic qualifications and the establishment of NVQs, and the formation of a three-track system in the 1990s with the introduction of GNVQs as a middle track.

The fifth phase began with the publication of the Dearing Report in 1996. Figure 2 contrasts the position of post-compulsory education and training in England, Wales and Scotland at this time. Each letter E shows the position of England on one of the dimensions of unification: the further to the right, the closer it was to a unified system. On balance the English system was still tracked, but it had features of a linked system on some dimensions. For example, tracking was weaker in respect of the dimensions of 'purpose and ethos' and 'progression to higher education'. This reflected the fact that many A level and GNVQ students shared similar aspirations about their future destinations. The overlap in functions of schools and colleges, and the growing tendency for academic and vocational courses to be offered by the same institution, led us to classify England as linked with respect to the dimension of 'local institutions'. The Department for Education and Employment (DfEE) was formed in 1996, combining education, training and employment policy within a single department – an example of England being unified with respect to the dimension of 'government and regulation'. On the other dimensions the English system remained tracked; most reforms up to this point had been internal to particular tracks or aimed at the introduction of new tracks. By the mid-1990s qualifications had become increasingly important as the focus of debates and policy. The English system was developing a national framework for 16-19 qualifications which formalised tracking but also provided a basis for developing a linked system (Spours et al, 1998a). Calls for unification continued, either in the form of a unified system, or in the form of a linkages strategy focusing on the idea of an overarching qualification framework. These calls embraced a range of models of unification, from grouped Baccalaureate models to open, flexible, unit-based frameworks.

In his review Sir Ron Dearing tried to balance the conflicting priorities of the Conservative government and education professionals with his desire to produce reforms capable of being further developed by another government. The proposals can be divided between those which promote a track-based strategy and those which support the development of linkages between the tracks. The recommendations which promoted tracking included the proposals to:

• clarify the distinct purposes of the three tracks or 'pathways';
• rationalise provision of courses offered in more than one track;

- strengthen each pathway, for example, by introducing tougher or more consistent A level standards, by simplifying GNVQ assessment, and by relaunching YT (Youth Training) as National Traineeships.

Other recommendations promoted linkages between the tracks. These included proposals for:
- a national qualifications framework with a single set of levels;
- a three–unit one year Advanced Subsidiary level (the 'horizontal AS');
- GNVQs, currently 12 units, were to be broken up to facilitate mixing; they were to be available as double awards (12 units), single awards (6 units) and, later, half awards (3 units), equivalent respectively to two, one and half an A level;
- a stand–alone key skills qualification available in all three tracks;
- overarching National Certificates and a National Advanced Diploma to encourage breadth and parity of esteem between academic and vocational learning;
- the merging of NCVQ (National Council for Vocational Qualifications) and SCAA (School Curriculum and Assessment Authority) and the encouragement of mergers between academic and vocational awarding bodies.

The review represented a weak linkages strategy (Spours and Young, 1996), but with variation across the dimensions of our framework. Its approach to the dimensions of content and process, such as the curriculum, was strongly track–based; but its approach to certification – the national framework – was linkage–based, and its approach to governance and regulation (the merging of NCVQ and SCAA and the Examination Boards) was unified.

NCVQ and SCAA merged in 1997 to form the Qualifications and Curriculum Authority (QCA). The new Labour government, elected in the same year, consulted over Dearing's main proposals, based on a document, *Qualifying for Success*, whose main themes were 'quality and standards', 'flexibility and breadth', 'key skills for all' and 'the feasibility of an overarching certificate' (DfEE, 1997).

The government's response to the consultation was cautious. It accepted some proposals (a horizontal AS level, a six–unit single award GNVQ with the possibility of half awards in the future, a stand–alone key skills qualification and the idea of qualifications linkages), but agreed to only small changes on others, such as coursework assessment and the extension of modularisation. A levels and GNVQ awards, not modules, would remain the building blocks of the system. It limited module retakes and deferred the unitisation of qualifications within a national framework and the creation of an overarching certificate.

Figure 2: The English, Welsh and Scottish systems at the beginning of the current reform phase

	Tracked system	Linked system	Unified system
Content and process			
Purpose and ethos		E W S	
Curriculum	E W	S	
Teaching/learning processes	E W	S	
Assessment	E W S		
System architecture			
Certification	E	W S	
Course structure and pathways	E	W	S
Progression to higher education		E W S	
Delivery			
Local institutions		E W S	
Modes of participation	E W S		
Staff	E W S		
Government and regulation		E W S	

The government's response is best understood in the context of its overall priorities which concentrated on raising standards in schools and getting the young unemployed back to work through the New Deal (Hodgson and Spours, 1999). It sought to resolve the potential contradiction between its 'schools standards' agenda and its 'lifelong learning' agenda by distinguishing between policies for the 16-19 age group and policies for adult learners (DfEE, 1998). Furthermore, it sought to combine more central regulation in relation to standards with a voluntaristic and demand-led approach to implementation and delivery. Schools and colleges would be free to choose whether they offered the new key skills qualification, the new AS and the new GNVQ single and half awards. To the extent that the reforms anticipated further moves towards unification, it was towards an open rather than a grouped model of unification. Three main interpretations of New Labour's proposals emerged: that they represented a sensible holding of the line to preserve A levels (Smithers, 1998); that they were politically safe, but lacking in vision and unlikely to work; and that they represented a further, albeit very modest, step towards a more flexible and unified qualifications system (Hodgson et al, 1998). While all three interpretations have some validity, the main aim of New Labour's approach to qualifications reform under *Qualifying for Success* has been to introduce stronger linkages than those proposed in the Dearing review.

The government continued to pursue unification along the dimension of government and regulation. It wanted more unified national organisational and regulatory structures in order to create greater coherence, to maintain and improve standards and to rationalise provision. Its 1999 White Paper *Learning to Succeed* extended this process into the funding and planning spheres, by announcing a new system of national and local Learning and Skills Councils (LSCs) as the basis for a single funding mechanism for school sixth forms, colleges and work-based training (DfEE, 1999).

The government's approach to the reform of post-compulsory education and training has been driven less by a vision of a (more) unified system than by the desire to manage more effectively a marketised education and training system (see Chapter One by Ball, Maguire and Macrae, and Chapter Four by Bartlett and Rees of this volume). It aims not only to replace the Training and Enterprise Councils but also to extend the standards agenda being prosecuted in schools to all post-16 education and training outside the universities. However, Ofsted is being appointed to inspect all 16-19 provision with a separate Inspectorate for adult learning. *Learning to succeed* is thus maintaining the policy separation between 16-19-year-olds and adult learning.

Debates and policy developments in Wales

The main debates and policy developments leading up to the Dearing Review covered Wales as well as England. In Figure 2 we classify the Welsh system in 1996 as broadly similar to that of England at this time, but we take account of two distinctive features of the government's policy in Wales. First, the Welsh Office supported the development of a national credit framework (CREDIS) which now covers most non-advanced Further Education (FE) provision in Wales. Most of the FE curriculum was modularised at the same time. We therefore classify Wales as linked rather than tracked on the dimensions of certification and student pathways. Because of modularisation Welsh 16-19 education, at least that provided in the colleges, was also somewhat more open than that of England (this is not shown in Figure 2). Second, education and training remained in separate departments of the Welsh Office, and before 1997 the responsibilities for regulating academic and vocational qualifications not only belonged to different bodies – ACAC (the Curriculum and Assessment Authority for Wales) and NCVQ – but were further divided because the former body had a remit for Wales only while the latter covered England, Wales and Northern Ireland. We therefore classify Wales, at the beginning of the current reform phase, as less unified than England on the dimension of government and regulation.

The small scale of government in Wales, and the relative density of its policy networks, made the separation of education and training policy less important. The more significant trend has been the continuing development of an increased capacity for separate policy making in Wales, with the devolution of policy responsibilities and the creation of Welsh bodies for funding, inspection, regulation and other quasi-governmental functions. Debates about education and training have increasingly developed a Welsh character, especially with the report of the government-appointed Education and Training Action Group (ETAG, 1999) which aimed to set an agenda for the National Assembly for Wales. However, a separate capacity for policy making does not necessarily result in divergent policies: the ETAG proposals for a National Council for Education and Training for Wales, and for local Community Consortia for Education and Training, were subsequently mirrored in *Learning to Succeed*'s proposals for a system of Learning and Skills Councils in England.

Although most elements of the government's policies in response to Dearing and *Qualifying for Success* applied to Wales as to England, there was at least one significant difference. In its Green Paper *Learning is for everyone*, the Welsh Office expressed its strong support for a 'seamless' framework for all post-16 qualifications (Welsh Office, 1998). This builds on the work of CREDIS and the parallel Higher Education Credit Initiative. While this framework would leave the qualifications themselves unchanged, it marks a more decisive move than England has yet made towards an open linked qualifications system at 16-plus. In contrast to England, the lifelong learning agenda in Wales embraces the whole of post-compulsory education and training. As a result, policies and debates in England and Wales may be starting to diverge. Wales may move more rapidly towards unification as the National Assembly for Wales develops its own strategy, influenced by the ETAG report and by other reform proposals such as the Institute of Welsh Affairs' (IWA, 1999) proposal for a Welsh Baccalaureate.

Debates and policy developments in Scotland

Recent developments in Scotland can also be understood in terms of a series of phases, although these do not match the phases described for England (Howieson et al, 1997). The first four phases were introduced, respectively, by the government's 1979 consultative document on 16-18 education (SED, 1979), by the Action Plan which proposed the national modular system of vocational education introduced in 1984 (SED, 1983), by calls for reform of the post-compulsory curriculum, and by the 1992 Howie Report which proposed a two-track post-compulsory system starting at 15 years (SOED, 1992).

By the early 1990s Scotland represented an open or flexible version of a linked system, with variation across the different dimensions (see Figure 2). The provision of most post-compulsory education through relatively short (120-hour) 'academic' Highers courses and even shorter (40-hour) 'vocational' National Certificate (NC) modules made the system particularly flexible in respect of subject choice and progression; hence our classification of the Scottish system as 'unified' with respect to student pathways. NC modules were widely available in schools and most post-compulsory students took Highers and NC modules in combination. On most of the other dimensions Scotland could be classified as a linked system, reflecting weaker tracks than in England.

In 1992 the Howie Committee concluded that the current system did not adequately cater for the increasing range of students staying on in education (SOED, 1992). It proposed a track-based reform strategy, based on academic and vocational tracks starting at 15 years. This would have reversed the direction of change in the Scottish system, which had been moving towards an open model of unification; Howie's proposals would have moved it back towards a grouped model of tracking. The public consultation over the Howie proposals revealed agreement on the need for reform but almost universal opposition to tracking.

The current reform phase in Scotland was introduced by the government document *Higher Still: Opportunity for all* (Scottish Office, 1994) which announced the introduction of a unified system for post-16 education, initially scheduled for 1997 but later postponed to 1999. The unified system is based on 40- or 80-hour units, usually grouped into 160-hour courses, available at five levels. Units and courses cover the range of academic and vocational subjects, but are designed on common principles. Units are internally assessed, with an additional external assessment for courses. *Higher Still* is an open model of a unified system, with no centrally prescribed core courses or curriculum requirements, although core skills are embedded in courses and units where appropriate. Students may, however, take specified combinations of courses and/or units leading to Scottish Group Awards (SGAs).

Scotland is thus set on its strategy towards an open unified system, but with three important qualifications. First, the Scottish strategy emphasises particular dimensions: it is unifying the system architecture (especially certification), the form of governance and regulation, and (to a lesser extent) the content and process of the curriculum, but it is not unifying institutions or modes of delivery. Second, the conservatism of Scottish education creates a risk of strategy drift: instead of unifying academic and vocational learning *Higher Still* could simply lead to the takeover of the vocational by the academic. Third, *Higher Still* only embraces two of the three post-compulsory tracks; the work-based route remains outside *Higher Still*, except to the limited extent to which SVQs may contribute to SGAs.

Scotland's strategy for unification is being taken a step further forward through the Scottish Credit and Qualifications Framework. This will consist of a common language and a framework of credit points and levels for all post-compulsory programmes and awards including *Higher Still*, SVQs and higher education qualifications (COSHEP et al, 1999). If *Higher Still* embodies a unified system strategy for school- and college-based learning, the Framework embodies a linkages strategy for connecting

Higher Still with all other post-16 learning, including the work-based route.

In the short term, at least, the establishment of the Scottish Parliament in 1999 may make less difference to the direction of post-16 policy in Scotland than the establishment of the Assembly in Wales. The main lines of Scottish policy were already well-established. After numerous controversies and a threatened teacher boycott which was only averted at the last minute, the implementation of *Higher Still* was scheduled to begin less than two months after the Parliament and its Executive assumed power. The policy-making initiative continues to rest with the Inspectorate and the Executive, which is staffed largely by officials from the former Scottish Office. *Higher Still* is increasingly under the control of the Scottish Qualifications Authority (SQA), the unified body created in 1997 from the merger of the main academic and vocational qualifications awarding bodies. The main foci of policy attention for the first few months of the Parliament were school education and social exclusion among school leavers and adults, not unification. However, in the longer term the constitutional changes may slow the pace of unification. In the first place, central government in Scotland no longer needs to establish its legitimacy by asserting its Scottishness and pursuing policy differences for their own sake. Second, different ministers and departments of the Scottish Executive are responsible for school and post-school education respectively. This partially reverses the unification achieved in 1996 when education and training were brought together under the Scottish Office Education and Industry Department (SOEID). *Higher Still* straddles the two departments, and this may inhibit the development of the strategic view necessary to pursue further unification, especially if the Enterprise and Lifelong Learning Department (responsible for post-school education) is distracted by its enterprise function. Third, as the new democracy develops, the legitimacy of the Inspectorate's leadership is increasingly being challenged; policy making may become less consensual and more 'political'. The consequences for unification are hard to predict but there are signs of a renewed educational conservatism infused by academic values and a preoccupation with standards.

Comparing developments in England, Wales and Scotland

At the beginning of the current reform phase Scotland was a linked system whereas England and Wales were tracked systems on many dimensions. Scotland was the most open system, and England the least, although by comparison with most European countries all three had relatively open systems. There were differences in the institutional and policy context in each country, including the size and centralisation of the systems and their educational policy cultures. Moreover, by early 1998, when this project ended, the three countries were at different stages of the policy process. England and Wales were still debating the choice of policy strategy, while Scotland was developing and implementing a strategy that had already been determined.

Nevertheless, all three countries have been moving away from tracking towards a linked or unified system. In this respect they resemble most other countries in Europe. Only Germany has continued to pursue a track-based strategy and it would appear that such a strategy can be viable only in a country with a strong system of work-based training. England and Wales are pursuing linkages strategies whereas Scotland is pursuing a unified system strategy, subject to the qualifications noted above. The Scottish model of unification is the most open of the three, and the English model the least. The more open models adopted in Scotland and Wales reflect the fact that qualifications policy has not differentiated between 16-19-year-olds and 19-plus-year-olds to the same extent as in England. In England policy for 16-19 qualifications remains dominated by the gold standard of A levels and the reluctance of successive governments to endorse any policy that might appear to undermine it.

In terms of their positions on the tracked-unified system continuum, the three countries' strategies broadly reflect the range across European countries. The main difference we have noted so far is the greater openness of the British strategies. When we look at the different dimensions of unification the shared 'Britishness' of the three systems and their policy strategies becomes more apparent. First, British strategies for unification are certification-led. Second, the unification of governance and regulation (including funding) has progressed further in the three British systems than in almost any other European country. Third, work-based learning is more marginal to the strategies of all three systems than in many European countries; British strategies for unification focus on full-time education and risk marginalising the work-based route. Finally, in all three British systems policy strategies have increasingly responded to pressures and problems internal to the education and training system; these have been created by the system's expansion, by its increased complexity and by the greater interdependence of its component parts and dimensions. External pressures for change, such as the changing needs of workplaces, have been less important influences on policies for unification in Britain than in many other European countries.

The strategies for unification described in this section, together with the institutional contexts and debates, constitute what we call the 'national policy environment' of each country. Drawing on our conceptual framework and our analysis of the national policy environments of England and Scotland, we identified key themes and issues for more detailed study. In the next section we summarise our conclusions on three of these themes and issues.

Key policy issues

The role of regulatory and awarding bodies

The Scottish Examination Board (SEB) and the Scottish Vocational Education Council (SCOTVEC) merged in 1997 to form the SQA. In England the QCA was formed out of a merger of SCAA and NCVQ, and the main academic and vocational awarding bodies were brought together to form three unitary awarding bodies (Spours et al, 1998b). These mergers concerned two key dimensions of the unification process in each country: government and regulation, and certification. We contrasted the mergers in the two national policy environments: that of Scotland, characterised by a unified system strategy and a single body combining awarding and regulatory functions, and that of England, with a linkages strategy and a more complex set of distinctions between regulatory and unitary awarding bodies.

Our study confirmed, first, that England and Scotland remain qualifications-driven systems. The reform of qualifications was one of the main driving forces for national organisational change. Second, the emerging roles of the QCA and SQA reflected the different position and movement of each system on the continuum of tracked, linked and unified systems. In Scotland, the early role of the SQA has been tied to *Higher Still* and the introduction of the Scottish Credit and Qualifications Framework; in other words, it reflects Scotland's movement towards an open unified system, at least for school- and college-based education. In England, the initial emphasis of the QCA has been on creating greater alignment and consistency of standards across different qualifications; it can be seen as taking the English system into an early part of a linkages stage of development.

Third, there are different assumptions, approaches and debates about regulation and awarding functions in the two national policy environments. In England, there is a clear distinction between the role of the regulatory body and that of awarding bodies working within a legally defined nationally agreed framework. There is a professional consensus that there should be more than one awarding body to preserve diversity and choice for schools, colleges and employers. In Scotland, even before the creation of the SQA, there was only one main awarding body for each type of qualification. The distinction between regulatory and awarding functions was imported from England at the same time as SVQs, to maintain comparability with arrangements south of the Border. The SQA inherited a 'public administration' culture in contrast to the culture of 'markets and regulation' of its equivalents south of the Border.

Fourth, initial evidence suggested that bringing together regulatory and awarding bodies provided a strong driving force for the unification of qualifications systems, although this happened in different ways in the two national policy environments. In Scotland the formation of SQA represented a relatively balanced fusion of the academic, paternalist culture of the SEB and the vocational, entrepreneurial culture of SCOTVEC, and it took the Scottish qualifications system in an open and unified direction. In England the formation of QCA was initially seen by some as an unequal marriage between SCAA and NCVQ, with the academic culture of SCAA dominant. This now appears to be an oversimplification; QCA has rapidly evolved to develop a distinct corporate identity of its own. The movement towards a more unified regulatory and awarding system has been a more diffuse process in England, due to the size and complexity of the regulatory body, the QCA, and its relationship with the three major awarding bodies which compete with each other and operate as semi-commercial organisations.

Our analysis raises an important theoretical and policy question: how does the dimension of government and regulation, which is currently the most unified of the system dimensions, at least in England and Wales, interact with other system dimensions? Current evidence suggests that the unification of national bodies can be a driving force for unification along other dimensions, provided that these bodies share the vision of moving towards a unified system and create educational and policy alliances through a gradual and evolving reform process. There are risks that both the QCA and the SQA could develop strongly unified regulatory strategies which conflict with other dimensions of the system, for example, the needs of local institutions.

Core and key skills

The national policy environments place great importance on the development of key skills (in England) or core skills (in Scotland). Indeed, core/key skills are one of the few respects in which the current reforms appear to be responding directly to external demands, especially from industry. Core/key skills also have a potential unifying role: they may comprise a component of the curriculum of all learners; their purposes may relate both to employment and to higher education; and they may prefigure the more process-oriented concepts of learning which could characterise a unified curriculum of the future. However, this unifying role and its practical implications could be very different in the context of a linkages strategy, where core/key skills add a common element to programmes with different content, pedagogy and assessment approaches, than in the context of a unified system when they would form part of an integrated curriculum (Young et al, 1998).

In both England and Scotland approaches to core/key skills tend to reflect a deficit concept of the learner, and the perceived need to remedy the failures of compulsory schooling. This is in contrast to policies elsewhere in Europe, where programmes to promote generic skills are based on analyses of the skill demands of new industries and are exemplified by the German idea of 'work process knowledge' and the Dutch notion of the 'core problems' of different occupational sectors (Kamarainen, 1998). However, the deficit concept of core/key skills may be less influential in Scotland than in England where key skills are largely associated with overcoming poor literacy and numeracy standards and where a narrower approach to competence has underpinned their assessment. This has culminated in Dearing's proposal for a stand-alone key skills qualification, available to all post-16 learners regardless of their course of study, to be launched in September 2000.

The different histories of core/key skills in England and Scotland, and their links with different unifying strategies, have given rise to different formal definitions in the current reforms in the different countries. In Scotland the five core skills of communication, numeracy, information technology, working with others and problem solving have equal status. In England, the first three of these have the title of 'key skills'; these are the skills that will be assessed by the proposed new key skills qualification. The wider key skills (which include 'improving own learning and performance' as well as those used in Scotland) have a lower priority on the grounds that no satisfactory way of assessing them has been developed.

The most important difference between English and Scottish policy is in their different approaches to delivering core/key skills. *Higher Still* 'embeds' core skills by incorporating them into the design of units or courses wherever the subject matter and assessment arrangements make this appropriate. In addition, qualifications taken prior to *Higher Still* are 'audited' for core skills; the *Higher Still* certificate includes a core skills profile based on previous qualifications taken by the student as well as *Higher Still*. Stand-alone core skill units are available, but mainly to fill gaps left by embedding and auditing. In England, the embedding of key skills is less developed because of the existence of a separate key skills qualification; the emphasis is on the three main key skills which are seen as more easily assessable than the wider key skills. Opportunities for attaining the three main key skills are signposted within A levels and GNVQ specifications but how far this is taken remains at the discretion of the delivering institution. This contrast reflects the different unifying strategies: linkages in England and unified system in Scotland. If, as in England, key skills are added to separate tracks in the context of a strategy to preserve the distinctiveness of these tracks, the concept of key skills is one which defines them in terms of process, independent of the content of learning. If they are developed as part of an integrated curriculum it is far easier to operate a concept of core/key skills which stresses the relationship being process and content and the application of generic skills and knowledge in particular contexts.

There are related differences in approaches to the assessment of core/ key skills. The English assessment model for key skills was originally designed in NVQ performance outcomes terms, but now includes an element of independent assessment. Moreover, where key skills are delivered independently of content, the reliability of stand-alone assessment becomes more critical; this partly explains the focus on the three more 'measurable' skills in England, described above.

In neither country are core/key skills compulsory for all post-16 students. However, the embedding approach in Scotland makes it more likely that students will pick up core skills as a matter of course. One consequence of this difference is that English policy makers are looking for ways to encourage the delivery, take-up and completion of the new key skills qualification through incorporating it in criteria for inspection and university entrance and, in the future, through funding mechanisms. There has been less emphasis on extrinsic incentives of this kind in Scotland.

The work-based route

The work-based route, including apprenticeships and YT programmes, is an important feature of post-compulsory provision throughout Great Britain. Nevertheless it has not featured to any significant extent in debates or strategies for unification in either England or Scotland (Howieson et al, 1998b).

Despite their different unifying strategies for full-time provision, the two countries pursue a similar linkages approach to the work-based route. In Scotland, the choice of a linkages rather than unified system approach to the work-based route is partly explained by the fact that work-based qualifications (SVQs) are not fully under Scottish control. Training policy was formulated on a British-wide basis until 1994 and SVQs, like NVQs, continue to be based on occupational standards that are UK-wide. Instead of being included in the unified system of *Higher Still*, SVQs will be linked with *Higher Still*, together with higher education qualifications, in the Scottish Credit and Qualifications Framework. Specified SVQs may count towards an SGA; this represents, however, only a limited form of linkage, since substitution will be restricted to specific SVQs which will count only towards the optional section of the SGA.

The integration of NVQs into a national qualifications framework in England and of SVQs into the Scottish Credit and Qualifications Framework raise similar issues. These arise from their basic characteristics concerning their relationship to national occupational standards and their competence-based nature. To include S/NVQs in either framework will mean resolving a number of difficult issues, including the variation in their size and the lack of a volume measure based on time. Both issues pose major problems for the incorporation of competence-based occupational qualifications into a unitised and credit-based qualifications system.

The policy of developing closer links between the work-based route and full-time provision, and facilitating progression between the two, is being facilitated by the creation of National Training Organisations, which, unlike their predecessor bodies, have an educational as well as a training remit. In all three British systems more unified funding arrangements are being proposed. In Wales the ETAG report proposed a 'unified framework' of national and local bodies "to integrate the planning, commissioning and resourcing for all publicly funded education and training programmes post-16, including work-based training" (ETAG, 1999, p 8). In England, the Learning and Skills Councils (LSCs) proposed in *Learning to Succeed* will end the organisational separation of the work-based route under the TECs, and will lay the basis for the development of common learning plans for each locality which will attempt, among other things, to link full-time and work-based learning.

Modern Apprenticeships and possibly National Traineeships offer the potential for a more linked work-based route model. Some employers may take advantage of the smaller qualification blocks (for example three-unit GNVQs) and key skills qualifications to be introduced in England in order to create broader training programmes. In Scotland some employees are likely to take *Higher Still* units, if not courses, when they attend college. However, Modern Apprenticeships schemes are variable in their content and have produced poorer completion and attainment rates than originally anticipated (Middlemas, 1999). These problems point to the need for further reform of work-based programmes to give a larger role for colleges offering broader vocational qualifications. Such developments could signify a less distinctive work-based route and the emergence of something more like the French model of alternance.

Work-based qualifications are being incorporated in a linked system, alongside full-time qualifications, but there is a reluctance to incorporate them – at least for the time being – in a unified system. In Scotland as well as England there is a widespread desire to retain S/NVQs as distinctive qualifications to safeguard the delivery of occupational competence, to maintain industry ownership and to avoid domination by educational interests. In Scotland it has been argued that SVQs are not strong enough to preserve, within a unified system, the principles that they represent and so should remain outside it. This does leave the question whether strong work-based qualifications and a strong work-based route can be developed in Britain. It is clear that unification, whether by means of a linkages or a unified system strategy, will not in itself solve the problems of the work-based route. Underlying problems also need to be addressed, such as employer voluntarism and low levels of investment in training; low skill demands; the lack of some of the necessary infrastructure and supports; and the nature of the youth labour market in Britain (Evans et al, 1998).

Unification as a policy process

Cross-national trends

Our European comparisons pointed to a tendency for countries to adopt strategies which involved moving either from tracked to linked systems or from linked to unified systems (Young and Raffe, 1998; Lasonen and Raffe, 1998). Our empirical base is too limited for us to say if this is a universal trend, and if so whether it will continue until all countries have developed unified systems. At this stage we can draw only two conclusions with confidence; that many countries are moving towards unification; and that, as post-compulsory education systems expand, new divisions are emerging. The renewed interest in overcoming exclusion can be seen as an attempt to overcome these new divisions.

One reason why it is difficult to identify a general trend is that unification has typically proceeded over a number of steps and stages whose long-term outcomes are uncertain. Many countries' unification strategies are explicitly incremental. In Scotland *Higher Still* was presented as a step in an evolutionary process of reform, rationalising existing provision and consolidating earlier reforms (Scottish Office, 1994). In Wales proposals for a Welsh Baccalaureate made slow progress initially because they were expressed in terms of a direct replacement of existing qualifications and as a set of principles which would have been difficult to implement through an incremental approach (Raffe et al, 1998c). The ETAG report and early indications from the Assembly suggest that an evolutionary approach is more likely to be adopted. In England, the *Learning For the Future Project* argued that the transition from a tracked to a unified system would have to be through one or more transitional 'framework' stages, similar to the model of a linked system described above (Richardson et al, 1995). The reform proposals following the *Qualifying for Success* consultation also envisage reforms over several stages, although the steps are small and there is no explicit government recognition that a unified system is even a long-term goal (Hodgson and Spours, 1999).

An incremental approach to unification carries a risk of strategy drift. If it proceeds through a relatively consensual process of policy change, it may lose sight of any radical vision that may have inspired it in the first place and thus fail to challenge the assumptions and practices of the existing system. The more evolutionary, consensual and consultative process in Scotland, compared with England, has had its advantages but has underplayed the changes involved and has made fewer attempts to confront conservative 'academic' values in Scottish education. It has focused on the internal problems of the education system more than on the changing needs of society and the economy. Moreover, in an open voluntaristic system an incremental approach makes it even harder to guarantee the outcomes of policies; these depend on the decisions of providers and the choices of individual students and end-users of qualifications such as higher education institutions and employers.

An incremental approach also raises the question of whether the values, goals and 'vision' underlying unification need to be fully spelt out from the start, or whether, like the system itself, they should develop incrementally over the stages of the reform.

Introducing a unified system

Two of us (Raffe and Howieson, 1998) applied our conceptual framework to analyse the policy process of developing a unified system in Scotland. We hypothesised that policy making for a unified system may need to be a more linear and top-down process than other types of policy making. It applies a consistent set of principles and criteria to the whole system, and therefore requires more detailed prior specification of objectives, and greater central coordination of the change process, than reforms which accept greater variation across different parts of the system. The experience of *Higher Still* confirmed this hypothesis: it was a centrally led, managed process, and the consultations, although genuine, were exercises in a form of 'democratic centralism' in which those who lacked the ability of centrally-based policy makers to take a view of the whole system found it hard to play a constructive role. As the chapters by Ball, Eraut and their colleagues demonstrate, the perspective of the individual institution or learner can be very different from that of the central policy maker. Only as *Higher Still* approached the implementation stage did participants at the local and institutional level start to play a major role.

However, the linear, top-down character of the policy process partly arose from the fact that the reform was certification led. A unifying policy that involved other dimensions of unification, such as methods of teaching and learning, might be able to proceed in a less linear and more bottom-up fashion.

McPherson and Raab (1988) identified a decline in value-consensus among members of the Scottish education policy community, and suggested that policy makers increasingly responded to this by leaving the values underlying policy implicit. This was true of *Higher Still*, which was initially presented not as the expression of a vision of post-compulsory education in the future, but as a technical solution to problems of the current system. It might appear to be unnecessary to make explicit statements of the values and priorities of an open unified system, since such a system allows students, providers and end-users scope for determining their own priorities. Conversely, it may be particularly difficult to reach agreement on the design principles which should underlie such a system, since the system imposes a common set of criteria on a wide range of issues and stakeholders, with much less scope for variation or exemption than a linkages approach. It is therefore difficult to achieve consensus on the details of a unified system, and this helps to explain the Scottish Office's low-key, non-visionary presentation of *Higher Still*. In addition, it did not want to frighten a teaching profession already suffering from 'innovation fatigue' and complaints about morale and workload; furthermore, it did not want to draw attention to the different strategies followed north and south of the border. Some commentators have argued that the lack of an explicit vision obstructed the progress of *Higher Still*.

Unifying through linkages

England presents a somewhat different situation with respect to the policy process of unifying academic and vocational learning. The 'policy community' is more diverse and fragmented; the system is far larger and more complex; the system from which current reforms must evolve is less flexible and more divided; policy for post-compulsory education and training has been subject to more explicit forms of political intervention than in Scotland; and as a corollary to the former points, policy has evolved in the context of more radical alternatives proposed by academics and other sections of the professional education community. The policy process has been less consensual and more contentious and has frequently polarised around the future of A levels, and to a lesser extent around support for or opposition to the NVQ system. A unified system has been a more explicit part of the debates, as have a variety of attempts to spell out the steps and stages that might be needed to get there (Richardson et al, 1995; Spours and Young, 1996). During the early 1990s two versions of a unified system emerged, which correspond to our distinction between grouped and open models. One emphasised the development of unified Baccalaureate-type awards (Finegold et al, 1990; Jenkins et al, 1997); the other focused on the development of a flexible, unitised and unified qualifications framework (AfC et al, 1994; JACG, 1997).

There are, however, at least two parallels with policy developments in Scotland. Partly in response to the cautious approach adopted by the New Labour government, the more radical variants of a unified system that were widely discussed in the early 1990s have at best been relegated to a back seat. Second, whereas reform proposals in the early 1990s were presented as elements in an explicit attempt to modernise the British economy and the major institutions of British society, more recent proposals have been pragmatic responses to internal problems of the system such as the lack of alignment between existing qualifications and the need for comparability of standards. This trend towards focusing on the internal problems of the system could be seen either as a loss of vision or as a consequence of the acceptance of unifying ideas by the Conservative administration in its later years and by the Labour government elected in 1997.

In England the new Labour government began by attempting to construct a new consensus around cautious, incremental steps towards a more linked qualification system. However, *Learning to Succeed* may indicate a move to a more unified approach, at least on our dimension of government and regulation. Conversely we have seen growing tensions in the Scottish consensus on moving towards a unified system. Value choices which could previously be left implicit are coming out into the open; conflicts are emerging over the precise form which a unified system should take, and how it should arbitrate between different vested interests. Wales is closer to the English position, but with the important differences of a more homogeneous and closely knit policy community and less opposition to unification from vested interests.

Conclusions

In this concluding section we briefly consider the future of unification and the implications for convergence or divergence within the UK. We reassess our conceptual framework, and explore the implications of current developments for the learning society.

Our comparative studies suggest that as post-compulsory education and training becomes more complex policy makers find an increasing need for a 'system' perspective, but not necessarily one based on the idea of a unified system. The trend away from tracking appears nearly universal, although this may be expressed in different ways: in moves towards a fully unified system, in linkages and various forms of 'mixing' of studies, or in the integration of academic and vocational learning within tracks rather than across tracks. The position of work-based provision within more unified systems, and the most effective strategy for combating social exclusion, remain unresolved issues (Young and Volanen, 1998).

The focus of our research was primarily on contrasting developments in England and Wales with those in Scotland. In England the future of unification remains uncertain. Qualification reforms remain constrained by a reluctance to consider any fundamental reform of A levels. The recommendations following *Qualifying for Success* signal a desire to keep the tracks rather than to transform them, but to link them more closely in order to promote the consistency of qualifications and greater flexibility. The *Learning to succeed* proposals, on the other hand, may signal a continuing process of unification of government funding. Wales, from a position where it was in important respects part of the same system as England, is using its increased autonomy to develop a more open and more strongly linked system. Scotland is more clearly committed to an open version of a unified system, but its lack of an explicit vision may lay it open to strategy drift, and the separation of school from post-school education in the new administration may make it even harder to regain the original concept of unification that some associated with *Higher Still.*

No simple generalisation about convergence or divergence is possible because this depends on the dimensions of unification that are examined. There is potential for the Scottish and English systems to diverge, but in a wider European comparison both systems appear likely to retain recognisably 'British' features, such as their openness in the sense described above.

We now reassess our conceptual framework in the light of our research. Our distinction between different types of systems and different unifying strategies proved useful in interpreting the broad policy strategies of England and Scotland and many of the issues that they raised. Our distinction among the dimensions of unification led us to analyse unification as an incremental process which can take place unevenly across different dimensions. The distinction between open and grouped systems helped us to contrast different models of unification and to examine some of the distinctive implications of an open system. We tested our framework on a case study of Wales, where it cast some light on current debates and the potential for divergence from England.

At the same time our research suggests a number of directions in which our conceptual framework needs to be developed. First, the dimension of 'government and regulation' embraces several sub-dimensions which need to be analytically separated. The merging of government departments formed an important part of the context of our research. With respect to regulation, we have demonstrated its importance as a factor driving unification. Funding is a powerful instrument of government control, and increasingly of unification, which merits further study.

Second, we have argued for an incremental model of change. There is a need to conceptualise different models of incremental change and how changes on one dimension might influence those on others.

Third, there is a need to go beyond unification as a rejection of academic/vocational divisions and to explore new possibilities for relating academic and vocational learning.

Fourth, we have become aware of the importance of distinguishing between types of unified system, but our concept of an open system and related notions such as flexibility require elaboration.

Fifth, elsewhere we have set our conceptual framework within the context of social and economic changes (Raffe et al, 1998b; Lasonen and Raffe, 1998), but these changes have remained part of the context. That is, the conceptual framework has not focused on the relationships between systems of post-compulsory education and training and the social and economic context within which they are located. There is a need for a complementary conceptual framework for analysing the changing relationships between post-compulsory education and social and economic changes.

This brings us to our final theme. Unifying academic and vocational learning is not an end in itself but arises as part of a broader process of social change and of policies with the long-term goal of achieving a learning society (Young et al, 1997; Young and Volanen, 1998; Young, 1998). The developments we have described in England, Wales and Scotland have a number of positive implications for the creation of a learning society. To the extent that they support wider participation, more common standards, balanced programmes of study and improved achievement in initial education and training, these unifying developments may produce more successful learners in a better position to continue learning throughout adult life. They build on the relative flexibility and openness of the British systems, which already provide some of the potential foundations for a learning society; in Wales and Scotland, at least, they go some way towards the development of a single more inclusive system for all post-16 learners, adults as well as 16–19-year-olds. They are starting to break down many of the obstacles to a learning society that we summarised at the beginning of this chapter.

Nevertheless, there is much further to go. The emerging flexible frameworks for lifelong learning remain far from seamless, especially in England. Institutional barriers, funding barriers and age barriers persist. No worthwhile vision of the learning society can ignore the enormous potential for learning provided by the workplace, especially when this is integrated with learning in other settings (Coffield, 1998); yet even certified work-based learning remains marginal within the current unifying policies, let alone the less formal kinds of learning at work described by Michael Eraut and his colleagues in Chapter Seven. The pressure for unification has largely been top-down, whether driven by a centrally defined model of a unified system as in Scotland, or by the quest for rationalisation and consistent standards as in England; we have yet to see how these developments will be reflected in the responses of institutions and of individuals. It also remains to be seen how far unification can challenge the individualised and marketised model of learning analysed by Ball, Maguire and Macrae in Chapter One. Above all, the persistence of academic/vocational divisions reflects assumptions about the limited capacity to learn of those for whom vocational programmes are thought appropriate; if anything, these assumptions are gaining rather than losing currency. If a learning society is to be more than a form of rhetoric, it must mean a society permeated by learning relationships, both at work and in the community, and efforts to promote it must confront such assumptions. Unification is not primarily a means to a more efficient system, but a change in purpose, direction and the distribution of resources; in other words it is part of creating a new kind of society based on different assumptions about the potential of human beings.

Notes

[1] This chapter is a product of the Unified Learning Project, funded by the Economic and Social Research Council (L123251039) as part of its research programme on *The Learning Society*.

[2] The order of the authors' names is rotated across the different publications of the Unified Learning Project, to reflect their equal contributions.

[3] The Swedish model offers two academic and 14 vocational programmes; each has a modular structure and many modules are, in principle, interchangeable between programmes. See Raffe et al (1998a).

References

AfC (Association for Colleges), The Girl's School Association, The Headmasters' Conference, The Secondary Heads Association, The Sixth Form Colleges Association, The Society for Headmasters and Headmistresses in Independent Schools (1994) *Post-compulsory Education and Training: A Joint Statement*, London: AfC.

CBI (Confederation of British Industry) (1998) *Qualified to compete: Creating a world-class qualifications framework. Human Resources Brief*, London: CBI.

Coffield, F. (ed) (1998) *Learning at work*, Bristol: The Policy Press.

Coffield, F. (1999) 'Lifelong learning as social control', *British Educational Research Journal*, vol 25, no 4, pp 479-99.

COSHEP, SOEID, QAA, SACCA and SQA (1999) *Adding value to learning: The Scottish Credit and Qualifications Framework*, Glasgow: SQA.

David, J and Jenkins, G. (1996) *The Welsh Baccalaureate Cymru*, Cardiff: Institute of Welsh Affairs.

Dearing, Sir Ron (1996) *Review of Qualifications for 16-19 Year Olds*, Hayes: SCAA Publications.

DfEE (Department for Education and Employment) (1997) *Qualifying for Success: A consultative paper on the future of post-16 qualifications*, Sudbury: DfEE.

DfEE (1998) *The Learning Age*, Cm 3790, London: The Stationery Office.

DfEE (1999) *Learning to Succeed*, London: The Stationery Office.

ETAG (Education and Training Action Group for Wales) (1999) *An education and training action plan for Wales*, Cardiff: ETAG.

Evans, K., Hodkinson, P., Keep, E., Maguire, M., Raffe, D., Rainbird, H., Senker, P. and Unwin, L. (1998) *Working to Learn: A work-based route for young people,* Issues in People Management No 18, London: Institute of Personnel and Development.

Finegold, D., Keep, E., Miliband, D., Raffe, D., Spours, K. and Young, M. (1990) *A British 'Baccalauréat'?*, London: Institute for Public Policy Research.

Hodgson, A. and Spours, K. (1999) *New Labour's new educational policy agenda: Policies and issues for education and training from 14+*, London: Kogan Page.

Hodgson, A., Spours, K. and Young, M. (1998) 'Broader and broader still', *Times Educational Supplement*, 16 May.

Howieson, C., Raffe, D., Spours, K. and Young, M. (1997) 'Unifying academic and vocational learning: the state of the debate in England and Scotland', *Journal of Education and Work*, vol 10, no 1, pp 5-35 (ULP Working Paper 1).

Howieson, C., Raffe, D., Spours, K. and Young, M. (1998a) 'Group awards and overarching certification and the unification of academic and vocational learning', *Unified Learning Project* Working Paper 6, CES (University of Edinburgh) and PSEC (Institute of Education, University of London).

Howieson, C., Raffe, D., Spours, K. and Young, M. (1998b) 'Unifying academic and vocational learning: the position of the work-based route', *Unified Learning Project* Working Paper 8, CES (University of Edinburgh) and PSEC (Institute of Education, University of London).

IWA (Institute of Welsh Affairs) (1999) *The Welsh Bac: From Wales to the world*, Cardiff: IWA.

JACG (Joint Associations Curriculum Group) (1997) *The next steps towards a new curriculum framework post 16*, Wigan: JACG.

Jenkins, C., David, J., Osmond, J. and Pierce, J. (1997) *The Welsh Bac: Educating Wales in the next century*, Cardiff: IWA.

Kamarainen, P. (1998) *Interim Report on the CEDEFOP projects 'Key Skills' and 'Coaching Networks'*, Thessaloniki: CEDEFOP.

Lasonen, J. (ed) (1996) *Reforming upper secondary education in Europe*, Finland: Institute for Educational Research, University of Jyväskylä.

Lasonen, J. and Raffe, D. (1998) 'Comparisons of post-16 education strategies to promote parity of esteem between vocational and general education in Europe', Paper presented at the CEDEFOP/DIPF Conference on *Comparative Vocational Education and Training Research in Europe*, Bonn.

Lasonen, J. and Young, M. (eds) (1998) *Strategies for achieving parity of esteem in European upper secondary education*, Finland: Institute for Educational Research, University of Jyväskylä.

McPherson, A. and Raab, C. (1988) *Governing education: A sociology of policy*, Edinburgh: Edinburgh University Press.

Middlemas, J. (1999) 'Modern apprenticeships: achievements so far', *Labour Market Trends*, September, pp 487-92.

NCE (National Commission on Education) (1993) *Learning to succeed*, London: Heinemann.

Raffe, D. and Howieson, C. (1998) 'The Higher Still policy process', *Scottish Affairs*, no 24, pp 58-76 (ULP Working Paper 9).

Raffe, D., Arnman, G. and Bergdahl, P. (1998a) 'The strategy of a unified system: Scotland and Sweden', in J. Lasonen and M. Young (eds) *Strategies for achieving parity of esteem in European upper secondary education*, Finland: Institute for Educational Research, University of Jyväskylä.

Raffe, D., Brannen, K., Croxford, L. and Martin, C. (1999a) 'Comparing England, Scotland, Wales and Northern Ireland: the case for "home internationals" in comparative research', *Comparative Education*, vol 35, no 1, pp 9-25.

Raffe, D., Howieson, C., Spours, K. and Young, M. (1998b) 'The unification of post-compulsory education: towards a conceptual framework', *British Journal of Educational Studies*, vol 46, no 2, pp 169-87 (ULP Working Paper 2).

Raffe, D., Howieson, C., Spours, K. and Young, M. (1999b) 'Issues in a "home international" comparison of policy strategies: the experience of the Unified Learning Project', in F.J. Coffield (ed) *Why's the beer always stronger up North? Studies of lifelong learning in Europe*, Bristol: The Policy Press.

Raffe, D., Spours, K., Young, M. and Howieson, C. (1998c) 'Unifying academic and vocational learning: current policy developments in Wales', *Unified Learning Project Working Paper 10*, CES (University of Edinburgh) and PSEC (Institute of Education, University of London).

Richardson, W., Spours, K., Woolhouse, J. and Young, M. (1995) *Learning for the future: Interim report*, CES (University of Warwick) and PSEC (Institute of Education, University of London).

SCE (Scottish Commission on Education) (1996) *Learning to succeed in Scotland*, Edinburgh: Church of Scotland.

SED (Scottish Education Department) (1979) *16-18s in Scotland: The first two years of post-compulsory education*, Edinburgh: SED.

SED (1983) *16-18s in Scotland: An action plan*, Edinburgh: SED.

Scottish Office (1994) *Higher Still: Opportunity for all*, Edinburgh: HMSO.

Smithers, A. (1998) 'View from here', *Independent*, 9 April.

SOED (Scottish Office Education Department) (1992) *Upper secondary education in Scotland*, The Howie Report, Edinburgh: HMSO.

Spours, K. and Young, M. (1996) 'Dearing and beyond: steps and stages to a unified 14-19 qualifications system?', *British Journal of Education and Work*, vol 9, no 3, pp 5-18.

Spours, K., Young, M., Howieson, C. and Raffe, D. (1998b) 'Regulation, awarding bodies and the process of unification in England and Scotland', *Unified Learning Project* Working Paper 4, CES (University of Edinburgh) and PSEC (Institute of Education, University of London).

Spours, K., Young, M., Lazar, A. and Levrat, R. (1998a) 'Linkage approaches to post-16 education reform: the case of the English and French systems', in J. Lasonen and M. Young (eds) *Parity of esteem in European upper secondary education: Post-16 strategies*, Finland: Institute for Educational Research, University of Jyväskylä.

Welsh Office (1998) *Learning is for everyone*, Cm 3924, London: The Stationery Office.

Young, M. (1998) *The curriculum of the future*, London: Falmer Press.

Young, M. and Raffe, D. (1998) 'The four strategies for promoting parity of esteem', in J. Lasonen and M. Young (eds) *Parity of esteem in European upper secondary education: Post-16 strategies*, Finland: Institute for Educational Research, University of Jyväskylä.

Young, M. and Volanen, M.V. (1998) 'Mapping the national strategies: a commentary', in J. Lasonen and M. Young (eds) *Parity of esteem in European upper secondary education: Post-16 strategies*, Finland: Institute for Educational Research, University of Jyväskylä.

Young, M., Howieson, C., Raffe, D. and Spours, K. (1997) 'Unifying academic and vocational learning and the idea of a learning society', *Journal of Education Policy*, vol 12, no 6, pp 527-37 (ULP Working Paper 3).

Young, M., Howieson, C., Raffe, D. and Spours, K. (1998) 'Core and key skills as a unifying strategy: Anglo-Scottish comparisons', *Unified Learning Project* Working Paper 5, CES (University of Edinburgh) and PSEC (Institute of Education, University of London).

THREE

Skill development in higher education and employment

Elisabeth Dunne, Neville Bennett and Clive Carré

Introduction

Higher education has changed radically over the last decade, and is still in the process of change. Some argue that it is in a state of crisis – in terms of funding, quality, the management of academic time and priorities, the conception and management of teaching and learning, and, fundamentally, in terms of purposes. Analysts, such as Barnett (1994) and Scott (1997), conceive the latter as a crisis of knowledge, initiated by the increased role of the state and employers in the determination of the higher education curriculum, and exemplified by the increasing emphasis on so-called transferable skills. The latest major vision statement on higher education supports this shift in purpose, by portraying the new economic order as placing an increasing premium on what it calls 'key' skills – seen as necessary outcomes of all higher education programmes (Dearing Report, 1997).

The last decade has seen a shattering of long-held assumptions about university and academic autonomy, as public and political interest in quality, standards and accountability has intensified efforts for reform. These reforms, underpinned by the ideological and philosophical approach of a conservative government and now being pursued by the present government, have had a major impact on higher education institutions. "The search for economy, efficiency and value for money assumes a degree of management totally foreign to the traditional democratic and collegiate culture of the universities" (Green, 1994).

Nevertheless, the Committee of Vice Chancellors and Principals (CVCP) has advocated the inclusion of personal or key skill acquisition in higher education, as illustrated by their joint declaration of intent with the Confederation of British Industry (CBI) and the Council for Industry and Higher Education (CIHE) (1996). In this declaration it was asserted (although it is not clear what evidence has been used to underpin these statements) that most British people, most educators, and most students now believe that it is one of higher education's purposes to prepare students well for working life. A joint national effort was also agreed by the three parties, to ensure that students in higher education develop attributes thought useful for success in employment and future life, that is, the "general personal and intellectual capacities that go beyond those traditionally made explicit within an academic or vocational discipline" (CVCP, CBI, CIHE, 1996).

As outlined by Drummond et al (1997), many universities have accepted the implications of the political and economic agenda, at least at the level of policy, the majority having institutional policies and central directives which assert their commitment to skills development. Yet this acceptance, indeed advocacy, of the role of the state and employers in the determination of higher education curriculum, remains antithetical to some. Barnett (1994), for example, decries the shift to a situation in which society is framing the character of higher education, arguing that the state now identifies the forms of knowing and development that it sees as worthwhile, a situation in which academics become state servants, fulfilling the state's agenda. He further claims that transferable skills are a means of disenfranchising discipline-based academics of their expertise. A similar scepticism, although for different reasons, is apparent among university tutors. Many believe it is not part of their role to provide skills for employment; they have little sympathy for the newly emerging definitions of quality in higher education, nor for the current climate of accountability in British universities (Gubbay, 1994).

A review of both national and international literature suggests that a consensus has emerged with regard to diagnosing the needs of the future economy and the prognosis of the skills base necessary to confront it. The central role of higher education in developing that skills base seems equally clear (see Mayer, 1992; Otala, 1993; Stasz et al, 1996). Unfortunately, in achieving this agreement, prescription seems to have outrun conceptualisation. Little or no thought has been given to the theoretical or empirical base of the skills deemed necessary or to underlying implicit assumptions about transfer.

The study

It was against this backdrop that the study reported here was undertaken. The overall aim of gaining enhanced understandings of skill acquisition in higher education and employment in order to inform, and subsequently to improve, provision, was completed in two stages. The first stage was designed to map the field by providing a clarification of contemporary policies, practices, priorities, conceptions and expectations within both higher education and employment settings. The second stage was to ascertain and evaluate employer-led skills initiatives within the context of higher education.

The first stage required information from four different sources – teachers in higher education, their students, employers and early-career graduates.

- With regard to university teachers, key questions concerned their knowledge and understanding of skills; how they conceived skill development and its place in the curriculum of higher education; and how they planned, delivered and assessed skills. Further areas were explored, such as if, and how, the planning and teaching of skills were differentiated from disciplinary knowledge; and what constraints, if any, impeded their teaching of skills.
- The extent to which the teaching of skills is effective – or is perceived as effective – depends, in part, on the attitudes and motivation of the student body. It was therefore important that data be acquired from students on their understandings of skills, the importance afforded to them, their perceptions of the quality of skills teaching, and of their own learning in this context.
- Employers have led the push for the inclusion of key skills within the higher education curriculum but there is remarkably little information about policies and practices designed to sustain or enhance these skills in employment settings. It was therefore important to ascertain the perceptions of employers on the role of skills in recruitment processes, policies on training and continuing skill development, and the means by which graduates are socialised or enculturated into particular organisational structures and settings.
- Employees' perspectives may, however, differ considerably from those of their employers. In order to ascertain employees' perspectives, the study focused on the first two years of graduate employment. The questions of central concern here included the opportunities and contexts provided for the use of existing skills, the type and usefulness

of any training provided for their development, and the value and perceived transferability of the knowledge and skills acquired while at university.

The data for the second stage of the study, on employer-led initiatives in higher education settings, were acquired from evaluations of two very different initiatives:
• the Team Development programme funded by BP;
• the Shell Technology Enterprise Programme.

Conceptualisation

Given evident confusion about the skills required of graduates, the first necessary task was to review the current terminology and conceptualisation of skills. The research project was set up in terms of 'core skills'. However, it became clear that this term was but one of several related terms, such as transferable, personal, common or key skills; or personal, core or generic competences; or personal attributes. Each of these terms was used to label sets, or lists, of skills deemed important by employers and government. Such skill labels seemed prone to rapid, and unpredictable, change. The lists contained different numbers and combinations of skills, although there was some agreement about the importance of communication, numeracy, teamwork, technology and problem solving. What the lists also have in common is that they are theoretically and empirically threadbare, and have rarely, if ever, contained the perceptions of those who are expected to deliver these skills in higher education.

This failure to involve university teachers has engendered further confusion not least because, for them, the term 'core skills' typically connotes those skills that are central to their discipline. These are distinct from personal transferable skills, which tend to be defined as cross-disciplinary and generic, such as effective note taking and organising study time. The term 'core skills' thus has contested meanings. Consequently we have chosen, in the interests of clarity and consistency of reporting, to use the word 'core' to refer to disciplinary skills. For the purpose of the present study, the term 'generic' is used to represent those skills which can support study in any discipline, and which can potentially be transferred to a range of contexts in higher education or the workplace.

There remains the problematic assumption that generic skills transfer easily from one context to another. Our analysis of the research on transfer suggests that this assumption is not tenable. The evidence indicates that transfer is unlikely to occur unless intentionally taught for, and that teaching for transfer requires high levels of pedagogical skill (see, for example, Blagg et al, 1993).

The analyses outlined above underpinned the development of two models necessary to the achievement of our research aims and intentions – one to identify patterns of skill provision, and the other to describe generic skills. A difficulty in the description of generic skill acquisition lay in the variety of contexts for provision and in the complexity of overlap between disciplinary learning and generic skills. A model was therefore developed in order to clarify analysis of skill provision, in terms of knowledge and skill outcomes and teaching practices. It distinguishes five areas of course provision: disciplinary content, disciplinary skills, workplace awareness, workplace experience and generic skills, as shown in Figure 1.

Figure 1: A model of course provision

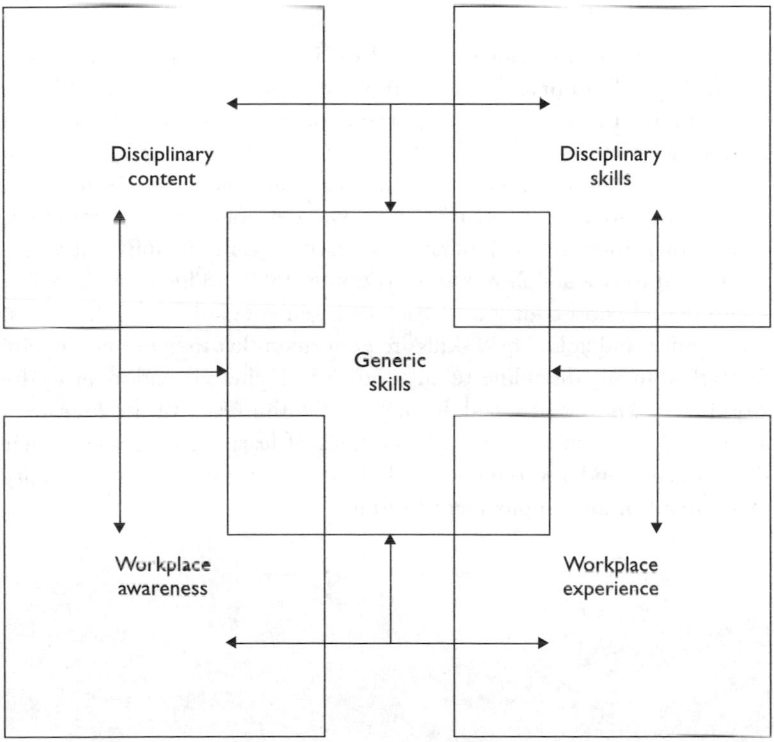

In this model, substantive and syntactic knowledge bases are portrayed as interdependent, in line with epistemological, psychological and curriculum analyses (Schwab, 1964; Anderson, 1983; Fenstermacher, 1996). The relationship between core and generic skills is more complex, however. In some disciplines, generic skills are taught as core skills, for example communication and presentation skills in departments of drama and law, whereas in others these same skills are taught as generic, often in separate 'bolt-on' courses. The central element of the model (generic skills) is thus shown intruding into the other four elements. Disciplinary knowledge and skills, and generic skills, can be acquired through work experience, either through direct placement in the workplace or through some kind of simulation. The development of workplace awareness and the use of work experience are represented by the bottom elements of the model. The connections between these elements indicate potential links, given different course purposes and intentions. There is no assumption about directionality, so disciplinary knowledge can, for example, be acquired in the institution for subsequent use in the workplace, or vice versa.

The validity of the model is based on its isomorphism with current psychological theories of learning, contemporary scholarship in epistemology, the agendas of employers and government, and modes of course provision in higher education. The utility of the model rests on its ability to identify patterns of course provision, considered later.

A second model – of generic skills – was developed from the findings of an earlier study, in which of all the departments in one university were scrutinised for their skill provision (Dunne, 1995). This is presented in Figure 2 and consists of four broad management skills – of self, others, information and task. These skills are generic in that they can potentially be applied to any discipline, to any course in higher education, or to the workplace. The set of sub-skills included within each of the four areas are intended to serve as a set of examples of learning outcomes, rather than as a rigid and unvarying set of skills to be achieved in each university department or any employment setting.

Figure 2: A framework for the development of generic skills

Management of self

- Manage time effectively
- Set objectives, priorities and standards
- Take responsibility for own learning
- Listen actively and with purpose
- Use a range of academic skills (analysis, synthesis, argument etc)
- Develop and adapt learning strategies
- Show intellectual flexibility
- Use learning in new or different situations
- Plan/work towards long-term aims and goals
- Purposefully reflect on own learning
- Clarify with criticism constructively
- Cope with stress

Management of information

- Use appropriate sources of information (library, retrieval systems, people etc)
- Use appropriate technology, including IT
- Use appropriate media
- Handle large amounts of information/data effectively
- Use appropriate language and form in a range of activities
- Interpret a variety of information forms
- Present information/ideas competently (orally, in written form, visually)
- Respond to different purposes/contexts/audiences
- Use information critically
- Use information in innovative and creative ways

Management of others

- Carry out agreed tasks
- Respect the views and values of others
- Work productively in a cooperative context
- Adapt to the needs of the group
- Defend/justify views or actions
- Take initiative and lead others
- Delegate and stand back
- Negotiate
- Offer constructive criticism
- Take the role of chairperson
- Learn in a collaborative context
- Assist/support others in learning

Management of task

- Identify key features
- Conceptualise issues
- Set and maintain priorities
- Identify strategic options
- Plan/implement a course of action
- Organise sub-tasks
- Use and develop appropriate strategies
- Assess outcomes

Findings

The findings of the study are now considered briefly prior to a discussion of their implications. Full details are presented in Bennett et al (2000).

Teachers' conceptions and practices

We know little about the nature of the beliefs and conceptions of teachers in higher education since previous studies have been few and theoretically unsophisticated. Conceptions have typically been categorised into a crude teacher-centred versus student-centred dichotomy, and the usual conclusions drawn are that teachers have limited conceptions of both teaching and learning, and that their conceptions are very difficult to change (cf Biggs, 1996; Trigwell and Prosser, 1996).

Given our over-arching aim of providing findings relevant to changing or improving the teaching of generic skills, a sample of teachers who deliberately included these skills in their teaching was selected. They came from 16 departments, including a range of vocational and non-vocational disciplines, in four universities. Two of these universities were 'pre-1992' (and more traditionally academic and research-led); two were 'post-1992' and were to some extent more vocationally oriented.

Since all these teachers were recommended by their respective institutions for their good practice in skill development, it might therefore have been supposed that they would be conversant with the contemporary debate on skills. From interviews, however, this appeared not to be the case. Most, from whichever institution, were unclear about the definitions of, and assumptions underpinning, generic skills. They were also unfamiliar with the notion of transfer of learning. It was apparent that the majority was unaccustomed to articulating or examining their beliefs about teaching and learning. Beliefs were largely implicit, such that many found it extremely difficult to discuss either how students learn or the purposes of higher education.

In general, their stated beliefs were not good predictors of their promotion of generic skills in practice. However, where skill teaching is explicit, where there is little disciplinary content because of a focus on processes, where a course is named, for example, 'transferable skills', and where such skills are assessed, teachers are more likely to support a utilitarian approach to higher education, and to be aware of employer requirements of graduates. Generally, commitments to particular teaching approaches are associated with different expertise or motivations, which in turn can be mediated by such contextual influences as modularisation, departmental policies or large group sizes. Hence practices may, but do not always, provide evidence of beliefs about higher education.

In the earlier study by Dunne (1995), it was found that staff providing skills-based courses in a traditional university often felt isolated, unsupported, and criticised for attending to teaching rather than to research. Similar comments were made in this study, together with statements highlighting that there is no extrinsic reward for working at teaching: "I suspect my colleagues would say there is very little recognition for teaching. You don't get chairs for being innovative in the curriculum or for producing really successful programmes, but that is another big agenda". This pressure seemed to be as great in at least one of the 'new' universities as in the 'old'. Developing skills-based courses was also considered time-consuming, demanding greater attention to the planning of outcomes and processes of learning than more traditional modules.

Patterns of course provision

The practices of the sample teachers were ascertained by analysis of the course planning documentation, interviews about teaching intentions, approaches, tasks, and assessment procedures, together with several observations of the teaching of the selected courses. These data were analysed with regard to the model of course provision described in Figure 1, the outcome of which was a typology comprising six patterns, shown diagrammatically in Figure 3.

Pattern 1: skills provision is within the distinctive substantive and syntactic knowledge of the discipline, with discipline-based skills seen by the course providers as the core skills of the subject. Generic skills such as group work, communication, library use, and so on, may be used or encouraged to enhance the academic study, but are of an incidental nature.

Pattern 2: substantive and syntactic knowledge of the discipline is developed through the acquisition and use of particular generic skills. The latter are the *means* by which learning of the disciplinary knowledge is encouraged and enhanced. Disciplinary and generic skills are considered of equal importance.

Pattern 3: there is an emphasis, explicitly, on students acquiring generic skills as an *outcome* rather than as the means to develop disciplinary knowledge. Disciplinary knowledge provides a context for learning.

Pattern 4: the focus is exclusively on generic skills, to the extent that the disciplinary knowledge and skills acquired or used could be only tangentially related to disciplinary study, or could be of the students' choice.

Pattern 5: the focus is on substantive knowledge and its application, particularly in those subjects that are vocational. Insight into the workplace is through occasional contacts with employers, visits to the workplace or through simulations. There is also some provision for generic skills.

Pattern 6: here there is an emphasis both on generic skills and raising awareness about the requirements and constraints of the world of work. The context for skills utilisation and development is 'real' work experience in a workplace setting. The focus on disciplinary knowledge and skills, or on generic skills, will vary depending on the purpose of the experience.

Figure 3: Patterns of course provision in higher education

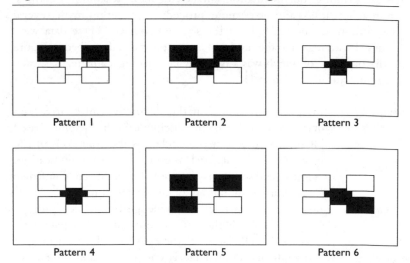

Pattern 1   Pattern 2   Pattern 3

Pattern 4   Pattern 5   Pattern 6

Observation of classes and feedback from students suggested that, at least in the modules that we were invited to investigate, generic skills are being taught with some rigour. The patterns indicate that this is done in many different ways, whether within the context of the discipline or the workplace, and with different emphases. As such, they provide models of practice for teachers wishing to incorporate generic skills within their courses. Although this research project focused in depth on only a small number of modules, there is little doubt from interviews with heads of departments and senior staff that Pattern 1 – that is skills being incidental rather than explicit – is the most common across the four institutions. Patterns 2, 3 and 4 reflect a more deliberate and explicit approach to skill development, and such modules are becoming increasingly prevalent in each of the institutions studied. It is worth recording, however, that, in the modules observed, an explicit focus on generic skills was almost always intended as providing a foundation that would be central to effective learning throughout a student's time in higher education, rather than as a preparation for work. First year students were introduced to generic skills so that they could use, practise and develop them in new contexts, in particular within disciplinary study. Generic skills courses were seen as an investment by those who taught them. Their rationale comes from within higher education and their major purpose is the enhancement of student experiences in higher education. Only in those disciplines where some part of the degree programme provided professional training (such as in pharmacy), or in modules emphasising, for example, career-related skills, was there a marked emphasis on the world of work (Patterns 5 and 6).

In terms of generic skill provision, there was little difference between each of the institutions. Although each was able to offer access to a variety of examples of skills teaching, it became apparent that explicit attention to such skills – even when strongly promoted by the institution – was not widespread and not universally valued. Although each university had different policy and strategy plans in relation to skill development, these being most explicit in the 'new' universities, there seemed little difference when it came to implementation. Teachers who promoted skills in each institution often felt that they were not fully supported by their colleagues and that skills were generally seen as less important than disciplinary knowledge.

Employer initiatives

Development and evaluation activities were undertaken with two employer initiatives on the teaching of generic skills in higher education – the Shell Technology and Enterprise Programme and the BP programme on

Team Development in Universities. The Shell Technology and Enterprise Programme (STEP) has, over the last decade, been supporting a major programme of undergraduate vacation placements in small and medium enterprises (SMEs) across the country. The purpose of this is to encourage work-based skill development. A further aim is to erode the barriers to the employment of graduates in small and local companies, so that graduates perceive them as places that offer careers, and employers in such companies perceive the benefits of recruiting graduates.

British Petroleum (BP) has been sponsoring a Team Development in Universities programme over the last five years – an initiative to promote the use of team skills so that graduates are better prepared for the workplace. Industrial experts have worked in 10 universities to provide students with an experience of teamwork, and to provide academics with the kinds of ongoing professional development in teaching skills advocated by the Dearing Report (1997).

The focus of our study with STEP was on the development of assessment and accreditation procedures for skills acquired by students in the workplace. For the Team Development programme, the focus was on a comparison of courses with different groups of students and on the integration of team skills into curriculum study.

The data highlight that both programmes are widely valued by those who participate in them. The Shell project addresses and supports the needs of employers and offers opportunities that are not normally available within higher education. The BP programme is becoming increasingly collaborative and integrated within the curriculum of several of the university departments where it has been welcomed. Both programmes, however, are hampered by widespread resistance among academics to development and change, and by university administrative systems that do not always easily support new initiatives.

A major difficulty in the STEP scheme, however, was finding students a placement in a small company. Student demand far exceeds places and this tends to be the case for any kind of sandwich course, long or short, and even vacation placements. This situation may well get more difficult with the likelihood of increasing numbers of students responding to the requirement to gain employment-related skills. The issue of quality of placements may also be one that needs further consideration.

The BP Team Development programme is likely to be most effective when the curriculum and the learning processes expected of students have been designed specifically to promote teamwork. A major problem is that many university teachers are used to more didactic teaching methods rather than facilitative, interactive and student-centred ways of working. Nevertheless the study demonstrated that the course run by trained academics was as well received by students as were the courses run by trainers. However, there remains a real need for the training of a 'critical mass' of university teachers who are able to facilitate this type of learning.

Both these initiatives highlight that major employers are prepared to fund initiatives in higher education that extend beyond a relationship premised on recruitment needs, and that demonstrate a commitment to enabling higher education to meet the increased demands being made on it for skill outcomes. However, the impact of such programmes will only be maximised where universities are working consistently to change their culture of teaching and learning, and where employers in general are prepared to support the kinds of learning they argue are so important.

Student conceptions

Students' beliefs and conceptions about teaching and learning generic skills were acquired from interviews with focus groups. Each group was made up of some four to six volunteer students studying the sampled modules in each institution, the total number involved being just over 200. A questionnaire survey gained responses from over 400 students taking these same modules (a return rate of between 11% and 87% per course, depending largely on whether their teacher had timetabled sessions during which questionnaires could be completed and collected or whether students worked more independently and were less easy to contact).

Data from the questionnaire survey, reinforced through observations and interviews, showed that familiarity with, and definitions of, terms like personal transferable and core skills varied widely. Not surprisingly perhaps, students who had studied modules where these terms had been emphasised showed most familiarity; nevertheless even among this group definitions were unclear, and there was some confusion between transferable and core skills.

When asked about the purposes of gaining a degree, almost 80% cited job and career prospects, although only half stated that this was the single most important factor, the majority of these being in 'new' universities. Few students mentioned the importance of 'key' skills, and seemed somewhat confused about what employers thought were the benefits of graduate education. About a third mentioned the acquisition of disciplinary knowledge, and another third cognitive development and personal management skills, which included maturity of thinking, the ability to argue, having commitment, discipline and aspirations. Few identified core or generic skills in this context, and only 15% mentioned career or job-related skills as a perceived benefit to employers. Ironically, they did recognise that employers saw these skills as lacking in graduates.

University careers services are concerned that students should be aware of employers' emphasis on skills, and that they should take career development seriously throughout their degree. However, there is evidence of considerable ignorance in this respect. Over half the students did not know who was responsible for career management in their university, and none cited the careers service in this respect – possibly because the careers service has traditionally remained reactive rather than proactive. The majority of students participating in this research were in their first or second years (third year students were less likely to be involved in skills-based courses), and were thus less likely to have been involved with the careers service. A few modules did, however, encourage links with careers even for first year students.

All students reported a diet of lectures, individual work, and seminars/tutorials in their degree studies, and the majority also experienced team or group work and project work. Few had been involved in student-led activities. The skills that they believed they had developed most from their courses included presenting information, taking responsibility for their own learning, using appropriate sources, carrying out agreed tasks, managing time effectively, identifying key features of a task, gathering information, listening actively, respecting other viewpoints and dealing with criticism. Not all such skills were deemed important. Managing time was seen as the most important, and listening actively the least.

Of importance to course developers is the finding from the interviews that despite the perceived benefits of courses which included generic skills, students would not have chosen a skills-based module if it had been optional. Students report being committed to their chosen discipline and tend to opt for what is perceived as being a traditional degree scheme. Students also reported being instrumental in their approaches to their studies, that is, what is assessed is what counts. So assessment is likely to provide the main motivation for student involvement, whether the orientation is disciplinary or generic. When skills processes are emphasised by teachers, but assessment is of syntactic and substantive knowledge, students are less likely to perceive the significance of generic skills. When skills remain embedded and implicit within disciplinary study, students are least likely either to recognise them or to be eloquent, or even interested, in their description. Finally, skills courses are likely to be more acceptable if introduced early in the degree programme.

Employers and employment

Employers have been very successful in influencing central government policies on the purposes of higher education, as can be seen in the Dearing Report (1997), which argued for a growing interdependence between institutions, the economy, employers and the state. Employers' organisations have provided enthusiastic support for skill development in higher education, exemplified by the 'wish lists' that have emanated from a plethora of employer surveys over the last decade (for example, QHE, 1993,1994; Harvey et al, 1997). However, these surveys have not provided a clear understanding of employer purposes, the contexts for which skills are deemed necessary, or perceptions of the differential role of employers and higher education in the training and development of skills.

These issues were the foci of our data collection in employment settings. The human resource directors of 24 major national and international companies were interviewed on recruitment practices, modes of employee enculturation into the organisation, and in-house training. Twenty-four graduates in their first two years of employment (in a mix of large, medium and small companies) were also interviewed about the opportunities and contexts provided for the use of their existing skills, the type and usefulness of in-house training, and their perception of the transferability of the skills acquired in their university career. Ten of these graduates were followed up one year later to ascertain changes in their development and use of skills.

Employers' perspectives

Recruitment procedures were uniformly rigorous, often lengthy, and provided ample opportunities for candidates to show their capabilities. The initial skill requirements tended to be similar across companies, with selection criteria reflecting the competencies later identified for training and appraisal. Competition was severe, with employers selecting as few as one per cent of applicants. Those selected were generally trained over a two-year period, incorporating generic skill development structured around work experiences. As such, skill development was situated within specific functions and contexts. Some companies extended training to include community work and outdoor adventure training on the grounds that these activities enhanced skill transfer, such as in teamwork and problem solving. However, other employers were highly sceptical of such activities.

The skills prioritised in training were remarkably similar across employers despite their very different purposes. Training was seen as a balance between individual development and company needs, and typically included four distinct groups of skills: knowledge and intellect, personal effectiveness, interpersonal and communication, and business acumen and management style. The claimed advantage of these is that they are easily understood, and observable, by supervisors and employees alike. Line managers were involved in the formal assessment of both technical and generic skills, often against defined competencies. However, the training of these managers to monitor the progress of graduate employees was not well developed, although progress was being made by some employers to design and implement self-appraisal systems.

Some companies also provided opportunities for self-learning, sometimes associated with personal development files to record reflections and achievements. Guided practice, by peers acting as working coaches, and the training of trainees themselves to help other trainees learn, further aided the sharing of expertise.

A common weakness is the lack of evaluation of the learning acquired from training courses sited away from the workplace, organised either internally or externally. At best, evaluation is limited to personal or group reflection on the course. In general, managers assume that training has been effective, rather than ascertaining any changes in knowledge or performance as a consequence of that training, or attempting to build on the new skill or knowledge required.

Recruitment, training and the enculturation of new graduate employees into ways of company working were all affected by the company culture and management philosophy. For example, in some companies changes in the structure of the organisation had altered the relationship between management and staff. Procedural guidelines, previously imposed from the top, now gave greater power to staff, and had resulted in a more open, flexible structure in which employees were trusted to take on wider and different roles. Lessening central control was also perceived as leading to the 'empowering' of individual workers to develop their own learning. Explicit advice about company culture, and ways of fitting into it, were provided at induction, although the duration and purposes of induction varied greatly. Indeed, in some companies, it was unclear what purposes were being served by this process.

Employee perspectives

Content analyses of the interviews with graduate employees revealed a rich mixture of common and unique perceptions. One of the most important was that although a common vocabulary was used to describe skills, what was being practised was quite different because of the variety of tasks, and the unique contexts in which they were undertaken. The clearest example was 'communication skills', which included a wide range of verbal activities including chatting, using the telephone and dictaphone, as well as higher order skills such as interviews with clients and colleagues, together with a variety of writing skills.

Some graduates thought that they had acquired skills at university, as part of their disciplinary study, that were directly relevant to their work; for example, studying English enabled them 'to read and write critically'. Others thought that the subject matter was of secondary importance, and the value of a degree was training in, for example, 'being methodical', or 'to learn more effectively and to get higher order mental skills'. Those who had had work experience as part of their degree appreciated the direct relevance to their employment of the skills that they had gained. One graduate demonstrated an interesting change in perception over the first year of employment – from believing degree content to be irrelevant, to understanding the usefulness of what it had offered.

Among the factors that graduates thought important in determining opportunities for the development of skills were the culture of the organisation and the working environment. Where the organisational culture was described as rigidly hierarchical, training was restricted to following procedures as to how a particular task might be executed. In other cases a greater degree of autonomy allowed decision making to be left to the discretion of the graduate, and there were many more opportunities to develop skills through arranging their own training.

Aspects of the working environment that were deemed important included the size and nature of the work groups, which varied enormously. A few graduates worked alone, hardly moving from their offices, and at most dealt with senior colleagues. Others had many more opportunities to develop skills of negotiation, managing others, working as part of management teams, or dealing with the public, adapting every day to different situations.

Finally, although there was a range of beliefs about transfer of skills, many took an implicit 'situated' perspective, arguing that the value of skill development was seen as relating to preparation for using specific skills in a specific context.

Overall it was clear that the graduates' job demands and their work environments gave rise to very different practices, and these practices, together with their personalities, shaped their perceptions of the skills they were using and developing. In other words generic skills are heavily context dependent, a finding which may have important implications for teaching and learning in higher education.

Changing practice

Higher education

The aim of our study was to inform practice, with a view to its improvement. Central to the achievement of improvement in the planning and delivery of curriculum are the teachers themselves, as Fullan (1991), among others, has argued. Richardson et al (1991) also show that genuine changes can only come about when teachers think differently about what is going on in their own classrooms, and are provided with practices which match their different ways of thinking. Their argument is straightforward – no lasting curriculum change is possible without a prior change in teachers' behaviours, attitudes and beliefs. This is no easy feat, however. The most effective staff development strategies identified at school level require opportunities for teachers to confront the assumptions and beliefs underpinning their own practices (Fullan and Hargreaves, 1992; Bennett et al, 1997). But approaches of this kind tend to be resource hungry, and also assume a level of pedagogical knowledge that is unlikely to be widespread among academics, most of whom have experienced little or no training in teaching. The effect of this was apparent in the lack of knowledge about teaching and student learning, and also in their abilities to reflect on, and articulate their beliefs. Many of these teachers were also surprisingly cautious about implementing change, despite the fact that they had been selected because they had been involved in such efforts.

Part of this caution, and the lack of any clear relationship between their beliefs and practices, were a consequence of contextual factors and constraints outside their individual control. Those mentioned included the research assessment exercise, which took the focus away from teaching and course development, teaching quality assessments, institutional and departmental policies regarding curriculum delivery and assessment, such as modularisation, and increasing student numbers.

Evidence from research in schools on achieving effective innovation shows that attempts to change individual teachers are likely to fail unless there is support and a similar willingness among colleagues, together with appropriate supportive policies within the institution itself. Another project within *The Learning Society Programme* (Hannan et al, 1999) presents the same picture from an analysis of innovators in higher education, where a large number of interviewees commented on resistance by departmental peers. In other words, attitudes, conceptions and practices are mediated by situational or contextual factors, most immediately at the departmental level. Some of the findings from our interviews with teachers leave little grounds for optimism in this respect. Many reported that their attempts to change or innovate were not supported by their colleagues, and that there was little evidence of planning for future change at the departmental level. Tradition, in both the old and new universities of our sample, and particularly with regard to assessment practices, appears to die hard. In the words of one academic: "There is a heavy element of tradition here, so that lots of things are going unquestioned. We do it the way we do it because we do it that way ... kind of circular." Lack of departmental and institutional support, and indeed active resistance, were also evident in some of the evaluations of the STEP and BP schemes.

Silver (1998) suggests that innovations of any kind encounter their main difficulty at departmental level, but argues that this is not restricted either to higher education or to this nation. The international literature on higher education abounds as much as that of industrial practice with discussion of underlying conservatism, and Silver quotes De Woot (1996) to the effect that "change in our universities is slow and difficult because of our culture. Whatever does not come from inside, what is not in our habits or traditions, is too often regarded with distrust or simply ignored" (pp 22-3). Departments, in turn, are willing or unwilling victims of institutional policies with regard to such broader curriculum structures as modularisation and assessment, and these in turn impinge on teacher intentions, and the manner in which they are able to plan for progression and continuity across course levels. The influence of centralised decision making was clearly apparent in our data, and in that of Silver (1998), where some staff report that changes were implemented under duress.

Although institutions are often seen to constrain innovation, they are increasingly unable to act autonomously. Several interrelated macro influences bear on institutional policy decisions concerning the teaching and learning of skills. One of the most powerful of these, the Higher Education Funding Council for England (HEFCE), has been instrumental in operationalising government policies to increase student numbers while at the same time driving down unit costs. This has had a predictable impact on institutions. According to Laurillard,

> ... the pressures being brought to bear have nothing to do with traditions and values. Instead, the pressure is for financial input to go down, and some measurable output to go up. There is an appetite for reform from within higher education ... but it moves slowly as we all scurry about in response to the increasing external pressures which exercise their own peculiar forms of change. (Laurillard, 1993, p 4)

In recognition of this, HEFCE currently funds a range of initiatives designed to enhance students' learning experience and employment prospects. Institutions are being encouraged to develop learning and teaching strategies which may reflect their relationships with employers and encourage the development of what are termed 'employability' skills. HEFCE also provides a fund for the development of teaching and learning in subject-based projects that address employability to varying degrees, and similar initiatives have been approved by the Welsh and Scottish Funding Councils.

At governmental level the Dearing Committee made the specific recommendation that all institutions should increase the extent to which programmes help students to become familiar with the world of work, and help them reflect on that experience. In its response, the government endorsed the view of the Committee, and implicitly the exhortations of employers, that enhanced employability should be one of the objectives of higher education, and has since supported a range of projects to encourage the spread of key skills and work experience. The Quality Assurance Agency is another powerful influence through its audit of teaching quality and appraisal procedures, as well as its programme of work on establishing and clarifying standards and qualifications. Similarly, professional Lead Bodies are able to impose their views through their accreditation procedures.

It is obvious that no university teacher is an island, but is inescapably moulded and constrained by departmental, institutional and national policies. Therefore in considering strategies for change each of these levels must be considered.

Achieving institutional change is complex, and there is little guidance available on innovation in higher education. There is a dearth of literature on the topic, and what is available is, as Silver (1998) reports, concerned either with description of, or proposed strategies for, initiatives, or with discussion of the adaptation of new technologies to the needs of an expanded and more diverse higher education system under severe economic constraints. He concludes that innovation is conditioned by institutional or systemic structures, departmental or disciplinary cultures, individual history, and priorities, and that deliberate change at any level has policy, cultural and ideological contexts.

Change efforts can be instigated by individuals, as our data show, but bottom-up initiatives of this kind, although admirable and often ground-breaking, do not provide an effective model for change across an institution, as research on innovation in schools has too often shown. Neither will institutional initiatives succeed simply through centralised exhortation. They require a concerted and integrated approach which recognises that the first necessary stage is a shift in teacher attitudes towards the innovation. Hord et al (1987), for example, document seven stages of teacher concern which occur through the change process, and which require appropriate response for effective change to occur.

Selling the teaching of key or generic skills is unlikely to be straightforward because, as Barnett (1994) and others have claimed, what is at stake for some is the nature and authenticity of a university education, structured around the primacy of substantive knowledge. As already outlined, some teachers in our sample, although innovative in the delivery of generic skills, justified their change on achieving improvements in student learning in traditional degree programmes, in the belief that enhanced generic skills improve performance across the range of traditional academic activity. Hence the motivation for change is governed by traditional conceptions of higher education rather than by external demands.

Change initiatives will need to be complemented by models of implementation, whereby teachers can come to understand, and judge, the diverse range of teaching approaches which have been successful in skill delivery. It is in this context that the model, and resultant patterns, of course provision generated in this study have proved useful in staff development efforts. Further, the theoretical perspective underpinning the model, together with the findings from associated empirical studies, provide a powerful justification for direct workplace experiences, or simulations of this, particularly in vocationally oriented degree schemes, not only to achieve domain specific knowledge and skills, but also to ensure their transfer. They also provide direct support to employer demands, and the Dearing recommendation, for extension of work placements in order to help students towards success at work, to improve links and to bridge the skills gap. However, our concerns about the quantity and quality of placements still hold.

Nevertheless the logic of placements can be overstretched. If knowledge and skills acquisition and use are largely domain or context specific, then for work experience to be optimal it would have to be located in a setting closely related to that of subsequent employment. In some disciplines such as medicine, education, social work or engineering, this could be reasonably achieved, but what kind of work placement would be optimal for a history, classics or English graduate? The STEP scheme provides an example of a successful placement scheme for just such students with its emphasis on generic skills. But the characteristics of an optimal placement for such students are still not known. Are all placements of similar value irrespective of their focus, length and degree of student choice?

With regard to innovation, the proposed Institute for Learning and Teaching in higher education (ILT) could provide a real stimulus for change efforts. It would therefore be a pity if it prioritises pedagogical developments, say, in interactive technology, as initial responses suggest, rather than concentrating on more basic, but more important, issues such as understandings of how students learn, of the role of assessment and feedback in student achievement and motivation, and of the necessity for teaching for transfer. These would seem to be crucial given our data on the lack of understanding by university teachers of how students learn and the lack of evidence on teaching for transfer. The available literature on transfer implies clearly that effective teaching for transfer requires deliberate planning, delivery and assessment, with objectives made clear to learners, and opportunities for practice in varying contexts. Thus the impact of the ILT would be increased if these aspects of pedagogy are built into their criteria for membership, and if institutions match this by offering appropriate courses in pedagogy, as well as providing incentives for staff membership.

In the absence of verified models of effective implementation, the CVCP, CBI and CIHE joint paper (1998) invites each university and college to reflect on the following four questions:

- How far does the teaching and learning practice in all courses reflect the general intentions of its 'mission statement' and strategic plan? If the two are not consonant, which needs to be changed?

- How can academics get appropriate recognition, promotion and reward for good work and innovation in developing skills courses?
- Are departments encouraged to learn from each other? Does the institution as a whole seek out good practice to adopt? Against whom does it benchmark? Have learning partnerships been established?
- Could the institution work more closely with local employers and further education colleges to extend the scope for work-related education?

These are sensible questions for any institution to consider, but they will not, in themselves, change pedagogical practice. Any consideration or guidance on strategies for change, or models of change, that take into account the broader institutional influences on practice are lacking here.

Employment

The importance of contextual influence is also reflected in our data from employment settings. One of our major findings with regard to graduate employees is that, although there appeared to be agreement among employers about the generic skills they prioritised, the skills actually needed and used, as well as the way they are defined, depend crucially on the characteristics of the work context. The term 'communication' is a prime example of this, with the requirement for and the nature of such skills varying widely across work contexts and tasks. Here lies the problem of transferability, since some graduate employees who were known to be able to argue a point of view in an undergraduate tutorial, reported being ineffectual when communicating with clients. The problem lies, in part, in the ambiguity of the label, since, as Barnett (1994) argues, this is a multi-dimensional skill, with a uni-dimensional label. Thus whatever skill training new graduate employees have had in their higher education, it is likely that they will lack – at least on entrance – the propensities for the varied, yet contextualised, communication demands of their company.

Although the focus of the comments above has been on communication skills, it should be noted that the graduate employees pointed to the fact that other generic skills such as team working and problem solving have little meaning outside specific work contexts. In other words, global generic descriptors hide enormous variation in actual skill use. These sentiments are echoed by the director of another project within *The Learning Society Programme*, Michael Eraut (1996), who claims that use of the same terminology does not prove that the skill itself is identical in each sector or even readily transferable. He also suggests that it is intrinsically improbable that problem solving could mean the same when applied to a student completing the first level of higher education as when applied to a senior manager of a company. Stasz et al (1996) also concluded that such general terms as problem solving and communication are too broad and ambiguous to be of much use to employers for either recruitment or training.

Our findings in this area mirror those of American research. Stasz et al (1996), for example, concluded that workplaces are socially constructed and reflect the decisions of people; skills can only be understood from the perspectives of people within a particular context. More specifically, Stasz and her colleagues (1996) showed that generic skills varied with work context. The characteristics of problem solving, team work and communication are related to job demands which in turn depend on the purpose of work, the tasks which constitute the job, the organisation of the work and other aspects of the work context.

Studies in Australia present a similar picture. Billett (1996) reviews those which have addressed the degree to which the knowledge required for skilful performance is generic or specific to the particular situation, and concludes that situational factors are significant enough to suggest that generic statements of performance are abstracted from, and invalid indicators of, actual performance. Beven and Duggan (1995) assessed the extent to which some of the national key competences (ie skills), such as problem solving and using mathematical ideas and technology, were indeed generic. They, too, concluded that, although some could be described as generic, the degree of applicability to each site, and the degree of success achievable, varied according to the specific context. They also found, as did Resnick (1987), that generic skills may be impossible to apply if the user lacks domain specific knowledge; in other words, the completion of workplace tasks is dependent on the capacity of workers to have domain specific, as well as generic, knowledge and skills.

These findings, in common with ours, fit neatly with theories of situated learning and cognition. This perspective is critical of approaches in which the activity and context in which learning takes place are regarded as ancillary to learning, and distinct to what is learned, since what is learned is thereby separated from how it is learned. This in turn defeats the goal of providing useable, robust knowledge (Brown et al, 1989). Instead, proponents of situated learning perspectives argue that the activity in which knowledge is developed and deployed is not separable from, or ancillary to, learning – it is an integral part of what is learned. "Situations ... co-produce knowledge through activity" (Brown et al, 1989, p 32).

Approaches such as cognitive apprenticeship are based on the above theoretical analysis (Collins et al, 1989). This technique supports learning by enabling students to acquire, develop and use cognitive tools in authentic work contexts, in a similar way to craft apprentices acquiring and developing the tools and skills of their craft through authentic work at, and membership in, their trade. Through this kind of authentic activity, knowing and doing become interlocked and inseparable. Billett (1996) advances a similar view about how individuals construct knowledge through participation in everyday activities in the workplace, based on the belief that learning is inherent in an individual's everyday thinking and acting, and that situations and social partnerships influence the knowledge that is structured. Eraut et al (1998) also investigated, from the perspective of social learning theory, knowledge embedded in the normal activities of the workplace and how it was acquired. They found that the most important sources of learning were what they called the microculture of the workplace, that is, the challenge of the work itself and the interactions with other people in the workplace.

These findings certainly provide theoretical support for the current initiatives on graduate apprenticeships and work experience, but real concerns must, on the basis of our data, remain regarding their effective implementation, particularly in smaller and medium sized enterprises.

Our findings on employer training appear to conform, implicitly at least, to a situated view of learning. Although the generic skills sought, and trained for, were somewhat similar – as would be expected from the homogeneity of employer wishlists of skills – development of these tended to be situated in particular work and task contexts. Several concerns emerged from these data, including the lack of training of line managers, whose job it was to monitor performance against often elaborate competency frameworks. Eraut et al (1998) comment on the recent literature on human resource management that highlights the role of the manager as staff developer, conceived in terms of appraisal and target setting, planned development opportunities, mentoring and coaching. Aspects of this role, such as mentoring and coaching, were rare in their sample of managers, and were equally rare in the settings that we studied.

A second concern was the lack of assessment of training outcomes. In most companies there was no formal evaluation of learning outcomes or of changes in job performance. In general, managers simply assumed that training had been effective. Druckman and Bjork (1994) also report from their studies in the United States that measures of post-training job performance are often missing, or of questionable validity. Further, training tended not to capitalise on the incoming strengths of graduates or focus on their weaknesses, appearing to take no account of skills identified at assessment centres. In other words, there was no indication of the development of tailored courses for new trainees. The fact that the person responsible for recruitment often had no responsibility for training may explain this.

In more general terms, Rajan (1997) shows – both from research in the UK and from an international survey – that the kinds of broad training in generic skills which could underpin employability are simply not being offered by most employers; and that British managers are the most guilty of providing short-term non-developmental training. In sum, employers' attitudes remain long on intentions and short on deliverables. Our findings in large national and international companies do not conform to this picture, but in our limited sample of small and medium sized enterprises the picture does seem to be very different.

Our results, showing that training, induction, and work practices were all influenced by the organisational culture, echo those of Druckman and Bjork (1994) who reported that they were struck by the key role of the organisational context in which performance occurs. They claim that, without an organisational culture that fosters the changes needed to implement innovation, proposals for change, however credible their source or convincing the evidence, will have little effect.

Organisations are, of course, subject to some of the same outside influences experienced by higher education institutions. Here, however, the influences are more diverse, including world markets and competition as well as national priorities. We collected no data on these influences, but the espoused movement away from centralised organisational structures, for example, seems more related to increased demands for efficiency as a result of international market pressures, than to internal considerations.

Implications and an agenda for future action

The study reported here set out to gain better understandings of generic skills in higher education and employment, in what turned out to be a shifting policy landscape. The implications of our findings for the effective implementation and utilisation of these skills are considered below in the form of an agenda for future action. These, too, are the issues – many of them complex – that need to be pursued, clarified and further researched if we are to call ourselves a learning society.

1 The discourse on generic skills, and all its variants, is confused, confusing and under-conceptualised. Employers and policy makers alike have been seduced by the slogans, with scant consideration of their definition, characteristics, transferability or utility. Yet the unity of future action on skills, whether it be in higher education, employment, or partnerships of both, as advocated in Dearing, can only follow unity of thought and understanding. Future discourse must therefore be grounded in the theoretical underpinnings of skills and their relationship to domain specific knowledge and skills, as suggested in our model.

2 Allied to the above is evidence of the lack of a common language of skills between higher education and employers. It seems to be assumed, by politicians at least, that this will be ameliorated by the improvement of links and collaborations with business, particularly in the provision of work-based learning opportunities. Here, the political rhetoric is high on the 'what' and low on the 'how'. In a recent speech, the Secretary of State for Education and Employment spelt out what must be done to equip students to meet the needs of employers and reach their full potential. They included: a minimum period of work experience for each student; a requirement that every student study a module giving them insight into the world of work; and a graduate apprenticeship scheme integrating higher level study with work-based learning. What was not spelt out is how this might be achieved at an acceptable level of quality.

Although work-based experience is theoretically justifiable, careful note needs to be taken of research on work experience and placements. More does not mean better. There is considerable variation in the effectiveness and acceptability of these programmes. Recent studies show that the best schemes are jointly planned, incorporate close guidance of experiences, and continued joint support by both workplace and university supervisors. In such circumstances students claim to have developed more generic skills and to have had more satisfying experiences (cf Martin, 1997). However, this is not achieved without careful planning and institutional support. It may also not be feasible to provide close supervision of students in the workplace if there is an expectation that large numbers of undergraduates should participate in such experiences.

3 If higher education is to play a full part in raising the level of generic skills, then a continuing process of training and professional development for academics will be required. There is little evidence, even from university teachers committed to the development of these skills, that their espoused or actual theories of teaching are underpinned by understandings of learning theory, or that they intentionally teach for transfer. Although the Department for Education and Employment (DfEE) is currently providing funding for a host of development and dissemination projects which have led to the availability of practical strategies for implementation (cf the website at www.keyskillsnet.org.uk), these studies are largely uncritical and atheoretical. Similarly, there seems little indication that the Institute for Learning and Teaching has any clear strategy or theoretical orientation for generic skills teaching. The absence of central policy initiatives in training is surprising given the perceived importance of skills to economic performance. In their absence, it seems that institutions themselves must take on the role of primary developer and provider.

4 Taking the role of training provider is just one of multiple roles institutions must take on if there is to be effective implementation. The practical strategies provided by the DfEE are useful in this respect since they highlight the need for clear and unambiguous central and departmental policies on the development of generic skills, incorporating systems of monitoring and flexible assessment regulations. For many teachers there will also have to be a shift in beliefs as a necessary prerequisite of appropriate training, a shift that for some might be more palatable if better linked to career prospects.

5 This study has, inevitably, identified issues on which there is a need for further research. The most urgent is that of 'transfer' – an area that we were unable to pursue sufficiently within this project. Given the centrality of transfer in theories of learning, and in the assumptions of employers and policy makers, it is surprisingly under-researched.

There is a similar need to elucidate empirically aspects of generic skills. The following list of issues requiring further study gives suggestions but is by no means exhaustive:
- the differential impact of vocational and non-vocational courses on skill transfer and use;
- the extent to which some skills transfer more easily than others;

- the effect on skill development of placements of differing length and format;
- the differential effectiveness on skill development of work placements and simulated work contexts;
- the importance of domain specific knowledge in skill use and transfer;
- the effectiveness of work-based skills training on job performance.

6 Improving the nature and quality of discourse, of training, and of institutional policy making are all essential, but all require an ingredient which to date has been sadly lacking – the utilisation of a defensible theory of learning. Simply put, theories provide the rudder for effective policy implementation. Without it, policy direction is unplanned, random or likely to end on the rocks. Theories of situated learning provide an appropriate theoretical underpinning for understanding the role, and transfer, of skills in context, for providing the rationale for such policy initiatives as workplace learning and graduate apprenticeships, and for informing teaching approaches. Yet consideration of any kind of theory is non-existent in any of the literature on policy formulation or enactment.

Coffield reiterates this point when arguing that government plans to create a new culture of lifelong learning are proceeding without a theory of learning, or even a recognition that one is required.

> To ask a politician, a civil servant or a professional specialising in education what their theory of learning is and how it helps them improve their practice tends to produce the same kind of embarrassed mumblings which result from a direct question about their sexual orientation. (Coffield, 1999, p 493).

He concludes that no *Learning Society* can be built on such atheoretical foundations. We concur with this. Without a theoretical understanding of how students and graduate employees learn, of how the setting or context mediates what and how they learn, of institutional and organisational change, and crucially, of what is to be learned, the Dearing prescriptions for the role of higher education in economic development, and in lifelong learning, will simply not be realised.

References

Anderson, J.R. (1983) *The architecture of cognition*, Cambridge, MA: Harvard University Press.

Barnett, R. (1994) *The limits of competence: Knowledge, higher education and society*, Buckingham: Open University Press/Society for Research in Higher Education.

Bennett, N., Dunne, E. and Carré, C. (2000) *Skills development in higher education and employment*, Buckingham: Open University Press/SRHE.

Bennett, N., Wood, E. and Rogers, S. (1997) *Teaching through play: Teachers' thinking and classroom practice*, Buckingham: Open University Press.

Beven, F. and Duggan, L. (1995) 'A conceptualisation of generic skills and context – dependent knowledge and a methodology for examining practice', in J. Stevenson (ed) *Learning in the workplace: Tourism and hospitality*, Centre for Skill Research and Development, Griffith University, Australia.

Biggs, J. (1996) 'Enhancing teaching through constructive alignment', *Higher Education*, vol 32, pp 347-64.

Billett, S. (1996) 'Knowledge, learning and work: a synthesis of research at Griffin University 1994-6', Paper presented at ANTRAC Conference, Melbourne, Australia, July.

Blagg, N., Ballinger, M. and Lewis, R. (1993) *Development of transferable skills in learners*, London: Employment Department and N. Blagg Associates.

Brown, J.S., Collins, A. and Duguid, P. (1989) 'Situated cognition and the culture of learning', *Educational Researcher*, vol 18, pp 32-42.

Coffield, F. (1999) 'Breaking the consensus: lifelong learning as social control', *British Educational Research Journal*, vol 25, no 4, pp 479-99.

Collins, A., Brown, J.S. and Newman, S.E. (1989) 'Cognitive apprenticeship: teaching the crafts of reading, writing and mathematics', in L.B. Reswick (ed) *Knowing, learning and instruction: Essays in honour of Robert Glaser*, Hillside, NJ: Erlbaum, pp 453-94.

CVCP (Committee of Vice-Chancellors and Principals), CBI (Confederation of British Industry) and CIHE (Council for Industry and Higher Education) (1996) *Helping students towards success at work: A declaration of intent*, London: CIHE.

CVCP, CBI, CIHE (1998) *Helping students towards sucess at work: An intent being fulfilled*, London: CIHE.

Dearing Report (1998) *Higher education in the learning society*, London: HMSO.

De Woot, P. (1996) 'Managing change at university', *CRE-action*, vol 109, pp 19-28.

Druckman, D. and Bjork, R.A. (1994) *Learning, remembering, believing: Enhancing human performance*, Washington, DC: National Academy of Sciences.

Drummond, I., Nixon, I. and Wiltshier, J. (1997) *Transferable skills in higher education: The problems of implementing good practice*, Draft project paper, Universities of Hull and Newcastle.

Dunne, E. (1995) *Personal transferable skills*, Final Report, University of Exeter.

Eraut, M. (1996) 'The new discourse of vocational education and training: A framework for clarifying assumptions, challenging the rhetoric and planning useful, theoretically informed research', Paper presented at the ECER Conference, Seville, Spain, August.

Eraut, M., Alderton, J., Cole, G. and Senker, P. (1998) *Development of knowledge and skills in employment*, Research Report No 5, Brighton: University of Sussex, Institute of Education.

Fenstermacher, G.D. (1996) 'The knower and the known: the nature of knowledge in research on teaching', *Review of Research in Education*, vol 20, pp 3-56.

Fullan, M. (1991) *The new meaning of educational change*, London: Cassell.

Fullan, M. and Hargreaves, A. (1992) *Teacher development and educational change*, London: Falmer Press.

Green, A. (1994) 'A psychological approach to identifying transferable skills and transfer skills', in D. Bridges (ed) *Transferable skills in higher education*, Norwich: University of East Anglia.

Gubbay, J. (1994) 'A critique of conventional justification for transferable skills', in D. Bridges, *Transferable skills in higher education*, Norwich: University of East Anglia/Eastern Region Training and Enterprise Council.

Hannan, A., English, S. and Silver, H. (1999) 'Why innovate? Some preliminary findings from a research project on Innovations in Teaching and Learning in Higher Education', *Studies in Higher Education*, vol 24, no 3, pp 279-89.

Harvey, L., Moon, S. and Geall, V. (1997) *Graduates' work: Organisational change and students' attributes*, Birmingham: Centre for Research into Quality, The University of Central England.

Hord, S., Rutherford, W., Huling-Austin and Hall, G. (1987) *Taking charge of change*, University of Austin, Texas, AZ: ACSD.

Laurillard, D. (1993) *Rethinking university teaching: A framework for the effective use of educational technology*, London: Routledge.

Martin, E. (1997) *The effectiveness of different models of work-based university education*, Curriculum Development Unit, Royal Melbourne Institute of Technology, Australia.

Mayer, E. (1992) *Employment related key competences for post compulsory education and training: A discussion paper*, Melbourne: The Mayer Committee, Australian Education Council.

Otala, L. (1993) 'Trends in lifelong learning in Europe', Paper presented at a TEXT Conference on the theme of *Accreditation of in-company training*, Dublin, September.

QHE (Quality in Higher Education) (1993) Update 6, *The Newsletter of the Quality in Higher Education Project*, Birmingham: University of Central England.

QHE (1994) Update 7, *The Newsletter of the Quality in Higher Education Project*, Birmingham: University of Central England.

Rajan, cited in E. Keep (1997) 'There is no such thing as society: Some problems with an individual approach to creating a learning society', Paper presented at ESRC Learning Society Conference, January, Bristol.

Resnick, L. (1987) 'Learning in school and out', *Educational Researcher*, vol 16, no 9, pp 13-20.

Richardson, V., Anders, P., Tidwell, D. and Lloyd, C. (1991) 'The relationship between academic teachers' beliefs and practices in reading comprehension instruction', *American Educational Research Journal*, vol 28, no 3, pp 559-86.

Schwab, J. (1964) 'The structure of the disciplines: meanings and significances', in G. Ford and L. Purgo (eds) *The structure of knowledge and the curriculum*, Chicago, IL: Rand McNally.

Scott, P. (1997) 'The crisis of knowledge and the massification of higher education', in R. Barnett and A. Griffin (eds) *The end of knowledge in higher education*, London: Cassell.

Silver, H. (1998) *The languages of innovation: Listening to the higher education literature*, Working Paper 1, Innovations in Teaching and Learning in Higher Education Project, University of Plymouth at Exmouth.

Stasz, C., Ramsey, K., Eden, R., Melamid, E. and Kaganoff, T. (1996) *Workplace skills in practice: Case studies of technical work*, RAND, Santa Monica, CA, National Centre for Research in Vocational Education, University of California at Berkeley.

Trigwell, K. and Prosser, M. (1996) 'Congruence between intention and strategy in university science teachers' approaches to teaching', *Higher Education*, vol 29, pp 443-58.

FOUR

The variable contribution of guidance services in different types of learning societies

Will Bartlett and Teresa Rees

Background

In recent years, labour markets have had to adapt to the twin pressures of globalisation and technological change. Increasingly, labour market participants are making frequent job changes in the course of their working lives. In the UK, the previous Conservative government's policy actively promoted the deregulation of the labour market, reducing the level of employment protection previously granted to the workforce. Companies 'downsized' and 'delayered', reducing their core of permanent workers and increasing their employment of part-timers and contract workers. Indeed, it has been argued that flexible employment contracts are bringing about the 'death of career' (Collin and Watts, 1996) and a dramatic reshaping of the employment relationship. Watts has referred to this process as the 'Careerquake' (Watts, 1996).

These changes have not, of course, affected all sections of the labour market with equal force. Overall, there has been little change in the average duration of job tenure (Burgess and Rees, 1997). However, the overall pattern disguises seismic shifts in career patterns among different segments of the labour force. Job security for male workers, measured by median length of job tenure, fell by 20% between 1975 and 1993, and labour turnover has risen dramatically for older workers and less skilled men (Gregg and Wadsworth, 1995). The decrease in length of job tenure for men has been offset by an increase in the length of job tenure for women, but this is in a context in which women in any case have a much higher share of part-time and temporary work. While a core of permanent employees has been insulated from these effects, there is much greater instability among the secondary labour market participants in part-time work, self-employment and other forms of 'atypical' work. Even within the core labour force, there is evidence of change. Comparing the recessions of 1980–82 and 1989–92, Inkson (1995) found that the proportion of managers changing jobs each year increased from 21% to 30%, while 'discontinuities' in managers' career paths due to job severance were an increasingly common experience among managerial personnel. If job mobility becomes a more central component of post-fordist society, in contrast to the supposed traditional progression up a hierarchical career ladder, so the importance of life-long careers guidance will increase.

Furthermore, changes from one job to another increasingly involve transitions between different types of jobs with different skill requirements, and between employment and retraining, rather than simple lay-off and re-hire into the same place of employment, or even into the same industry or occupation. The transition between jobs in the flexible labour market is intrinsically connected with periodic entry and re-entry into spells of education and training. In conjunction with the rapid expansion of adult education opportunities, the role of lifelong guidance is rapidly moving up the policy agenda to support the development of a *Learning Society*.

We distinguish in our research between two types of guidance: educational and vocational. Both form part of the generic activity which we refer to as 'career guidance' ('career' rather than 'careers' to emphasise the variable nature of career paths through a lifetime of shifting employment and training experiences). Educational guidance has a direct bearing on the development of the *Learning Society* by assisting individuals to improve their choices of educational and training activities in which they may invest their time, money and energy. A recent report by the Educational Counselling and Credit Transfer Information Service (ECCTIS, 1998) has revealed that many students attending undergraduate courses at UK universities have made poor choices of degree subjects, with over one fifth of second year students wishing they had chosen a different course of study. Improved educational guidance services are needed to assist individuals to make better choices not only about the variety of jobs on offer at the end of a course of education or training but also about the effectiveness and suitability of such courses themselves. Effective vocational guidance is also needed to reduce job search costs to job seekers by providing them with information and advice about career paths and vacancies. By enhancing the process of job search, vocational guidance can reduce the frictional unemployment that arises when there is a mismatch between job offers and the supply of labour.

The structure of the guidance system in the UK

In our research we were concerned to map the broad range and roles of all-age career guidance services in the UK. The guidance scene was changing dramatically during the period in which the research was being carried out, as a consequence of the 1993 Trade Union Reform and Employment Rights Act. As in other areas of public service, such as health, education and community care, there was an attempt to introduce market-type forces, or 'quasi-markets' into the provision of guidance services (Watts, 1998). In the case of the careers service this was achieved through competition for the right to supply statutory guidance services on an area basis (contracting out). Careers services were removed from the control of Local Education Authorities (LEAs) and privatised. They were funded on the basis of a contract specified directly with the State (the Department for Education and Employment [DfEE] through the Regional Government Offices). This change in the management of the careers service was similar to the quasi-market reforms which were introduced in many parts of the public sector in the 1990s[1]. By 1997, all the LEA careers services had been converted to private companies or partnerships and contracted out. Most were transformed into partnerships of LEAs and Training and Enterprise Councils (TECs), or Local Enterprise Companies (LECs) in Scotland. In a few cases, however, new private providers have entered the field and in those areas the careers companies retain a separate identity from the TEC. Nearly all the new careers companies are limited by guarantee, often with a non-profit status, although some were established as companies limited by shares with a for-profit orientation.

The development of a learning society with a focus on lifelong learning implies a need for the creation of institutions capable of supporting transitions throughout life between work and a variety of learning experiences. It is in this context that the delivery of adult guidance services plays a key role, and is a primary focus of the research reported in this chapter. In the UK, there is a fundamental difference in the way that guidance services are provided to young people on the one hand and adults on the other. The provision of guidance to young people (ie those in full time education and for a short time after leaving) is a statutory responsibility of the careers companies, and is set out in their core contract. This funds 85% of their budget through a capitation formula based on the number of school pupils in an area, augmented by a target-based element of funding covering the remaining 15%, linked to the number of 'action plans' achieved with the client group. However, guidance services for adults are non-statutory, and the extent to which they are provided by careers companies is dependent on their strategic objectives.

At the same time, there are a number of other important providers, including the TECs, the Employment Service (especially through its network of Job Clubs), a range of voluntary sector providers, and private organisations specialising in the provision of outplacement services and recruitment. Some special groups such as ex-offenders and demobilised military personnel are provided with separate arrangements through the Probation Service and the armed forces outplacement division. The activities of these organisations are described in more detail in Hawthorn (1996) and Bartlett and Rees (1999).

Another key locus of activity is in higher education (HE) and further education (FE) (Watts, 1997). The research indicated that the HE sector is significantly better resourced than the FE sector, although the pattern of provision even within the HE sector is highly variable (McNair, 1998). This inequality of provision has serious implications for equity and access, especially considering the increasing number of mature students who pass through the FE sector and who, as a group, must inevitably be one of the key targets of any programme of lifelong learning (Bartlett and Rees, 1999).

Impact of the guidance service reforms in the UK

We were also keen to identify the effects of recent quasi-market reforms on providers of new and emerging guidance services through a series of case studies. Our interest focused on the way in which the contracting out of the careers service had interacted with, and moulded local 'guidance networks'. We found that adult guidance services were more developed in areas in which the new careers companies were organised as LEA/ TEC partnerships. In these cases, the TEC often provided direct block funding to the careers company to support the provision of adult guidance services. This replaced the competitive quasi-market provision of services by TEC-funded providers. In cases where an independent company won the contract, this fusion did not take place; the TEC continued to act as an independent purchaser of adult guidance services on the local quasi-market. These two models of provision which have emerged since the implementation of the 1993 Act were clearly visible in our locality case studies.

Four English localities were selected as the case studies for this project: Bristol, Reading, Inner London, and Sheffield. The localities were selected on the basis of two main criteria: (a) the type of careers company which had been established and (b) the degree of tightness in the local labour market. The first criterion was designed to capture differences between careers companies by legal form. Two of the case studies were chosen to represent cases where incumbents had been converted into LEA/TEC partnerships, and two represent cases of new entry by newly established private sector careers companies. The second criterion was designed to provide variation in the labour market environment in terms of the level of unemployment. In addition a further locality in Scotland, Fife, was included to capture the Scottish dimension of guidance services.

Table 1: Case study areas according to selection criteria

	LEA/TEC (LEC) partnership	New entrant career companies
Low unemployment	*Bristol*	*Reading*
High unemployment	*Sheffield, Fife (LEA)*	*Inner London*

In all, 56 interviews were carried out in 1997 in the five case study areas. Interviewees included managers and guidance professionals in the new careers companies, the TECs and LEC, the voluntary, public and private sectors, and the Employment Service. Together with additional documentary evidence provided by the organisations contacted, they gave a detailed picture of the local guidance system in each locality (reported in detail in Bartlett and Rees 1999; Rees and Bartlett, 1999a). The main findings can be briefly summarised as follows.

While both Inner London and Sheffield suffer high levels of unemployment, Sheffield has a more developed adult guidance provision and enjoys a reputation for an active approach to the field. This is based on the commitment of the local TEC to fund services out of its reserves, the existence of a dedicated adult guidance division of the careers service, and a well-organised collaborative network of providers. The careers company was established in April 1995 as a non-profit company limited by guarantee with charitable status, and was set up as an LEA/TEC partnership. Both the LEA and the TEC nominate seven trustees to the board of the company to reflect stakeholder interests: schools, colleges, small and large employers, trade unions and training providers. Adult guidance is provided on a self-funding basis through a separate, specialised division. This division is funded by the TEC and by grants from the European Social Fund (ESF) and the Single Regeneration Budget (SRB). Indeed, European Union (EU) funding is a significant factor and provides about 35% of the income of the division. The company operates a drop-in careers library for adults who can obtain information and, who, if they live in the ESF area, are eligible for a guidance interview. The library is used by about 50,000 every year. The first guidance interview is free of charge and paid for by the TEC. Further guidance sessions are provided on a fee-paying basis to those earning over £300 per week, and free to the unemployed and those earning less than this amount. Psychometric tests are charged at almost £100, but are provided free to the same categories of clients. Outplacement counselling[2], is provided as a free service to companies employing less than 50 workers through ESF funding. Adult educational guidance is provided separately by the TEC through a Training Advice Centre. This unit employs three full time advisors and two information officers and about 4,500 people use the service each year.

The careers company has also established a network of local guidance providers and professionals who meet regularly in a Network Forum to exchange experience and ideas. This is especially useful for co-ordinating activity with the voluntary sector and local colleges and universities. Particular attention is paid to adults from disadvantaged groups. Outreach workers are employed to provide services to the local ethnic minorities who form 7% of the population. The integration of the company into the local guidance network, and the partnership between the LEA and the TEC has been highly successful and resulted in an accessible and high quality provision of guidance services for adults living in this locality. It should be noted that this collaborative approach did not spring up overnight but had been developed over a number of years prior to the reforms of the mid-1990s. Despite its success there is still a large unmet need for guidance and in the words of one careers company interviewee, "there is a need for core funding – why can't adult guidance be financed in the same way as young people's guidance?" This question points directly to an area of policy discrimination against adults.

In Inner London, unemployment rises above 15%, as compared to a national average[3] of 7%. There is a relatively large population from minority ethnic groups, and a concentration of asylum seekers and other disadvantaged groups. The careers company is a new entrant private company that is a subsidiary of a large company which holds the contract to provide guidance services in four areas. The shareholders of the parent company are a county council, some major financial institutions, and some individuals. The company provides guidance services for adults funded through contracts with the ESF, the SRB and the local authority. Target groups include the unemployed and people living in housing estates with high levels of social deprivation. However, there is no accessible high street 'shop' where adults can easily drop in to obtain service. The main information point is housed in the same building as the local job centre where unemployed people register for benefits. The adult educational guidance unit has remained under local authority ownership and management and struggles to retain its independence from both the careers company and the local colleges. The justification is a desire to provide unbiased and impartial advice. However, they too are located in the same building as the unemployment benefit office. This is likely to deter some potential clients, especially those seeking educational guidance. The Jobseekers' Allowance imposes a limit of 16 hours per week on attendance on a course of education or training. According to one interviewee, individuals may worry that, if they are seen to be looking for a course, they risk the loss of their Income Support and Housing Benefit. The interviewee argued that this effect was serious and presented an obstacle to the implementation of policies to promote lifelong learning.

The local TEC has a strong commitment to the provision of adult guidance. Working independently from the careers company, it delivers services through a network of independent providers who compete for the right to provide the service. Services are provided on the basis of fees to employed people and are provided free to the unemployed. In all, the TEC provides services to around 3,000 individuals per year. Targets are set to encourage providers to increase the number of fee-paying clients they serve. Other provision is fragmented among a plethora of voluntary and community groups. Local colleges work hard to plug the gaps but their primary focus is on attracting students onto courses rather than the provision of independent advice. Moreover, they struggle to attract funding from a diverse set of funding bodies.

In contrast to the two localities described above, Bristol and Reading both enjoy high levels of economic activity and low unemployment. Nevertheless they too differ from each other in the extent of provision of adult guidance services. In Bristol, the local careers service is a non-profit company limited by guarantee formed as a partnership between the local authority and the local TEC. It combines four separate branches serving distinct functions. One of these provides adult guidance on a consultancy basis to companies and also on a more limited scale to individuals on a fee-paying basis. The surplus from this branch funds the core guidance branch to provide free guidance services to adults, which is also subsidised by grants from the local TEC, the EU Konver programme (for redundant workers from defense-related industries) and from the DfEE. A city centre guidance shop provides highly visible services to the public, with a high proportion of adults among the users of the service. A third branch, funded by the TEC, provides services under the Education Business Partnership. The fourth branch covers training activities and aims to promote lifelong learning and career development. This branch is also funded from the TEC, under contract. In conjunction with local colleges it runs an open learning project targeted at people who have been out of education for some time, and a 'Return to Learn' scheme, based on the Rover and Ford Employee Development programmes. The latter subsidises employees to attend after-work courses; they are also subsidised by employers. Other activities of the branch include an outreach service through local guidance shops, a training programme for 'key workers' in small businesses, an open learning network and a National Vocational Qualification (NVQ) service for employers. In all these activities there is close collaboration with the local TEC that has a strong commitment to the provision of guidance services to adults. By integrating training and guidance services, the careers company is able to provide a relevant and accessible service that promotes both educational and vocational guidance to adults in an effective way.

By contrast, in Reading, which has similarly low unemployment (around 2%), the provision of adult guidance is extremely limited. The careers company is a new entrant company limited by guarantee. It undertakes a wide range of other education-related activities, both in the UK and abroad. It is an expanding company and through the contract bidding process has taken over the provision of guidance services in three other areas. This expansion is designed to protect the company against risk by the diversification of its activities. The company also claims there are economies of scale that allow it to improve the quality of its services provided to the core client group of school pupils and school leavers. However, it has taken a strategic decision to withdraw from the provision of adult guidance altogether and views it as an unprofitable market. The local TEC, although recognising the importance of adult guidance for both employees and the marginalised unemployed, struggles to obtain funding and is less willing to use its own reserves to finance adult guidance services than the company in Bristol. It has concentrated its efforts on pump-priming the local voluntary sector which provides services for the unemployed, women returners, disabled adults, minority ethnic groups and ex-offenders. However, these voluntary sector organisations are invariably small-scale operations. The TEC also works with the Training for Work programme, which provides pre-vocational training for the hard to employ, and funds a local telephone helpline. In the view of one TEC interviewee, however, the real area of need is among employees who have unmet career development needs and training needs. In his own words: "if the objective of a learning society is to develop skills, you don't do it by focusing resources on marginal groups. You have to do it by developing training for people in work".

A different approach to the provision of guidance services has been adopted in Scotland. Rather than universal competitive tendering for contracts, the Scottish Office chose to encourage local authorities and LECs to work together to bid for the careers service contract for their area. Hence, in Fife, the partnership which was awarded the careers service contract (Fife Careers) is made up of the local authority which has a long history of work on economic regeneration and social support, and Fife Enterprise (the Local Enterprise Company). Fife Adult Guidance and Education Service (FAGES) is based in the local authority's community education department and is one of the largest adult guidance providers in Scotland, reflecting the authority's concern with unemployment and community regeneration. Indeed, adult guidance is identified as a top priority for the council in its corporate objectives: it is seen as integral to its anti-poverty strategy.

The economy of Fife was, until recently, dominated by coalmining, defense industries and before that, textiles: all industries which have gone into major decline. Unemployment is 10% above the Scottish average. Inward investment has created some part-time jobs for women (such as call centres) but the substantial Hyundai project has been put on hold as a result of the crisis in the Pacific Rim economy.

Fife is characterised by partnership working among a range of organisations concerned with economic regeneration. Key actors in addition to FAGES, the local authority, Fife Enterprise and Fife Careers include the District Office of the Employment Service and Fife Training Information Services. This latter organisation, again based in the local authority, has its roots in the old Manpower Services Commission's Training Access Points scheme, set up in the late 1980s. The service provides independent computerised information on education and training courses throughout the UK through training information points in libraries, Jobcentres, colleges and careers services. There is also a free telephone enquiry service. Effort is put into listing up-to-date information on local opportunities including non-traditional, part-time, and short courses as well as open learning, in-house training and EU co-funded initiatives run by FAGES, such as First Steps and Route One for people returning to learning or the labour market.

FAGES coordinates the Fife Adult Guidance Network whose members all provide adult guidance, although for many it is as part of other activities such as community education, college courses, citizens' advice or placement for the unemployed. The network is now supported through funding from the Scottish Office: this is the only resource that the Scottish Office puts into adult guidance apart from the telephone helpline. In addition there are more informal, local guidance networks in the area and local planning groups for European projects.

The main sources of income for FAGES come from the local authority and the EU. Indeed Fife is one of the most successful adult guidance providers in the UK in terms of attracting EU funding. The active networks put FAGES in an advantageous position to apply for European funding. The focus on disadvantaged groups means that FAGES is eligible for many strands in the EU's Community Initiative EMPLOYMENT , such as ADAPT (for workers in declining industries) and INTEGRA (for the most disadvantaged) as well as other ESF monies under various objectives. There are close links with colleges that invite FAGES in to provide independent guidance and participate in their EU co-funded projects.

While the local authority sets no performance indicators for FAGES other than targets for European funding (which are normally exceeded), the service has set its own monitoring and evaluation systems in place. In addition, the Scottish Office has devised the Scottish Quality Management System for Education and Training (SQMS) and Fife is the first guidance service to implement this: it includes nine standards of organisational activity.

Hence, in some senses the institutional framework within which adult guidance is located in Fife is much more similar to the previous context within which careers services worked in local authorities. FAGES has a fair degree of autonomy in how it responds to needs in the area. There are no performance indicators or drivers working against providing a service for the most disadvantaged as there are elsewhere. If clients need a considerable amount of support to progress along various stages to the labour market, it is possible to provide this. The context of the service, within an ethos of community regeneration and anti-poverty strategies, and within a well-developed network of organisations, has facilitated cooperative working with a range of public sector agencies in what is a crowded playing field. The networking means it is more likely that adults receive independent advice as there is a culture of referral between agents. It has also facilitated maximum advantage to be taken of European funding: expertise has developed in making applications, handling the bureaucracy and managing the finances effectively in the way required by the European Commission, which makes working with such projects cost-effective.

Overall, the five locality case studies demonstrate that a key factor in determining the extent of provision of guidance services is the way in which the careers services and the TECs (LECs) interact in different cases, rather than on need as expressed by the state of the local labour market. Where interaction is close and collaborative, the transition to a contracted out careers service appears to have generated a dynamic and innovative approach to the expansion of guidance services for adults. This interaction appears to be best achieved in cases where there is a formal organisational partnership on which to base the work of the careers service. Elsewhere, in cases where such interaction is absent or made more difficult by the entry of independent careers companies without close links to the TEC structures, the provision of adult guidance is placed on a less coherent and more fragmented basis. Moreover, in such cases TEC-funded contracted-out provision is fragmented and small scale, and fails to benefit from the economies of scale which the large independent careers companies identify as important in their statutory activity. Thus, provision is unequal across localities and unrelated to labour market conditions, a highly unsatisfactory state of affairs.

Guidance systems in France, Germany, Italy and the Netherlands

In order to assess the relative strengths and weaknesses of the guidance system in the UK, we also carried out a series of case studies in four other EU member states: France, Germany, Italy and the Netherlands. We suspected we would find substantial variation in the organisation of guidance services.

France

In France, the guidance system for young people is highly centralised and professionalised, and provides a state-administered careers service (*Centres d'Information et Orientation*). For adults, there is a well-developed guidance system based around a number of different organisations, many of which are in the not-for-profit 'third sector', which in France forms a highly developed social economy (Danvers and Monsanson, 1997). Often these are social enterprises (*associations*) such as the *Retravailler* group of organisations that specialise in providing advice to women returners. This third sector provision is partly organised on a quasi-market basis. Examples include *AFPA* (*Association Nationale de la Formation Professionelle des Adultes* – Adult Vocational Training Organisation) which provides adult vocational guidance targeted towards the unemployed and handicapped and works under contract to the Ministry of Labour; the *Missions Locales* (*ML*), local multi-functional organisations which aim to provide guidance services together with other forms of social advice to young people in difficulty (*les jeunes en difficulté*), financed by formula funding from local authorities; and third sector providers which operate with either capitation payments or by competition for 'preferred provider' status with government agencies such as the government training agency *Agence Nationale pour l'Emploi* (*ANPE*).

AFPA integrates guidance into the training process. Occupational psychologists are employed to provide educational and career guidance services to around 150,000 clients either in the training centres or directly within firms. The *ML* provide an integrated service to help disadvantaged youth obtain access to housing, training, healthcare and income support, and to assist their 'social insertion' into society. Guidance is provided to disadvantaged young people as part of this process and is intended to overcome social exclusion which is recognised to be caused by a complex set of factors not restricted to unemployment or to low levels of education and training. The guidance services provided are supplemented by a process of 'social guidance' to redress social disadvantage. In 1994, there were 250 *ML* throughout France, and 5,000 employees and 900,000 young people between the ages of 16 and 25 received some form of assistance from these local organisations.

Typical of the third sector providers in the French social economy is the *Retravailler* organisation, which has 14 centres throughout France. It is an association under the 1901 Association Law, roughly equivalent to a voluntary organisation in the UK but with a more participative management structure. Guidance services are provided to adults over the age of 25, principally, but not exclusively to women returners to the labour market. Services are provided on the basis of a means tested fee, and funding is also derived from the ESF and various government programmes. The French Ministry for Women provides specific contract funding to the organisation. However, the funding base of these organisations is not secure, and in comparison with the more formal institutions (*ANPE* and *ML*) they can be regarded as niche service providers, highly dependent on contract funding in a competitive quasi-market.

A unique element of the French guidance system is the provision, under a law of 1978, for all employees to take a leave of absence once every five years for a period of training and 'skills assessment' (*bilans de compétence*). This is funded by a compulsory levy on employers with firms over a certain size. The payments are made into a central fund that then disburses money to providers that compete with each other for the right to provide the service. The keenly contested nature of the competition to provide skills assessment services is indicative of a quasi market form of organisation, in which collective resources finance services delivered by independent providers free at the point of delivery. Unlike the UK, it underpins a well-resourced national provision of guidance services to adults. The providers include *Retravailler* and other non–profit organisations such as the *Centre Interinstitutionel de Bilans de Compétence* (*CIBC*) which each focus on a specific segment of the quasi–market for adult guidance. The national training agency *AFPA* has also entered this market.

The main characteristic of the system is the way in which it tries to 'catch' disadvantaged groups by provision of specialised services for youth, women returners, and the unemployed, as well as employees looking for a career change. It involves funding from the employers, the state at local, regional and national levels, and, as in all other countries, money from EU programmes. It is also more comprehensive than the systems found in other countries studied. The drawback is the way in which the fragmented nature of provision generates inequality in levels of service between the various client groups, depending on the efficiency and coverage of the provider organisations involved. Focusing on specific client groups also risks overlooking people who are not identified as falling into one of the disadvantaged groups and cuts across the notion of guidance for lifelong learning.

Germany

In Germany, the core of the guidance services is provided by the state but housed within a system designed principally for initial orientation of young people and as a recruitment and placement service for employees and the unemployed (Chisholm, 1997). The guidance system has been closely linked to the system of dual education that provides twin-track education and training at school and in the workplace, and to the apprenticeship model of job entry. However, the state monopoly in the provision of guidance services has recently been ended. This, together with the growth of unemployment, exacerbated by the reunification of Germany, has led to the entry of a plethora of third sector and private sector organisations that offer a range of guidance services. The major growth has been in third sector provision aimed at disadvantaged groups, which combine some aspects of guidance with other activities, such as work preparation, confidence building and basic skills training. Those employed by these providers come from a range of career backgrounds and there is no state regulation or professional association governing the sector. Hence, while the core statutory services are highly centralised and regulated, other provision is diverse and uncontrolled. The performance indicators by which such organisations are judged by their funders relate to measurable outcomes like throughput, number of contact hours and market penetration. These drivers shape the nature of provision. There are no attempts to evaluate the impact of the service provided beyond 'tick and bash' accounting mechanisms.

Italy

The Italian guidance system is quite different from that found in either Germany, with its well organised state bureaucratic approach, or France, with its more pluralistic combination of state provision for young people and quasi-market provision for adults. The Italian system is characterised largely by its absence, in the sense that there is little or no state provision of guidance for either group. This is somewhat surprising given the high level of public expenditure in Italy, relative to GDP. However, the state in Italy is 'weak', it is highly decentralised with significant autonomy given to regional governments. In the past, more attention has been given to the provision of subsidies to state-owned industries and to setting up regional resource centres to support small businesses than to reducing frictions in the labour and learning markets. Another characteristic of the Italian labour market is the presence of powerful trade unions that have been able to promote highly protective labour legislation. This has led to extreme inflexibility in the labour market, involving employers in high lay-off costs. This partly explains the absence of an integrated guidance service: those lucky enough to find employment in the large companies or state establishments experience not the 'death of career', but its longevity. There has been little need for continuous career guidance in the Italian economy, nor for initial guidance, in a labour market which still relies heavily on the basis of 'connections' rather than merit for job placement.

Nevertheless, pressed by the forces of globalisation, this is beginning to change and the rigidity of the system is beginning to loosen at the edges. As the labour market becomes more flexible, the need for guidance is rapidly increasing. Into this gap, new third sector guidance providers have begun to insert themselves (Borzaga and Chiesa, 1997). In our field research, we looked at a number of these newly emerging organisations in the North West Italian region of Piedmont. We found that the newly emerging providers are characterised by their strong connections with local and regional government, and with local business interests, as well as by the high degree of involvement of their clients. In the case of so-called 'social cooperatives' (*cooperatives sociale*) which operate in the welfare sector, clients are often members of the cooperative organisation. One such organisation, *Orientamento Lavoro*, belongs to the Italian equivalent of the *Retravailler* movement (known as *CORA: Centri Orientamento Retravailler*) and has been established in Milan as a mutual organisation. It has received free office space from the city council to provide guidance services to clients who become members of the organisation. *CORA* is a member of an umbrella group *Donne e Formazione*, which, as its name suggests, provides guidance and training services mainly to women returners. Another social cooperative, *Orso*, is based in Turin and provides guidance services mainly to young people.

An example of another type of organisation, linked to and supported by local business organisations in partnership with local authorities, is *PromoLavoro* [sic] based in the town of Novara, mid-way between Milan and Turin. This is a private limited company that provides information, counselling and career development courses to its clients. As a private organisation, it is less constrained and more innovative than would be possible if it were a public sector agency. It is financed by the local Chamber of Commerce and the city council to provide guidance services free of charge to unemployed people in the locality, as well as to employees seeking a change of career. The organisation claims a 30% success rate in assisting clients to find new jobs compared to 5% at the local labour exchange. And in Rivoli, a town in the vicinity of Turin that has been affected by growing unemployment due to lay-offs at the local Fiat factory, a Centre for Employment Initiatives has been established as a cooperative organisation. This works closely with the local branch of the small business employers' organisation, *Confederazione Nazionale dell'Artigianato*, to provide a package of work and training for the unemployed in a form of decentralised 'Welfare to Work' programme. It, too, is organised on a local level and supported by local business.

Thus, in Italy, the emerging guidance system is much more fragmented and decentralised than elsewhere in Europe. It relies heavily on local initiative. But its principal characteristic and lesson for policy makers elsewhere is the way in which it demonstrates some successful experiences of locally based guidance services supported by combinations of local authorities and local business interests. The practice among some providers of integrating users and practitioners in social cooperatives is an innovative approach to improving access for disadvantaged groups and building social cohesion from the bottom up. Operating on the basis of inclusion and mutuality, they provide an important example of innovation in the provision of guidance services.

The Netherlands

The Netherlands provides an example of yet another mechanism for organising guidance services, based much more on a real market for guidance services than found elsewhere. Traditionally provided by the state through the Departments of Education (careers teachers) and of Employment (placement officers), a recent reform has led to the emergence of new private guidance companies (Meijers, 1997). This followed from cutbacks and rationalisation of the state-provided services linked to the reforms of the social security system carried out in the mid-1980s. These reforms were designed to encourage participation in the labour market by loosening it up and reducing welfare benefits. This created a system that is intermediate between the flexible labour market found in the UK, and the extremely rigid labour market found in Italy (Netherlands Bureau for Economic Policy Analysis [CPB], 1997). Schools were given block grants to buy in services of guidance professionals from the regional bureaux of the Education Department. In several regions schools decided to provide their own services in-house and the regional bureaux were closed. The employees set up their own private companies, which are now offering their services on the open market, but also compete vigorously for EU funding. Funding for the hard-to-employ disadvantaged groups such as drug addicts has been shifted from the Employment Service to the municipalities. Overall, the marketisation of guidance has resulted in a shift away from client-centred guidance to more labour market oriented work. It has also led to the Netherlands becoming one of the largest beneficiaries of European Programmes, such as LEONARDO DA VINCI.

Summary

The findings corroborate our initial hypothesis that there is substantial variation in the guidance systems among different EU countries. These range from:

- the highly centralised and state bureaucratic system found in Germany;
- the pluralistic French system, with its strong quasi-market provision for adults;
- the decentralised system in Italy, with its strong reliance on local initiative and involvement of local government, and local business interests as well as the client groups themselves; and, finally,
- the Dutch system, with its move towards open marketisation.

The UK system, as shown above, is yet again quite different, following the privatisation of the core career service for young people, combined with a patchwork development of adult guidance delivered by different combinations of TECs and the new careers companies in different areas.

This variability leads naturally to questions concerning the role of EU policy in relation to guidance systems for the emerging European single market, as well as for the possibilities for the coordination of an EU approach to the development of lifelong learning.

EU policy in the field of careers and educational guidance

The European Commission has been actively working on the development of an EU-wide guidance policy for some years. This has been prompted by the recognition of the need for guidance to support the development of the European Single Market, especially in relation to promoting EU-wide labour mobility, and the integration of the EU education and training systems (Rees and Bartlett, 1998, 1999a, 1999b; Rees et al, 1997, 1999). There is clearly a concern to ensure that a more integrated and wide-ranging guidance service should be provided. Indeed, the EC's White Paper on *Teaching and learning: Towards the learning society* (EC, 1995) makes the point that the citizen of Europe has more information available to assist in the selection of hotels and restaurants than in learning opportunities. However, the diversity of national guidance systems, combined with the EC's own arrangements for funding, mean that guidance is neither fully defined nor comprehensively delivered and EU policy has been developed in a fragmented manner.

In response to the emerging need for a more comprehensive approach, some new developments have been initiated. Largely in response to the development of the Single Market, a network of employment services from the member states known as the European Employment Services Network (EURES) has been established, and a computerised EU-wide jobs databank set up. Similarly, EU-wide computerised databases for education and training courses have been developed to which the public (in effect, largely job seekers) has access through their employment service. At the same time, close links are being developed between guidance professionals in higher education throughout the EU through the *Fédération Européen de l'Orientation Academique* network (*FEDORA*).

But the major element of EC co-funded adult guidance is delivered through its various programmes. These principally are ESF projects under the various objectives, the Community Initiative EMPLOYMENT, mentioned earlier with its strands targeting different disadvantaged groups such as ADAPT (those at risk of redundancy), INTEGRA (the most disadvantaged), HORIZON (disabled people), YOUTHSTART (young people) and NOW (women)[4]. In addition, guidance can be funded through the EC's action programme on education, SOCRATES, and on training, LEONARDO DA VINCI. Finally, there is scope for funding guidance through the Fourth Medium Term Action Programme on Equal Treatment for Women and Men. In all these programmes, guidance is provided as part of other activities, such as education, training, enterprise support, exchanges, employment projects and so on: it is not stand-alone. It also tends to be a minor part of the activity concerned. As a consequence, those providing guidance have not necessarily been professionally trained in guidance work. Indeed, they are more likely, primarily, to be educators, trainers or community development workers. Hence, what is provided under the name of guidance is highly variable, encompassing information, group work preparation for returning to work, advice, in-depth counselling and so on.

EU policy towards developing a European approach to guidance services has had to contend with, and work within, the wide variety of approaches taken towards the organisation of guidance services in the various member states. The intervention of and availability of funding from EU programmes has proved critical to the development of guidance services, especially for adults and disadvantaged groups in some member states. This is particularly the case in states where the guidance system is poorly developed (such as Italy), or where there has been a trend towards contracting out or privatisation of guidance services (such as the UK and the Netherlands). In France and especially in Germany, EU programmes and policies have been of more marginal significance.

The clear need is for a much more focused and systematic approach to the development of guidance services at the European level, which, however, will only come about in conjunction with the integration of the national guidance systems themselves. In Italy, the intervention of the EU is occurring in the context of something of a *tabula rasa*, and can be expected to be highly influential in shaping the emerging guidance system. Elsewhere, change will probably be more difficult. Nevertheless, if an integrated EU-wide labour market and a European version of the *Learning Society* is to be pushed forward, specific and focused policies will be needed to provide EU citizens with equal opportunities throughout the Union. The various EU programmes can be catalytic in this process, but there is also a need for more strategic thinking at the European level.

Policy options for the provision of adult guidance services in the UK

The comparative nature of the research, across localities in the UK and across countries in the EU, gives a broad perspective on the policy options for the management and financing of adult guidance services. As indicated above, the provision of adult guidance in the UK is location specific and highly variable from one area to another. In areas where there is a lack of integration of the local guidance system, provision for adults remains especially sparse. In England, local TECs and the voluntary sector have attempted to fill the gap, but their impact is often marginal. In some cases, careers companies and TECs or LECs have joined forces to provide a more integrated service. Almost everywhere, however, funding constraints have limited the extent of provision. Beyond the basic provision of free information, further guidance in individual counselling sessions, group sessions, psychometric testing, and other forms of support are offered on a fee paying basis (although where resources permit, sometimes with subsidies or free provision for disadvantaged groups). This model of free entry level information combined with fees for further guidance has become known as the 'Free Entry Pay to Stay' model, or FEPS. It underlies the introduction of a direct telephone guidance service as part of the new 'Learning Line' initiative. The adoption of this model by Government (unchallenged by the Green Paper, *The Learning Age,* DfEE, 1998) is justified on the basis of 'market failure' in the provision of information. Such market failure is alleged not to occur in the provision of the further elements of guidance services. The general proposition is that those who benefit from guidance services should pay for them. Potential beneficiaries include individuals whose job prospects are improved and whose job search costs are reduced, employers who benefit from reduced recruitment costs, and the state, which is helped by reduced benefit costs if unemployment is reduced. The government's position is that the main beneficiaries are individual job seekers. This position leads to the idea that the only case for free provision of guidance services by the state is in the area of information provision. Free information services in this model act as an entry port into further guidance provision to be offered at commercial fee rates. In our view, this approach needs to be critically re-examined. The asymmetries of information in the markets for labour and the quasi-markets for education and training are severe, but so are asymmetries of information in the markets for guidance. Individuals are no more likely to be able to judge the quality of counselling services on offer by guidance providers than they are able to judge the quality of services offered by providers of education, training or health services. The inability to judge quality undermines the market for guidance and calls for alternative arrangements.

Our international comparative research has therefore been designed to enable us to identify a number of alternative organisational and funding options (Bartlett and Rees, 1997). The *first* such option is finance by employers who stand to gain from having a well-informed and well-motivated supply of workers. One example of this is the employer levy system operated in France which funds the provision of skills assessments through a variety of providers, who compete to provide services to individuals who exercise their right to a leave of absence from work for guidance purposes. A possible route for the introduction of a variant of this system in the UK might be through the introduction of a guidance component for the Individual Learning Accounts proposed by the Labour government. In the version promoted by the Trades Union Congress (TUC) these would be financed by both employer and employee contributions (TUC, 1995, p 19).

The *second* option is finance though local partnerships, which bring together a variety of local interests to finance services for the local community, provided by non-profit organisations such as social cooperatives and voluntary sector organisations. Examples of this approach are the *Missions Locales* in France, and organisations such as *PromoLavoro* in Italy. It should be noted that various EU programmes often also support these types of organisations. Indeed, without it, their continued existence, or even their initial setting up, would often be problematic. In the UK, there are some initiatives that could be developed further along these lines. An example is the Sheffield Training Advice Centre, supported by ESF, local employers and the local TEC. However, the level of funding is insufficient for a comprehensive service and means-tested fees are also charged.

The *third* option is through integration of finance for education, training and guidance services. In France, the state-funded training agency *AFPA* is a provider of skills assessments, and delivers guidance alongside its training activities. In the UK, entry level guidance is provided in FE colleges financed through the Further Education Funding Council budget, but the independence of this guidance is questionable. We have already mentioned the relatively better resourced position of the HE sector.

The *fourth* option is through a state-funded quasi-market in which the state finances provision through competition between preferred provider organisations. As indicated above, the main example of this approach is found in France where the state employment agency, *ANPE*, contracts out the provision of adult guidance services on a competitive basis. In the UK, a quasi-market model has been introduced (in the provision of guidance services to young people) by requiring careers companies to enter into competition for service contracts. TECs also contract for adult guidance services with a range of providers, but as noted above, the TEC-managed quasi-market in the UK has resulted in patchy and fragmented provision.

The *fifth* option is through mutual or collective financing: social self-help membership organisations such as social cooperatives, Jobseekers' Clubs and voluntary organisations. This type of approach has recently also been identified by other research carried out by the DEMOS think-tank (Leadbeater, 1998). As we have seen, the main examples are found in Italy, but also elsewhere throughout Europe. Funding is provided by local authorities, local businesses, the ESF and through membership contributions of the clients. A typical example is the Milanese *Orientamento Lavoro* organisation. These third sector organisations have their echo in the UK through a variety of non-profit and charitable organisations, prominent among which is the EGSA association (Educational Guidance Services for Adults). The first EGSA was established in Belfast in the 1970s and later diffused throughout the UK, and a national association, National Association for Educational Guidance for Adults (NAEGA) has been established. The Belfast EGSA was set up by a group of social workers to help unemployed adults find suitable training and employment opportunities. However, although they provide a useful base on which to build, EGSAs require much more support if they are to continue to have any significant impact on the provision of adult educational guidance in the UK.

All these options for funding can be found in the various European countries that we have looked at in our research. We would argue that it is unlikely that an option based almost entirely on user fees and charges, as is being developed in the UK for adult guidance, would be capable of supporting the widespread diffusion of lifelong guidance required to support the needs of an emerging *Learning Society*. Exactly which alternative option could recommend itself as an alternative to the UK FEPS model depends very much on the vision of the *Learning Society* which drives policy making. It is to the definition of possible alternative visions which we turn to in the concluding section of this report, while leaving the final recommendations for new directions in policy to the policy makers themselves, who can hopefully find some useful ideas and 'guidance' from the findings of our research.

Conclusion: the development of lifelong guidance services for the *Learning Society*

In Rees and Bartlett (1999b), we identified three distinct models of the *Learning Society*. The first is the *'skills growth' model*. This emphasises the link between skill formation and economic growth. The improvement of the skills of the labour force is widely seen as a critical determinant of the international competitiveness of the economy. Rapid technological change requires continual retraining and re-skilling of the labour force to maintain an economy's position in the international pecking order. In this view, career guidance is instrumental and deterministic, providing a brokerage service for individuals in search of particular jobs or training courses.

The second is the *'personal development' model*, which is more concerned with facilitating individual self-fulfillment by provision of resources to enable individuals to make informed choices about their preferred modes of participation in learning and work. This model links more closely to the new view of career outlined above, and implies a more client-centred and voluntaristic role for the guidance services. The approach highlights a concern for equity, and the importance of individual self-fulfilment through the learning experience.

The third we have called the *'social learning' model* which emphasises the embeddedness of the learning process in the social and community context in which individuals are situated. This view stresses the role of social connectivity and the institutions of trust and cooperation in providing the foundations on which market-based economies can flourish and prosper (Putnam, 1993; Fukuyama, 1995). The role of collaborative learning and social capital, which draws on community resources and institutions, in promoting lifelong learning, has also been stressed by Schuller and Field (1998) in their related project on the relationship between initial education and lifelong learning within the ESRC *Learning Society* Research Programme. This model implies a more action-orientated role for guidance services in which guidance providers work alongside individuals rather than acting as independent experts. Examples can be found in the Italian experience with social cooperatives in which disadvantaged individuals work alongside guidance workers in a cooperative enterprise.

Coffield suggests that:

> These three models are a convenient device for making sense not only of much of the research conducted by the fourteen projects which make up *The Learning Society Programme*, but also of the new Labour government's vision for lifelong learning, as detailed in *The Learning Age*. (Coffield, 1999, p 9)

Clearly, these different conceptions of a *Learning Society* imply radically different approaches to policy (see Rees and Bartlett, 1998). However, in all three cases, there is a growing consensus as to the importance of career guidance for adults as an active and central element in its development. This is a view shared by the National Advisory Group for Continuing Education and Lifelong Learning which argues that "the provision of up-to-date, accessible and impartial information and advice will be essential if a strategy of lifelong learning for all is to be successful" (Fryer, 1997).

In the UK (as also in the EU), policy towards lifelong learning and lifelong guidance is clearly informed by the skill growth model. However, in our view, a wider conception of the learning society is needed, encompassing elements of the personal development and social learning approaches. The former could be promoted using our second financing option by an extension of the Individual Learning Accounts proposals to incorporate a guidance element, and including employer contributions as proposed by the TUC (see above), and drawing on the French experience with skills assessment. The latter could be supported by our fifth financing option, developing mutual and collective forms of organisation and funding, and could draw on experiences developed elsewhere, for example in the Italian social cooperatives.

The development of guidance services in the EU member states is crucial to the development of a *learning society*. However, as we have shown, funding sources, institutional arrangements, the levels of regulation of the sector and the drivers of provision vary considerably among and within the countries. Moreover, in the absence of a coherent policy at EU level, the provision of co-funding through programmes primarily targeted at other activities will continue to influence the nature and type of provision. The case studies within England and Scotland together with the experiences of the Netherlands, France, Italy and Germany illustrate the need for a coherent strategic approach to adult guidance services at EU, national, regional and local level[5].

Notes

[1] The marketisation of public sector services under the Conservative government in the UK in the 1990s involved applying market principles to publicly funded services. Hence, potential providers were invited to 'bid' for a contract to provide services, establishing 'quasi-markets'. Service level agreements incorporating targets and performance indicators were established. Quasi-markets remain a significant feature of service delivery in training, health and community care under the Labour government, as well as statutory guidance services for young people, although methods of contract allocation may change.

[2] Outplacement counselling is counselling provided by companies to employees who are about to be made redundant or those recently made redundant. Larger companies often devote substantial resources to this type of activity, but employees

of smaller companies rarely receive an equivalent benefit, so that the provision of a free service is a significant way of balancing the labour market chances of employees who are laid off from this sector.

[3] International Labour Organisation standardised unemployment rate for the UK, 1997, as reported in the Economic Commission for Europe, *Economic Survey of Europe 1999*, No 2, Table A10.

[4] The Initiative is being replaced by one called EQUALITY.

[5] The research was funded under ESRC grant number L123251007. We are grateful to Cathy Bereznicki and Tony Watts for their advice and assistance in carrying out the research on which this chapter is based. We are also grateful to Carlo Borzaga, Anna Chiesa, Francis Danvers, Nadine Monsanson, Lynne Chisholm and Frans Meijers who provided considerable assistance in the fieldwork phase in France, Germany, Italy and the Netherlands and for helpful discussions on the issues raised. Numerous guidance professionals spared time to talk to us about their work and organisations: we are very appreciative. Needless to say, any errors or omissions are entirely our own responsibility.

References

Bartlett, W. and Rees, T. (1997) 'The role of guidance services in the development of a learning society', Paper presented to the ESRC Learning Society Programme Conference, University of Bristol, 27-28 January.

Bartlett, W. and Rees, T. (1999) 'Adult guidance services for a learning society: evidence from England', in F. Coffield (ed) *Speaking truth to power: Research and policy on lifelong learning*, Bristol: Policy Press, pp 73-85.

Borzaga, C. and Chiesa, A. (1997) 'Counselling services in Italy', Paper presented to the International ESRC Project Workshop on Guidance Services and the Learning Society, Bristol, 11-12 September.

Burgess, S. and Rees, H. (1997) *A disaggregate analysis of the evolution of job tenure in Britain 1975-1993*, Centre for Economic Policy Research Discussion Paper 1711, London: CEPR.

Chisholm, L. (1997) 'Guidance services and the learning society: adult guidance and counselling services in Germany', Paper presented to the International ESRC Project Workshop on Guidance Services and the Learning Society, Bristol, 11–12 September.

Coffield, F. (1999) 'Introduction: lifelong learning as a new form of social control?', in F. Coffield (ed) *Why's the beer always stronger up North? Studies of lifelong learning in Europe*, Bristol: The Policy Press, pp 1–12.

Collin, A. and Watts, A.G. (1996) 'The death and transfiguration of career – and or career guidance?', *British Journal of Guidance and Counselling*, vol 24, no 3, pp 385–98.

Danvers, F. and Monsanson, N. (1997) 'Guidance services and the learning society: adult guidance and counselling services in France', Paper presented to the International ESRC Project Workshop on Guidance Services and the Learning Society, Bristol, 11–12 September.

DfEE (Department for Education and Employment) (1998) *The Learning Age: A renaissance for a new Britain*, Cm 3790, London: The Stationery Office.

EC (European Commission) (1995) *Teaching and learning: Towards the Learning Society*, Luxembourg: Office for Official Publications of the European Communities.

ECCTIS (Educational Counselling and Credit Transfer Information Service) (1998) *Lifelong learning: A survey of second-year undergraduates 1997/98*, London: ECTISS.

Fryer, R.H. (1997) *Learning for the twenty first century*, London: National Advisory Group for Continuing Education and Lifelong Learning.

Fukuyama, F. (1995) *Trust: The social virtues and the creation of prosperity*, New York, NY: Free Press

Gregg, P. and Wadsworth, J. (1995) 'A short history of labour turnover, job tenure and job security, 1975–93', *Oxford Review of Economic Policy*, vol 11, no 1, pp 73–90.

Hawthorn, R. (1996) 'Other sources of guidance on learning and work', in A.G. Watts, J. Killeen, J.M. Kidd and R. Hawthorn (eds) *Rethinking careers education and guidance: Theory, policy and practice*, London: Routledge, pp 173–85.

Inkson, K. (1995) 'Effects of changing economic conditions on managerial job changes and career patterns', *British Journal of Management*, vol 6, pp 183-94.

Leadbeater, C. (1998) *The employee mutual*, London: DEMOS.

McNair, S. (1998) *Supporting learner autonomy*, Sheffield: DfEE.

Meijers, F. (1997) 'Educational and vocational services in practice', Paper presented to the International ESRC Project Workshop on Guidance Services and the Learning Society, Bristol, 11-12 September.

Netherlands Bureau for Economic Policy Analysis (CPB) (1997) *Challenging neighbours: Rethinking German and Dutch economic institutions*, Berlin: Springer.

Putnam, R.D. (1993) 'The prosperous community: social capital and economic growth', *The American Prospect* (Spring), pp 35-42.

Rees, T. and Bartlett, W. (1998) 'Labour markets, learning and equality', in Target (eds) *The globalising knowledge economy – Challenges for small businesses*, Reports from the 1998 Cumberland Lodge Conference, Target and European Commission, pp 61-76.

Rees, T. and Bartlett, W. (1999a) 'Adult guidance services in the European learning society: a Scottish case study', *Studies in the Education of Adults*, vol 31, no 1, pp 5-20.

Rees, T. and Bartlett, W. (1999b) 'Models of guidance services in the learning society: the case of the Netherlands', in F. Coffield (ed) *Why's the beer always stronger up North? Studies of lifelong learning in Europe*, Bristol: The Policy Press, pp 21-30.

Rees, T., Bartlett, W. and Watts, A.G. (1997) 'Adult guidance and the learning society: the marketisation of guidance services in the UK, France and Italy', in F. Coffield (ed) *A national strategy for lifelong learning*, Newcastle: Department of Education, University of Newcastle, pp 159-76.

Rees, T., Bartlett, W. and Watts, A.G. (1999) 'The marketisation of guidance services in Germany, France and Britain', *Journal of Education and Work*, vol 12, no 1, pp 5-20.

Schuller, T. and Field, J. (1998) 'Social capital, human capital and the learning society', *International Journal of Lifelong Education*, vol 17, no 4, pp 226-35.

TUC (Trades Union Congress) (1995) *Funding lifelong learning: A strategy to deliver the National Education and Training Targets*, London: TUC.

Watts, A.G. (1996) *Careerquake*, London: DEMOS.

Watts, A.G. (1997) *Strategic directions for careers services in higher education*, NICEC Project Report, Cambridge: CRAC.

Watts, A.G. (1998) 'Applying market principles to the delivery of careers guidance services: a critical review', in W. Bartlett, J. Roberts, and J. Le Grand (eds) *A revolution in social policy: Quasi-market reforms in the 1990s*, Bristol: The Policy Press, pp 239-54.

FIVE

Changing patterns of training provision in the National Health Service: an overview

Jenny Hewison, Therese Dowswell and Bobbie Millar

Background

The focus of our *Learning Society* project was on the continuing education of nurses and allied staff working in the National Health Service (NHS). The project addressed issues relating to access and equity: factors which may encourage or inhibit progress towards a *Learning Society*. In this chapter we also examine the effects on participants of taking responsibility for their own learning by undertaking courses in their own time or at their own expense. This latter issue has been the focus of attention of policy makers and employers. Over the past two decades, motivated by a need to reduce the perceived burden of training on employers and the state, successive governments have encouraged a shift towards regarding post-compulsory education and training as an individual responsibility (King, 1993). It could be argued that in policy terms such a shift has the potential to be counterproductive in that it might systematically disadvantage certain sectors of the workforce previously targeted as training priorities: women and the less well qualified.

The shift of responsibility for continuing education and its consequences can be studied to good effect in the NHS. It is one of the country's largest employers, with almost a million employees and requires a varied, flexible and well-trained workforce. It is one of the major employers of women, 47% of the NHS workforce being nursing and midwifery staff who are predominantly female (NAHAT, 1995). Hence, studying continuing education in the health service allowed us to examine participation by a range of staff and to reflect on the implications of combining working and learning for individuals with differing employment and domestic circumstances. The study was carried out in the context of major changes both in the funding arrangements and organisation of health services, and in the provision of education and training for health service staff.

The changing policy context

Over the past 15 years private sector ways of working have been introduced explicitly into the supply of health services, and into the organisation and purchasing of continuing education and training (Humphreys, 1996). The reorganisation of the NHS and the attempt to encourage the development of a market in healthcare has been reflected in the reorganisation of training budgets. Within the NHS the decision to purchase healthcare is not made by the individual consumer and this separation of consumption and payment for services has been described as a 'quasi-market' in healthcare (Le Grand and Bartlett, 1993). Similarly, in the main, funding for continuing education has not depended on the purchasing decisions of individual students. However, recent changes in the funding and organisation of continuing education reflect an increasing influence of market forces or what Rees et al (1997), in another project within *The Learning Society Programme,* have described as an increased 'marketisation' of services. During the early 1990s, Regional Health Authorities allocated places on specialist courses through what were known as 'Working Paper 10' arrangements (DoH, 1989). With changes in the organisation of the NHS and with the abolition of regional health authorities, this function has now devolved to local consortia comprising representatives from hospital trusts, GP fundholders and other 'users' of training. These developments have tended to place more influence in the hands of employers who are now more directly involved in the process of commissioning education and have more direct control over training and staff replacement monies (Humphreys, 1996; Humphreys and Davis, 1995; Humphreys and Quinn, 1994). The current Labour Government is poised to extend the influence of employers as 'users' of education and training (*Nursing Standard,* 1999).

As well as reorganisation in the funding arrangements for pre- and post-registration education for staff, there have also been major changes in the provision of education. Although two decades ago most basic and continuing education for nurses and allied staff was provided 'in-house' by hospital schools of nursing, education at pre- and post-registration levels has now shifted to external providers, that is, higher education (HE) institutions. Most hospital trusts retain their own staff development department but many of their activities relate to health and safety training and essential skills training for staff such as moving and handling. While funding for external provision by HE departments has been safeguarded in the short to medium term, their longer-term future is less certain. In the future, hospital trusts may opt for more 'in-house' provision.

Like other HE departments, those providing continuing education for healthcare staff are under pressure to generate income via research and teaching. One form of such income generation is via new courses (such as degree courses) which are directly funded by individual students. The emergence of such courses means that there are at least two 'consumers' of continuing education and training, employers and individual students. The demands these two groups make in terms of the content, mode of provision and academic credit of courses, and the amount each are prepared to pay, may differ considerably. The fact that individual students have become purchasers of continuing education has led Humphreys to refer to the new developments in education and training in the NHS as a complex quasi-market (Humphreys, 1996).

Against this background of changing funding arrangements the continuing education and training of nursing and midwifery staff has been reformed and regulated by national professional and statutory organisations. The United Kingdom Central Council (UKCC) maintains a register of all nursing and midwifery staff in the UK and maintains professional standards for training via regulation of pre and post-registration education. The English National Board for Nursing, Midwifery and Health Visiting also has a role in maintaining standards in education and has had a major role in course validation and accreditation. By promoting a number of reforms these organisations have created an atmosphere where continuing education is a high priority for professionals working in the health service. Pre-registration education was rationalised and up-graded following major reforms in the late 1980s (UKCC, 1986). At the same time, education for enrolled nurses was phased out. Nurse education is now taken at diploma or higher diploma level. Further, while degree level programmes have been available since the early 1960s, the number of departments offering degrees in nursing and special registration programmes for non-nursing graduates has increased with the move into HE.

There have also been changes in post-registration continuing education and training and national guidelines have been introduced prescribing a minimum of five study days in every three-year period in order for nursing and midwifery staff to maintain their registration (UKCC, 1994). Such guidelines have created an atmosphere where continuing professional updating (and providing evidence of this) is a matter of priority. This situation has been exacerbated by the overall up-grading of qualifications. Most nursing and midwifery staff working in the NHS trained before many of the changes described above took effect and followed more traditional routes to registration. Before the 1987 reforms professional qualifications were not explicitly linked with academic accreditation. Thus, while the original intention of the reforms was to simplify pre-registration education by creating a single tier of qualified nursing staff, in the short to medium term this has not occurred. In effect there are likely to be nursing and other staff working at similar grades who have undertaken a variety of programmes of preparation and who possess a variety of academic qualifications. The existence of this variety creates pressure on all staff to upgrade their qualifications by virtue of the fact that experienced staff may be asked to supervise staff whom they perceive as more academically qualified than themselves.

Irrespective of their intrinsic worth, academic qualifications provide a simple selection device for recruitment and promotion. However, despite the introduction of national guidelines on the continuing education of qualified nursing and midwifery staff (UKCC, 1994), the obligations of NHS trusts are unclear with regard to the direct provision of training, release from work, staff replacement or funding for courses provided externally. Humphreys (1996) has argued that a tension has arisen from the NHS reforms of the 1980s and the concurrent activities of the professional nursing organisations. While the former has tended to increase the influence of the employers over education and training and serves thereby to act as a de-professionalising force, the activities of the professional organisations (along with the shift into HE) have served to increase the qualifications and status of nurses and thereby increase professionalisation. In the current political context, the influence of employing organisations is increasing. It is important to be aware of this changing educational context in order to interpret some of the findings described below.

Theoretical framework

Human capital theory and motivation to participate in training

The structural factors that shape labour market participation are often presented as individual choices. We argue that the same is likely to be true for training. Thus, a course might be available in an employee's own time and it would then be up to that individual to decide whether or not to take up this training 'opportunity'. As with employment, 'not taking the opportunity' is generally interpreted as a sign of lack of commitment to work. By these means, structural inequalities in access are turned into attributes of individuals. They cease to be problems and become useful selection devices in decisions relating to recruitment, promotion or availability of future training opportunities.

The theoretical framework underpinning the study was that of human capital theory. Green (1993) suggests that training decisions 'respond to economic incentives'. The theory predicts the circumstances in which training is more or less likely to occur. Some of the relevant factors relate to the individual's employment circumstances (for example working for a large or a small firm) but others are considered to be characteristics of the individual, for example how committed the person is to paid work.

Commitment to paid work is known to be influenced by domestic responsibilities. Analysis by Green (1993) of the General Household Survey revealed that women were less likely to participate in training than men. It was suggested by Green that part of this shortfall might have been explained by the fact that 'the attitudes and choices of people are likely to be affected by the opportunities they perceive'. That is, those with domestic responsibilities are less likely to put themselves forward for training because they perceive that the costs of participation (in terms of effects on other areas of their lives) are not outweighed by putative benefits such as career advancement. Within the NHS there is evidence to support this theory. In a study by Jackson (1994) 70% of women said that it was difficult for them to attend some kinds of training events. This study also emphasised that part-time workers were particularly disadvantaged regarding training; nearly all of these workers were women.

More recent work within *The Learning Society Programme* has criticised the human capital approach (Fevre, 1997; Coffield, 1999). Fevre and colleagues present evidence from a number of studies which suggests that human capital theory is inadequate in explaining the diverse motivations of individuals participating in training. They argue that training is often not regarded as an investment by individuals, but that on the contrary "... in the UK the usual idea has been that the users and hence the proper providers of education and training are employers and the state" (p 9). Hence, individuals rather than seeing training as an investment may perceive it as an obligation and under these circumstances the thought of individuals paying for training or undertaking it in their own time may be out of the question. Thus, pinpointing the users or consumers of education and training is not straightforward: while individuals may participate in training (and might thus be regarded as consumers) they may perceive that it is the employer that is the 'user' of this training and, under these circumstances, education would not be perceived as a personal investment. Others have argued in a similar vein, with particular reference to education and training in the NHS (Calpin-Davies, 1996). Fevre (1997) also argues that credentialism has often "been mistaken for investment in human capital" (p 11), and makes the distinction between training to do the job better and training to get a better job. In the former case the content of education and training is crucial, in the latter, content may be irrelevant.

These issues concerning motivation and the putative benefits of training were central in our study of training in the NHS as they have an important bearing on employee attitudes towards undertaking training in their own time and funding their own training.

Access and barriers to participation in training

There is a large literature on the factors associated with non-participation in training, some of it specifically relating to the nursing workforce (Bridge and Salt, 1992; McGivney, 1993; Maguire et al, 1993; Redshaw and Harris, 1994; Sheperd, 1995; Barriball and While, 1997) Within this literature responsibility for childcare is widely recognised as a factor constraining participation. Where individuals combine parenting and training they may need to develop strategies to avoid negative personal consequences. We gained additional insight into the factors involved by drawing on the theoretical and empirical literature on social roles and role strain. The most relevant work in this area concerns the effects on women of trying to combine paid work with family responsibilities. There is a substantial literature on this topic, with contributions from occupational psychology and management studies (for example Firth-Cozens and West, 1991; Davidson and Cooper, 1992), developmental psychology (Greenberger and O'Neil, 1993; O'Neil and Greenberger, 1994), sociology and social policy (for example Bielby and Bielby, 1989; Brannen and Moss, 1990), and other social science disciplines concerned with women and the family. The emphasis in much of this research has been on dual career families; that is, families in which both the man and woman have full-time, well-paid professional or managerial jobs.

From the perspective of human capital theory, two of the most useful aspects of the above work are how social roles influence the opportunities that people perceive to be open to them, and their response to those opportunities. The ways in which conflict between roles influences both perceptions and responses has been of particular interest. For example, a perceived opportunity in one role is not a real or practicable opportunity at all if taking it up involves damaging performance in another role. Thus, if the opportunity to seek promotion is likely to be associated with poorer performance in relation to an individual's role as parent, home carer or spouse, then the 'opportunity' may not be taken.

Our own previous work (Hewison and Dowswell, 1994; Dowswell and Hewison, 1995) has described the conflict between the demands of home and work. In that work the focus was on working mothers. In our current study in the health service we have added the demands of training as a third factor in the equation. Hence, the study has focused on the training opportunities and attitudes to training expressed by healthcare staff with and without childcare responsibilities. The nursing and midwifery workforce is predominantly female; however, we included male participants in our study. The number of men in the sample was too small to allow direct comparisons between male and female parents; nevertheless, we were interested in the perspectives of men on issues concerning work, training and childcare. We perceived at the outset that the study would have wider implications regarding psychological and practical barriers to participation in training by other groups of workers.

The study

Aims

Using healthcare as our arena, we focused on participation in continuing education and training of non-medical staff. We aimed to address a number of issues. First, we wished to document recent changes in the provision of continuing education and training with particular emphasis on the shift towards increased responsibility by individual staff to support (by time and money) their own continuing development. Second, we sought to describe the costs and benefits that participants take into account when deciding to enrol on courses either in their own time or that of their employers. A third objective was to describe the perspectives of participants undertaking courses in their own or in their employers' time. We were particularly interested in the way that domestic commitments shaped these perspectives. A fourth objective was to describe the experience of participating in continuing education and training on an individual's home, family and workplace. Fifth, we wished to describe the views of purchasers and providers of training on the shift towards increased responsibility for individual staff to support their continuing development, and last, we aimed to examine the implications of the findings for training policy.

Methods

To address these issues, we used a number of data collection methods.

Context

In order to document whether there had been any general shift from provision of training in employers' to employees' time we reviewed both the general literature in the area and a number of published prospectuses and yearbooks. This review provided us with contextual information at the national level, which was supplemented with data from the main external (HE) provider of continuing education for healthcare staff in our local area. Data on enrolment, funding arrangements, completion rates and demographic data on participants were collected for a number of courses. Where available, data was collected over two to five years. All records were held in anonymous form and the study received ethical approval from the College of Health Research Ethics Board.

Main fieldwork phase

We conducted interviews with 98 participants on a range of courses including a two-year course for enrolled nurses to upgrade their qualification (an open-learning course), degree level courses (part-time day and evening courses) specialist courses for nursing staff (full-time), a course in health promotion (open-learning) and a return to practice course.

Participants were identified after discussion with course tutors. We wished to include both men and women on a variety of courses where students were either self- or employer-funded or were undertaking training either in their own or their employers' time. We selected seven courses which offered variety in terms of such arrangements and in terms of academic level and content. The study was described at a scheduled course session to a cohort on each of the courses by the researcher (TD). Those willing to participate were contacted to arrange interviews. One hundred and ten students were approached and while there were only two direct refusals, for various reasons, it was not possible to arrange interviews with a further 10 students[1]. The sample also included nine participants attending a Return to Practice Course. As much of the interview dealt with issues concerning the participants' current workplace, this latter group will be excluded from the main descriptions and comparisons below. For the rest (89) all but three were employed within the health service.

The sample was thus not 'representative' in a statistical sense; courses were selected to provide variety rather than to 'represent' the selection of courses offered by the HE provider. As the interviews sought qualitative information on student experiences, our strategy was purposive and we sought diversity rather than statistical representativeness.

At the outset, we proposed to compare courses where individuals were attending in their own rather than in their employer's time (and where individuals rather than employers funded training). In the event this was not possible. We had not anticipated the extent of diversity which already existed in student funding arrangements. When we examined student records and when we interviewed course participants, it became clear that within the same course there were a variety of arrangements: individuals attending a part-time day-time course may have been wholly, partly or not funded at all by their employer. Similarly, some staff would be released from work to attend the course while some attended on their day off. Hence, comparisons were made *within* courses as well as *between* courses.

Interviews were carried out in a location most convenient to the participant, and most of the participants chose to be seen in their own homes. All interviews were carried out by the same researcher (TD). The interviews were semi-structured and recorded on audio tape; and to reduce the problems associated with technical failure, detailed notes were made during and after the interviews.

The interviews included a full training and work history. Participants were asked about the reasons for taking part in the course and the factors they had taken into account in reaching their decisions. They were also asked more generally about their attitudes to continuing education and training and about possible benefits they envisaged on completing the course. Participants were also asked explicitly about their preferences regarding training provision, for example whether they would have preferred alternative provision such as full-time rather than open-learning or vice versa.

The interview also covered issues relating to funding and release from work, the effects of participation on respondents and other family members and the types of support necessary to allow them to attend the course or to do coursework. Participants were also asked more generally about their commitment to work, parenting and other social roles. Throughout the interview we were interested in evidence of fit (or lack of it) between the ways in which training was provided and the expressed needs of participants.

Interviews included a mixture of open-ended and pre-coded (closed) questions. Standard methods of content analysis were used to post-code replies to open-ended questions (Silverman, 1993; Moser and Kalton, 1971). We were particularly interested in motivation and factors encouraging participation in training. Where participants expressed causal beliefs regarding the costs and benefits of training, such causal statements were coded using the Leeds Attribution Coding System (LACS: Stratton et al, 1988), a well validated and widely used coding system for qualitative data. Statistical analysis was carried out using SPSS (Statistical Package for the Social Sciences).

Non-participant interviews

We carried out a small number of interviews with NHS staff who had not participated in training during the last year (*n*=11). We had hoped to identify 'non-participants' via the participant interviews using a snowball technique. However, this approach was not successful. Students participating on courses were very reluctant to label their colleagues as 'non-participants'. In a climate where continuing education is of such high priority, not undertaking training was associated with stigma. We therefore contacted staff officers in two trusts who were able on our behalf to approach staff who had no recent training experience. Again, we sought a diverse rather than a statistically representative sample. These interviews covered the same topics as above with some questions recast in a hypothetical form. The aim of these interviews was to shed further light on those factors constraining or encouraging participation in continuing education and training.

Purchaser interviews

To provide contextual information interviews were carried out with training managers in NHS trusts. Managers were asked about:
- training policies, budgets and funding arrangements;
- the effects of training on service delivery (eg where staff are released from work it may have implications for other staff or service delivery);
- beliefs about the purposes of continuing education and training;
- links with external educational providers.

A total of 20 interviews were conducted with training managers and responses were analysed in terms of content. All but one of these interviews was recorded on audio-tape and transcribed in full[2].

Provider interviews

Interviews were also conducted with training providers (that is, staff in the School of Health Care Studies and staff with a designated training role employed by the trusts) to ascertain views on funding, policy changes, service constraints and liaison with service providers.

Findings

In the early stages of the research we carried out a review of literature relating to continuing education and training in the health service. This review provided a policy context within which to interpret our findings. Alongside this general literature review we examined yearbooks and national directories of training provision to determine the way in which general shifts in policy were reflected in changes in provision.

The results of this exercise were not easy to interpret. There was some evidence that for healthcare courses there was an increase in the overall number of courses being offered via 'open-learning' provision. However, along with changes in the mode of provision of courses, as described above, there have been more general changes in the content and structure of many courses. Hence, names of courses and the academic credit associated with particular courses have changed year by year and therefore it was very difficult to trace courses over time to decide whether a course that was previously offered full-time was later being offered via open-learning methods. Alongside changes in names, new courses emerge each year in response to the changing context and changing demand. For example, in the Leeds context one of the courses from which we drew part of our sample relied mainly on part-time (evening) taught provision and on self-directed learning which students undertook in their own time. However, the degree course we selected for study had been introduced in 1994; it did not replace an existing course but was designed to meet the demand for degree level qualifications by nursing, midwifery and allied staff. Thus, while it was not possible to trace such courses back over time to indicate whether there had been any actual shift in provision, the very existence of such courses reflects something of the changing context. This course was specifically developed to avoid the need for staff to seek release from work (or indeed funding from their employer) and was thus an explicit example of a course where the responsibility for learning lay with the individual rather than the employer.

Further evidence of this shift was provided by interviews with staff providing continuing education courses for nurses and midwives. For example, a midwifery tutor explained that a course that had previously been run full-time was now part-time. Although the course had been designed for students on day release, the reality of leave arrangements was more complex. As the tutor put it

> "The reality is that they come in on their days off to do the study ....
> There are three students from the same trust, the community midwife
> gets a day off, the hospital ones don't. The hospital midwives have to
> do more.... The budget isn't there to replace them. Some [midwives]
> can manage their own diary and still get the work done, but some can't
> do that."

Here was an example of a 'part-time' course where the experience of individual students was very different and where a proportion of students would be undertaking study entirely in their own time.

Demographic data

The sample included 81 women and eight men with an age range of 24–59. The mean age was 34.5, and all but four of the sample were white Europeans. Most of the sample were owner-occupiers with 93% living in their own homes and the rest in rented accommodation. In terms of education, half of the sample stayed on at school beyond 16 and most were educated to at least O level standard (84%) although 9% had CSEs as their highest qualification and 7% had no qualifications when they left school. The interview asked about children living in the household rather than whether participants had any children per se (hence, participants with children who had left home are regarded as not having childcare responsibilities as far as the analysis is concerned). Approximately half of the households included children (45 households – 51%) and of these, 38 households (44.7% of total households) required arrangements for childcare while the parent was at work. (If the youngest child was older than 14 then childcare arrangements were not always necessary.) Care was primarily provided by spouses (28%) and grandparents (28%). Seventy-seven per cent of the sample were living in a household with their partner, 9% with another adult and 13% in a household where they were the only adult.

Work patterns

Most of the sample worked full-time. Eighty-two per cent were in full-time employment (usually 37.5 hours per week although shift patterns meant that weekly hours varied). Thirty-eight per cent of the sample were working as registered nurses and 23% as enrolled nurses (hence the total proportion of nurses in the sample was 61%). Twenty-two per cent of the sample were working as midwives and 17% were working in allied professions (including audiology and radiography). The average length of experience in healthcare for this sample was 13.7 years (range 5–34 years). Sixteen per cent of the sample were paid on non-nursing grades. For the rest, 23% were employed at D grade, 40% at E grade and 21% at more senior levels[3].

Sixty-five per cent of the sample were working shifts rather than regular day-time hours. Sixty-one per cent of the sample were working in or around Leeds, the rest were spread across North and South Yorkshire, and a small number (6) travelled from the East Coast and Nottingham areas.

Mode of provision

The mode of provision varied on the courses examined. Forty-eight per cent of the sample were attending day time courses, 27% where the taught component was delivered in the evening and 25% attended courses where there was both day-time and evening attendance. All of the courses were run on weekdays. Fifty-five per cent of the sample attended courses that included clinical (work-based) placement. While 25% were attending full-time courses and had full-time secondment, 17% were attending part-time courses and the rest (58%) were attending part-time courses that relied primarily on self-directed learning or open-learning.

An important component in the participant interviews was the section relating to perceptions about the costs and benefits of taking part in training and this is the subject of much of the rest of this report. In terms of our theoretical framework and in view of the policy changes in the provision of continuing education for healthcare staff, the findings relating to motivations were particularly interesting. In the background section we suggested that training investments may be like other forms of investments and respond to economic incentives. That is, at the outset, we expected that motivations would relate primarily to perceptions about future benefits in terms of job choice, mobility and promotion. In the main, our findings did not support this expectation. We have used extracts from interviews to illustrate response categories.

Motivations to enrol on the course

There were a range of motivations for deciding to take part in the various courses and respondents frequently gave a number of reasons. The percentages for each reason therefore relate to the total proportion of the sample that mentioned (without prompting) that reason. Motivations were elicited by asking the question: 'Can you think back to when you started on the course. Why did you want to do any further education or training at all?' Student replies were coded in terms of content. As responses represented answers to a question asking 'Why ...' all were expressed as causal attributions. Eight broad categories were derived – in later analysis these have been grouped to allow simpler comparisons between groups.

Personal motivations

Fifteen per cent of respondents ($n=13$) described motivations relating to their sense of having missed out in the past or of having a 'chip on their shoulder' about not having gained a particular qualification earlier. Thus, in a sense, these individuals were trying to 'catch up' with where they thought they should be in terms of academic qualifications, and obtaining the degree or whatever was 'remedial' or part of a personal catching-up exercise. Extracts from interviews illustrate such responses.

"But I think one of the main reasons was feeling that I didn't achieve as well at school as I would have liked. It seemed like a chance to do it again although quite a number of years later." (Midwife)

"I want one [a degree] for personal reasons, possibly because I am the only one out of four who hasn't got one...."

Interviewer: "Do you mean in your family?"

"Yes, it is personal to myself. I mean I think I messed up when I was younger." (Staff Nurse – Grade E)

Twenty-eight per cent of respondents (*n*=24) described more positive personal reasons for undertaking the course. These individuals saw their own continuing personal development as important and wanted to take part in a course because they didn't want to get 'stale'. Some liked the stimulation of attending courses, or thought it was important to continue to learn throughout life:

"It is something I thought about really after doing the diploma and because they talked on there about how we have points at level two ... it didn't sound difficult to me to go on to the next level. Having got so far I thought I might as well keep going." (Staff Nurse Grade E)

Sixteen per cent of the sample (*n*=14) said that they were generally interested in the course (this group was distinguished from those that said that they were interested in the course as it related closely to their area of work – this group are discussed below):

"Interest really, for me. Because my midwifery course, that course really sparked an interest in me and I wanted to further that." (Midwife)

Work-related motivations

Seventeen per cent of respondents (*n*=15) mentioned reasons to do with their current job that prompted interest in the course – this was usually expressed in positive terms. These respondents perceived that they would be able to do their jobs better with increased knowledge about, for example, health education.

Twenty-seven per cent of respondents (*n*=24) mentioned motivations relating to promotion and 17% (*n*=15) talked about moving sideways to a different sort of work role.

While the above two categories described positive professional factors encouraging participation, there were also three broad categories that related to the work domain which tended to be more negative.

Thirty-three per cent of participants (*n*=29) identified aspects of their current job that they didn't feel they were doing well (for example teaching students) or that they were being overtaken by others in their immediate work environment:

> "As part of my job I actually assess the students .... So, I was told to do it I suppose, advised that it would be in my best interests to go on this course ... they built into my job that I would have a teaching and assessing input and therefore I ought to go and get a degree." (Nurse – Grade H)

Fifty-two per cent of the sample (more than half) mentioned the wider professional environment as a reason for taking part in the course. The expressions these staff used were "the way nursing is going now..." or "with the changes in the NHS".

> "When I was doing my nurse training, I knew the way nursing was going. I knew that courses would be springing up and I wanted to complete my training and get a degree.... It creates pressure that people have to do it when they resent having to do it when they're not inclined to. But the way that nursing's going at the moment, if you don't keep up to date and get some study you get left behind if you want promotion, if you want to get on, you have to be *seen* to do it." (Staff Nurse – Grade E)

> "I don't think career wise, I don't know, I can't see it making any, making an awful difference, you know. Maybe I am wrong but I feel that the way things are going in nursing, if I am going to stay in nursing really I need to have a degree because increasingly when you look in the *Nursing Times* for jobs and things now, particularly the more senior posts, they're like graduates you know.... I'm going to be in the NHS for a

number of years, I'm going to have to have a degree probably, so that's really why I decided to do it." (Staff Nurse – Grade E)

A category that was mainly used by enrolled nurses was the idea that "I felt my role had disappeared so I was 'forced' into it." (Sometimes members of this group said that they didn't really want to do the course at all.) These sorts of reasons also applied to nurses on the specialist courses, "you have to do this course to stay on this unit". These respondents did not feel that they needed to 'catch up' in a personal or broadly professional sense, but that they were 'pushed' into it by managerial/work organisation pressures; they identified their workplace environment (rather than the general professional environment or pressures relating to performing a specific role) as the source of pressure. A total of almost 46% (*n*=39) gave these sorts of reasons.

In order to simplify comparisons between groups, motivational response categories were merged to form four broad categories. As in the classification above, responses were grouped according to whether they related to the personal or professional domain. Within these two domains responses were either (i) future oriented or (ii) related to their present role, or to their past. In general, responses relating to the present and the past tended to be negative. Thus, participants identified gaps in their previous education and training, or referred to current pressures (either professional or personal) encouraging participation. In contrast, motivations relating to the future tended to be more positive and suggested optimism about the future and about future benefits (personal or professional) resulting from participation in the course. These positive responses were examples of where participants perceived they were responding to 'economic incentives' (for example promotion) in the model described by Green (1993). In some respects these categories are analogous with the proverbial 'stick and carrot'. While the stick would operate from behind, would be perceived in a negative light and would act as a *push* to encourage participation, the carrot would be held in front (the future), would be perceived positively (for example as an investment) and would thus act as a *pull* to participation. (These categories have been described in more detail in an earlier publication – see Dowswell et al, 1998a.)

One of the aims of the study was to assess the effects of having heavy domestic responsibilities on participation in training. For the sample already enrolled on courses it was possible to compare those with and without childcare responsibilities in terms of their motivations to take part in the course and in terms of the effects of the course on work and family life. So, did the presence of the children in the household influence motivations to take part in courses? Or, relating this question to our theoretical framework, did domestic constraints influence perceptions about opportunities?

Domestic responsibilities and motivations to take part in training

Of the 89 participants, 45 lived in households where there were children and 44 where there were no household members under 16. Examination of the motives encouraging participation for those individuals with and without children revealed that there were some significant differences between the two groups. (These findings are described in more detail elsewhere – Dowswell et al, 2000: in press.) While those with and without children were equally likely to be motivated by negative or *push* factors, it was interesting to note that those with children were less likely to perceive positive benefits from training. This group were less likely to perceive that training was an 'investment' in their future; that is, they were less likely to mention personal development, interest or optimism about promotion drawing (or pulling) them towards training.

Course funding and leave from work

In 58% (*n*=52) of cases the employer was paying the full course fee. Eighteen per cent of students (*n*=16) were paying the entire course fee themselves and in the remainder of cases (24%, *n*=21) students were paying some part of the fee. When asked about who should pay, only two respondents thought that the student should pay, 42% thought the cost should be shared and 54% (*n*=48) thought the health service/employer should pay.

Leave for the taught component of the course was provided for 62% of the sample (*n*=55). For the rest, leave was less than the taught time – 18 students had no leave whatsoever. For the open learning students the taught time was likely to form only a small proportion of the total time they were expected to put into course work.

The effects of participation on home life

Participants described various effects of participating in the course on home and family life. The findings relating to those students on the enrolled nurses conversion course have been described in more detail elsewhere (Dowswell et al, 1998b). Here we describe findings for the sample as a whole.

Fifty-five per cent of the sample (*n*=49) said that the course had impacted on family life and on relationships within families; and this was usually in a negative way. Organising childcare was not always easy for participants and several of the participants described guilt associated with their role as parent or guilt associated with asking 'favours' from friends or relatives in terms of childcare provision. Quotations from interviews illustrate these points.

> "I think I rely more on, certainly my eldest, I think to help out a bit more. Well, all of them but perhaps her more. I was going to say that I have let my house go a bit, you know what I mean by that, and I think perhaps the biggest change is that I feel as though I have less chance to spend time with the children, especially the youngest one at weekends. Because I tend to be racing round trying to do everything.... Fitting housework and things in that I would have done on my day off." (Nurse – Grade D)

> "If I am up to my eyeballs in it ... and if I have got to get an assignment in, my friend will say, oh bring them down. But I hate asking people. I hate putting on anyone else." (Staff Nurse – Grade E)

> "Although [husband] is really understanding, sometimes he can't understand when I've just got to get this particular work done, and he has just got to take the kids out of the way, and I think he feels a bit resentful sometimes that it has taken quite so much time up." (Midwife)

More than two thirds of the sample (69%) said that the course had affected home care. Most of these participants mentioned that their usual standards of home care and catering for their families had changed (for the worse). The following quotations illustrate responses to the question: 'Have you made any changes at home while you have been on the course?'

"Oh my God. Yes, my house has gone to rack. I just don't have time. I don't have time to cook, you know, really good full meals every single night, like I used to. It's just not a top priority any more." (Staff Nurse – Grade E).

"Oh yes! My housework goes to pot. I don't feel as though I have got any time." (Audiologist)

Participants described a range of strategies to cope with changes at home. Housework would be prioritised, for example, but ironing would be abandoned as a 'luxury' activity.

Sixty-eight per cent of the sample (*n*=60) said that the course had led to a reduction in leisure activities.

There were some interesting findings relating to the effects of the course on home life for those with and without children. First, there were *no* differences between groups in terms of the effects of the course on home care. Most of the sample talked about doing less housework and this applied to those without children just as much as it did to those with children.

There were differences, however, between those with and without children in terms of the effects of the course on other family members (including partners) and family care. Not surprisingly, those with children were much more likely to mention such changes.

Referring back to our theoretical framework it seemed that participants in training used a whole range of coping strategies to maintain their various social roles. We found examples of role expansion (the participant simply taking on additional work and responsibilities), personal role definition (letting the housework "go to pot"), and structural role definition (asking partners to increase their role in childcare). However, for a proportion of students these strategies were not always successful. Less than half of the sample (42%) said that they thought the course was fitting in reasonably well with home and family life. Forty eight per cent (*n*=43) thought that the course was a strain and 10% of participants (*n*=9) thought that the course was causing serious detrimental effect to their home and personal lives.

Manager interviews

Interviews were carried out with 20 NHS managers with specific responsibility for training in three NHS trusts in the Northern and

Yorkshire area. A number of issues were raised by managers which have particular importance in considering the development of a *Learning Society*. These include:

- identification of training needs;
- employer versus employee funding;
- release of staff;
- education and training on NHS premises;
- developing professions and demand for continuing education.

Identification of training needs

Most of the managers had fairly formal and seemingly clear strategies for identifying training needs. In most speciality areas a certain number of courses were compulsory or staff required frequent updating in order to maintain their skills. Such courses would include health and safety days or courses in specific skill areas such as moving and handling. In specialist areas certain staff would require regular courses, for example, in the administration of intravenous drugs. A further area that was considered essential for many nursing and midwifery staff included courses in teaching and assessing; and staff at certain grades would be expected to complete such courses. For all of these compulsory or 'essential' courses staff would be released from work to undertake courses, which would be provided in-house by the trust training departments (and would therefore be free to individual staff) or would be funded by trust training budgets.

Other courses that were regarded as essential for at least some staff in order for trusts to offer specialist services were also funded by the health service but were provided externally in HE institutions. Such courses would include full-time courses in areas such as neonatal nursing or intensive care. Experienced nurses working in these areas would be seconded full-time away from their normal work to undertake intensive study and clinical placements in specialist units. These courses have been funded at Regional/NHS Executive level via what are known as 'Working Paper 10' arrangements (DoH, 1989). In order to decide how many places are provided on such courses, managers in trusts made projections about future staffing levels and future service needs. As one manager explained, this was not always easy to achieve:

> "I have always found it to be a very difficult exercise because it was a five-year forecast and really to see that far into the future is quite difficult

...there was the 'black hole' forecasted in nursing which was supposedly supposed to hit us around '92 which it never did. For some reason, we are now having difficulty recruiting." (Departmental Manager)

Other types of courses provided 'in-house' within trusts were courses providing more generic work skills such as management or recruitment and selection.

The main means of identifying training needs described by managers were regular staff appraisal interviews. However, the idea that training was built on individual needs identified through such mechanisms was not supported by the evidence from our participant interviews. Indeed, when asked why they were attending the course, none of the 89 participants mentioned their staff appraisal interview. A number of managers did recognise that demand for 'non-essential' courses did tend to come from individuals rather than from any joint appraisal of service and individual needs by health service managers and their staff. This was seen as being particularly true for nursing staff. As one manager put it, training was initiated:

"... I suppose firstly by individuals because at the moment, particularly with nursing ... generally the academic level that nurses are meant to function at." (Nurse manager)

In this context where demand from individuals for certain sorts of courses is very high, the question of who should pay becomes critical.

Employer versus employee funding

While the bulk of continuing education and training for health service staff continues to be funded either by employers or by the NHS Executive, a number of courses have emerged which tend to be funded by individual staff.

On the question of who should pay for courses, the trust or the individual employee, the general consensus among managers was that it depends who benefits: if the service benefits then the service should foot the bill, if on the other hand the course tended to be of benefit primarily to the individual then that individual should pay. However, the decision about whether a particular course benefited the trust (and to what extent) was made by managers at ward level. Individual managers would have different views, and in any case, the judgement about 'who benefits' would not be a simple one.

In one of the three trusts where managers were interviewed there had been an attempt to grade training A-D in terms of priority in order to determine the amount of support an individual could expect from the employer. A potential difficulty with this policy was that it was left to individual managers to decide on the priority rating for a particular course. One manager recognised that this rating tended to depend on demand rather than on the intrinsic worth of a particular course, as, at the end of the day, only a certain amount of funding was available.

> "I think probably there is going to be a measure of conflict happening in the not too distant future purely because of the volume of people applying to go off studying. Again that's ... because, you know, nursing as a profession is promoting itself on its academic side and so the expectations are to continue studying." (Nurse manager)

Whether a course was regarded as a 'necessity' or a 'luxury' from the service point of view seemed to vary considerably across trusts and between individual managers within the same trust.

Release of staff

All of the managers were very clear that although training was important, the first priority of the service was the needs of patients. Meeting service needs and providing release for staff was generally managed at ward level and was usually unproblematic; however, this was not always the case. While none of the managers admitted that the service had ever been severely compromised because of low staffing levels due to the volume of training, there were occasions when sickness, maternity leave and release for training together caused staffing shortages. Where study leave was granted this was managed at the ward level and cover had to be provided within existing staffing resources. That is, staff would be expected to arrange the off-duty so that they would cover for each other. Occasionally study leave was cancelled as service needs were seen to have priority over training.

The issue of staff turnover and training was also mentioned by several managers. None of the managers felt that they could ask staff to sign a contract to say that they would remain with the trust after undergoing expensive trust-funded training. Such a policy was however regarded as desirable by some of the managers.

Education and training on NHS premises

Ostensibly, many continuing education courses are run under the auspices of external providers such as the local university. In practice, however, many courses (including most of those we studied) involve clinical placements in hospital and community settings with supervision and indeed teaching by NHS staff. This was also a cause of concern to managers and again, service needs had to be set against the training needs of staff on placement. Again, from the point of view of the managers we interviewed, service and patients came first.

Developing professions and demand for continuing education

We started the results section discussing major changes in nurse education and the implications of such changes for the nursing workforce. We end this section on the same note. Course participants and the managers we interviewed recognised that many staff felt that they had to undertake courses to 'catch up' with newly qualified staff. One manager identified a group that she perceived as 'keenest' on continuing education.

> "Those who trained perhaps seven or eight years ago.... The particular age group that perhaps just coincided with when, you know, nurse training changed over.... They're the ones that seem particularly motivated to either doing diplomas or degrees." (Nurse manager)

There would be experienced staff who had followed traditional training routes who were being asked to supervise less experienced but more academically qualified staff. Managers recognised that setting educational qualifications/credentials against experience in terms of decisions relating to, for example, promotion was not easy. As one manager put it:

> "I mean there's mainly this view that nursing has just gone too, too far really, education wise." (Nurse manager)

Policy implications

At the moment, healthcare staff are receiving mixed messages about continuing education and training. While there is a good deal of rhetoric and seemingly fairly general agreement from the nursing establishment, employers and indeed individual staff that continuing education is a 'good thing', there is less agreement on how much is needed, what (in terms of content) should be provided, who should pay and how achievement at any particular level should be recognised and rewarded. The current Labour government is also sending mixed messages about the most desirable direction for changes in pre- and post-registration training for nursing and other staff. In an interview in the *Nursing Standard*, Frank Dobson, the then Secretary of State for Health, admitted that the shift of nurse training out of the NHS and into HE had some advantages. Nevertheless, he deplored what he perceived as a widening gap between theory and clinical practice and called for increased involvement of the NHS in training. With regard to the upgrading of nurse education, Mr Dobson suggested that many perceived that nurse education had "gone academic". It was clear that the term 'academic' was used in a disparaging sense. (*Nursing Standard*, 1999, p 10).

The interviews with participants and with service managers in our study revealed that there was a mismatch in terms of what the two groups expected from continuing education. While managers claimed that they used forward planning and individual appraisal to put together what was an essential 'shopping list' in terms of staff competencies and updating, this was clearly geared around the need to deliver health services. We also found some evidence that managers regarded 'willingness to pay' as a sign of individual commitment. This finding has emerged in other research on NHS staff (Murphy, 1995). Paying for courses is thus regarded as a (desirable) attribute of individuals. The high cost of courses and lack of resources may on the other hand be perceived by individuals as issues relating to access. Again, there is a mismatch: what employers (may) perceive as a problem of attitude, individuals (may) perceive as a problem of access.

For individuals, in terms of motivations, continuing education seemed to be less to do with updating and developing work-related studies, and more to do with gaining academic credit. This was sometimes to gain promotion in their existing sphere of work, that is, an 'investment' or a recognition of 'economic' incentives (Green, 1993). More frequently, however, the 'push' for qualifications came from a sense of either personal inferiority or a perception about the relative position of health professions. These findings do not in general support human capital theory. As Fevre (1997) has noted, credentialism may be mistaken for investment in human capital, but it is not the same thing. The majority of students in our sample did not tend to undertake training to increase their knowledge and skills. They did not explicitly express a desire to do their jobs better. In this sense, they did not see their participation as an investment in their productive capacity; they simply wanted a qualification. Our evidence also suggests that the individuals who respond to pressures to gain such qualifications are then expected to 'pick up the tab'.

At the conclusion of our study the issue of funding was one which remained central and there were many unanswered questions. While it is clear that there are limited health service resources available to fund continuing education, there is a need to ensure that such education is targeted to achieve service efficiency. Using willingness and ability to pay for continuing education (and for the credentials that accompany it) as a means of selection or gauging the commitment of staff is unlikely to be efficient or just. Whether increased participation in educational activities by health service staff will produce greater efficiency in the delivery of health services is unknown. It is possible that increased participation increases the chances of promotion at the individual level, but whether this produces any benefit to patients is unknown.

We have referred to a number of mismatches in terms of the supply and demand for healthcare education. There is a need for individual healthcare staff, professional bodies, healthcare unions, providers of education, employers and indeed the wider stakeholders in healthcare education (patients, taxpayers and the government) to agree on the broad purposes of continuing education for healthcare staff. Agreement on this broad agenda would clarify who the main beneficiaries of continuing education are and this may well include individual staff. Such agreement, in turn, would clarify the issue of who should pay, what the content of courses should be and who is best placed to provide them.

Further, agreement is required on what constitutes a reasonable and an unreasonable demand for training to make on individuals' out-of-work time. In our study, staff with children were faced with particularly difficult choices: to enrol on a course and carry the social, financial and psychological costs, or to turn down the 'opportunity' of further training, and accept that their career would suffer as a result. The equal opportunities implications of lifelong learning policies must be explicitly addressed if this problem is to be resolved in the future.

One of the themes of *The Learning Age* (DfEE, 1998) is that individuals should be encouraged to take responsibility for their own learning, with support from government and employers. Support is generally discussed in terms of financial support, as in the concept of Individual Learning Accounts. Support in terms of time for learning has been relatively ignored in discussion to date. For some learner groups (for example the unemployed) time may not be in short supply; but for those seeking to continue learning while in paid employment, time may be an extremely scarce resource. A number of recent reports have shown that people in the UK often work long hours, and that women in particular have very little spare time when they seek to combine paid work with bringing up a family. The time implications of current lifelong learning policies must be re-examined if desired levels of participation are to be achieved.

In the context of the NHS, nursing is currently experiencing a crisis in the recruitment and retention of staff. Salary levels and other factors are clearly important, but people who have, or want to have, a family life as well as a career may also choose not to join (or stay in) a profession that makes such heavy demands on their out-of-work time. Training will always carry costs, but financial savings may be illusory if they result in human costs that are just too high.

The rhetoric of the *learning society* is upbeat and positive. It is about 'opportunities' and the benefits that learning can bring. Lifelong learning promises that there will be many such opportunities, following one after another, throughout an individual's career.

To many of the participants in our study, such a prospect would be a threat, not a promise. It was not that they lacked motivation to learn, but rather that learning opportunities were often offered on very disadvantageous terms. We argue that many groups of learners will need to be given a better deal if desired participation rates are to be achieved at an acceptable human cost. In a just and sustainable learning society, rhetoric and fine words must be followed by fair deeds.

Notes

[1] Reasons for failure to arrange or complete interviews included: (a) incorrect data on student telephone numbers or addresses and non-response to written communication (6); (b) students not being home at the time arranged for interview and non-response to follow-up communication (2); (c) health (1) or domestic (1) problems leading to interview cancellation.

[2] One manager interviewed in a work area did not wish the interview to be taped. Detailed notes were made throughout and following the interview.

[3] Nurses and midwives are paid according to their clinical grade. A newly qualified staff nurse would usually be employed at Grade D and would remain at this level until obtaining promotion to the more senior E grade. Ward sisters are frequently employed on F and G grades. Staff employed at H and I grades are often managers or clinical specialists.

References

Barriball, K.L. and While, A.E. (1997) 'Participation in continuing professional education in nursing: findings of an interview study', *Journal of Advanced Nursing*, vol 23, pp 999-1007.

Bielby, W. and Bielby, D. (1989) 'Family ties: balancing commitments to work and family in dual-earner households', *American Sociological Review*, vol 54, pp 776-89.

Brannen, J. and Moss, P. (1990) *Managing mothers: Dual earner households after maternity leave*, London: Unwin Hyman.

Bridge, H. and Salt, H. (1992) *Access and delivery in continuing education and training: A guide to contemporary literature*, Nottingham: University of Nottingham, Department of Adult Education and Employment Department.

Calpin-Davies, P. (1996) 'Demand for post-qualifying professional education in the health care sector in England', *Journal of Advanced Nursing*, vol 24, pp 800-9.

Coffield, F. (1999) *Breaking the consensus: Lifelong learning as social control*, Inaugural Lecture, February, University of Newcastle.

Davidson, M.J. and Cooper, C.L. (1992) *Shattering the glass ceiling: The woman manager*, London: Paul Chapman.

DfEE (Department for Education and Employment) (1998) *The Learning Age: A renaissance for a new Britain*, Cm 3790, London: The Stationery Office.

DoH (Department of Health) (1989) *Working for patients: Education and training*, Working Paper 10, London: HMSO.

Dowswell, T. and Hewison, J. (1995) 'Schools, maternal employment and child health care', *British Educational Research Journal*, vol 21, no 1, pp 15-29.

Dowswell, T., Bradshaw, G. and Hewison, J. (2000: in press) 'Domestic responsibilities and participation in continuing education: A descriptive study', *Journal of Advanced Nursing*, July.

Dowswell, T., Hewison, J. and Hinds, M. (1998a) 'Motivational forces affecting participation in post-registration degree courses and effects on home and work life: a qualitative study', *Journal of Advanced Nursing*, vol 28, pp 1326-33.

Dowswell, T., Hewison, J. and Millar, B. (1998b) 'Enrolled nurse conversion: trapped into training', *Journal of Advanced Nursing*, vol 28, pp 540-7.

Fevre, R. (1997) *Some sociological alternatives to human capital theory and their implications for research on post-compulsory education and training, patterns of participation in adult education and training,* Working Paper 3, Cardiff: School of Education, Cardiff University of Wales.

Firth-Cozens, J. and West, M.A. (eds) (1991) *Women at work,* Milton Keynes: Open University Press.

Green, F. (1993) 'The determinants of training of male and female employees in Britain', *Oxford Bulletin of Economics and Statistics*, vol 55, pp 103-22.

Greenberger, E. and O'Neil, R. (1993) 'Spouse, parent, worker: role commitments and role-related experiences in the construction of adults' well-being', *Developmental Psychology*, vol 29, pp 181-97.

Hewison, J. and Dowswell, T. (1994) *Child health care and the working mother,* London: Chapman and Hall.

Humphreys, J. (1996) 'English nurse education and the reform of the National Health Service', *Journal of Education Policy*, vol 1, no 6, pp 655-79.

Humphreys, J. and Davis, K. (1995) 'Quality assurance for contracting of education: a delegated system involving consortia of British National Health Service Trusts', *Journal of Advanced Nursing*, vol 21, pp 537-43.

Humphreys, J. and Quinn, F.M. (1994) *Health care education: The challenge of the market,* London: Chapman and Hall.

Jackson, C. (1994) 'Why women in the NHS don't get a share of the action', *Health Service Journal*, 7 April, pp 24-6.

King, D.S. (1993) 'The Conservatives and training policy 1979-1992: from a tripartite to a neoliberal regime', *Political Studies*, vol XLI, pp 214-35.

Le Grand, J. and Bartlett, W. (1993) *Quasi-markets and social policy*, London: Macmillan.

McGivney, V. (1993) *Women, education and training*, Leicester: National Institute of Adult Continuing Education, and Hillcroft College.

Maguire, M., Maguire, S. and Felstead, A. (1993) *Factors influencing individual commitment to lifetime learning: a literature review*, Employment Department Research Series, no 20, Sheffield: Employment Department.

Moser, C.A. and Kalton, G. (1971) *Survey methods in social investigation* (2nd edn), London: Heinemann Educational.

Murphy, M. (1995) 'Open learning: the managers' and educationalists' perspective', *Journal of Advanced Nursing*, vol 21, pp 1016-23.

NAHAT (National Association of Health Authorities and Trusts) (1995) *NHS Handbook* (10th edn), Kent: JMH Publishing.

Nursing Standard (1999) 'Frank talk' (report of an interview with Frank Dobson), 19 May, vol 13, no 35, pp 10-12.

O'Neil, R. and Greenberger, E. (1994) 'Patterns of commitment to work and parenting: implications for role strain', *Journal of Marriage and the Family*, vol 56, pp 101-18.

Redshaw, M.E. and Harris, R.N. (1994) 'Training and education for nurses working in neonatal care', *Journal of Advanced Nursing*, vol 20, pp 1023-9.

Rees, T., Bartlett, W. and Watts, A.G. (1997) 'Adult guidance and the learning society: the marketisation of guidance services in the UK, France and Germany', *Journal of Education Policy*, vol 12, no 6, pp 485-97.

Sheperd, J.C. (1995) 'Findings of a training needs analysis for qualified nurse practitioners', *Journal of Advanced Nursing*, vol 22, pp 66-71.

Silverman, D. (1993) *Interpreting qualitative data: Methods for analysing talk, text and interaction*, London: Sage Publications.

Stratton, P., Munton, T., Hanks, H., Heard, D. and Davidson, C. (1988) *Leeds Attribution Coding System (LACS) Manual*, Leeds: Leeds Family Therapy Research Centre.

UKCC (United Kingdom Central Council) (1986) *Project 2000: A new preparation for practice*, London: UKCC.

UKCC (1994) *The future of professional practice: The Council's Standards for Education and Practice following Registration*, London: UKCC.

SIX

Working and learning in Britain and Germany: findings of a regional study

Phil Cooke, Antje Cockrill, Peter Scott, John Fitz and Brian Davies

Introduction

In attempts to create a *Learning Society* the concept of multi-skilling plays an important role in relation to learning at work and organisational learning. This paper presents an overview of a project which was entitled 'Training for multi-skilling: a comparison of British and German experience'[1]. The following two sections outline the background to and theoretical conceptualisation of this study. These are followed by a discussion of the objectives and methodology. The main part of this paper presents the findings of this research and the conclusions that could be drawn from the results.

The Learning Society and multi-skilling: background and concepts

For some considerable time commentators both in the labour market and academia have been aware of a 'skills deficit' or low skills equilibrium in Britain. This implies the notion that Britain's labour force is less well trained, skilled and educated than that of competitor nations and, therefore, less able to compete in increasingly globalised markets. Concerns about the lack of appropriately skilled and trained workers in Britain, particularly at intermediate level, have existed at least for a decade (for example Finegold and Soskice, 1988; Keep, 1993; Steedman, 1998) and both the previous Conservative and the present Labour government have declared 'education and training' to be flagship policy areas. Both have produced a plethora of policy documents in this area and many new initiatives have been introduced. These initiatives have aimed primarily at increasing access to education, training and learning, such as *Investing in Young People*[2], *Learning Direct*[3], the *National Grid for Learning*[4] or the *University for Industry*[5] as well as initiatives directly geared at facilitating learning, education and training, such as the *New Deal*, *National Records of Achievement*, *Learning Cards* (planned), *Individual Learning Accounts*[6] (planned) and the current review of the *National Targets for Education and Training*, as well as new qualifications such as *National Traineeships*, *Higher Modern Apprenticeships* and new 'starter' qualifications aimed below NVQ level 2 (DfEE, 1998a; Welsh Office, 1998). This new framework geared at facilitating education and training also includes the launch of a network of National Training Organisations[7].

In the wider area of education, training and learning, the Labour government has continued and built on Conservative policies and initiatives almost without a conceptual break[8]. This includes a clear emphasis on using education and training to improve employability and the competitiveness of the British economy, although this has been somewhat tempered by the Labour government to include notions of learning being advantageous to society as a whole and as contributing to social cohesiveness. These New Labour policies also fit in seamlessly with current European Union (EU) policies where education and training play a key role in concerns for economic growth, social stability, and fear of social exclusion. As in Britain, these policies have moved away from an exclusive economic relationship towards a greater concern with social stability, albeit still economically determined (Brine, 1998). This dual focus of learning as being beneficial for the individual, on the one hand, and good for society in general, on the other, is evident in the government Green Paper *The Learning Age*:

> Learning helps create and sustain our culture. It helps all of us to improve our chances of getting a job ... [it] increases our earning power, helps older people to stay healthy and active, strengthens families and the wider community and encourages independence.... It helps [businesses] to be more successful by adding value and keeping them up-to-date. [it] develops the intellectual capital that is now at the centre of a nation's competitive strength. It provides the tools to manage industrial and technological change, and helps generate ideas, research and innovation ... [it] is essential for a strong community. In offering a way out of

dependency and low expectation.... We must bridge the 'learning divide' ... which blights so many communities and widens income inequality. The results are seen in the second and third generation of the same family being unemployed, and in the potential talent of young people wasted in a vicious circle of under-achievement, self-depreciation and petty crime. Learning can overcome this by building self-confidence and independence.[9] (Excerpts taken from the Internet version of the DfEE Green Paper, 1998a)

A pervasive theme in all recent government publications and policies concerning education, training and learning is the notion that a 'learning society' (sometimes the terminology varies and the concept is referred to as a 'learning age' or 'learning culture') has to be created and that this concept entails a society committed to learning throughout life (Dearing, 1996; Fryer, 1997). The creation of a *learning society* is perceived as a necessity because the increasing internationalisation and globalisation of the world's economies requires the increased competitiveness of the British economy, which can only be achieved by improved education and training, implying increased commitment by all to these concepts (Fryer, 1997). However, these assumptions have not gone unchallenged. Rees (1997b) maintains that the belief that an increase in training would benefit economic performance has been questioned, for example, by such commentators as Shackleton on the grounds that the returns from training are extremely difficult to calculate even at firm level, let alone for the national economy (Shackleton, 1992). Lindley (1991) is critical because he sees the utilisation of managerial strategies to be decisive factors in national economic performance; not skills supply per se. Moreover, Fuller and Unwin (1998) make the valid point that concepts such as 'lifelong learning', the 'learning society' and even the 'learning organisation' may make striking policy document rhetoric but do not reflect accurately work and learning in the real world.

As authors of this chapter, we acknowledge these complexities and debates, as well as the fact that the concept of a *learning society* is much wider than learning and training either when thought of in terms of an individual's employability or economic productivity in general. However, at the outset of this research it was clear that learning in and for the workplace would have to play an important role in present and future policy decisions and even a change of government would not change the pressures and challenges facing both British society in general and the economy in particular. Although the relationship between increased skill supply and improved economic performance may be less obvious than often maintained, it cannot be doubted that increased knowledge in the workforce at least offers the potential for better economic performance and improved competitiveness. It is on an exploration of this suggestion that this research project has been based.

The call for increased competitiveness by increasing the knowledge base of the workforce through education and training is not new. Indeed, Lundvall and Johnson (1994) argue that while "knowledge has always been a crucial resource in the economy" (p 23), fundamental changes in post-Fordist economies affect the demand for it in three ways. First, there is a need for broader participation in learning processes so that within firms, swift and efficient innovation processes must involve all levels in the firm. Second, multi-skilling and networking skills become of crucial importance, and third, the capability to learn and apply learning processes to production, sales and especially marketing becomes the most important dimension in the viability of the modern firm. Some commentators such as Warmerdam (1997) see the need for meso-level institutions — umbrella-training organisations of the kind described later in this paper — to promote training and the development of transferable skills required by individual enterprises but also across whole enterprise sectors.

Western European economies are facing a situation characterised by both unemployment and skill shortages. It is in this context that multi-skilling in the workplace has become increasingly important by adding to the skills base of the workforce. In both Britain and Germany increasingly fewer workers have to maintain economic productivity and to support spiralling social protection costs[10]. The numbers of people working in the most economically productive sectors such as manufacturing are shrinking both on grounds of changes in the age composition of the workforce and a reduction in size of these sectors, in contrast to the less economically productive service sectors. This implies that in the future lifelong learning, particularly in the form of multi-skilling in the workplace, will play an important role in 'neutralising age' (European Commission, 1998), keeping older people longer as active and productive members of the workforce, as well as generally providing the skills needed in an environment with rapidly changing technology.

However, the literature on the sociology of work and related areas shows that there is considerable debate about the precise meaning of the term multi-skilling and the extent to which it is used as a distinctive strategy within organisations. The theoretical grounding for contemporary conceptions of multi-skilling relies heavily on Atkinson's (1984) notion of 'functional flexibility', Piore and Sabel's (1984) idea of 'flexible specialisation', Kern and Schumann's (1984) parallel German terminology of 'new production concepts' and the more abstract notion of 'post-fordism' generally. Although these studies have different origins and implications, all of them imply that newly multi-skilled craft workers would assume an increasingly central position within the work organisation structures of Western economies.

Similarly, although much more practical than empirical, Cross (1985) developed an early seven-fold taxonomy of way-stations from single-craft working to the truly polyvalent worker, who would be equally skilled in a number of previously distinct crafts. This model had the benefit of classifying distinctions between different possible interpretations of multi-skilling. At the extremes, it is possible to perceive 'multi-skilling' as little more than a minor re-combination of existing tasks at one end of the scale or, alternatively, as the creation of entirely new hybrid occupations. Some of the confusion in the debate about these issues is the result of unclear terminology. As Incomes Data Services (IDS) (1994) rightly acknowledge, multi-skilling is not clearly defined and in consequence it is difficult to determine, for example, how it differs from the cognate concept of 'flexibility'.

IDS state that the term 'multi-skilling' is most commonly used with reference to skilled-level occupations but suggest that its use should not be limited in this way because companies themselves do not do so. We would concur with this and have used the term to encompass a wide variety of examples of horizontal and vertical forms of task integration[11] within organisations, although the main focus has been the acquisition of additional skills at intermediate level. Four main types and levels of 'multi-skilling' have been identified:

- *horizontal role integration:* new technical skills are acquired that are normally considered to be part of another occupation at the same skill level, for example the merger of parts of two craft-level occupations;
- *downward vertical role integration:* the assumption of additional technical skills that would normally be considered to be part of less skilled occupational categories in the same field, for example craft machinists becoming responsible for transporting materials or similar ancillary tasks;
- *upward vertical role integration:* taking on new technical skills usually associated with occupational categories of a higher skill level in the

same field, for example operatives becoming responsible for quality assurance documentation or for machine tool programming; and

• *social skills:* learning to work as part of a team with communication, problem solving skills, and so on added on to technical abilities.

Considering that all occupations involve the gradual accumulation of additional skills at varying speeds, the question arises whether multi-skilling is a distinct process or if it happens naturally in the course of organisational change and individual development. In its most obvious form it exists as a formal programme designed to consciously redirect the occupational profile and skill formation processes within the organisation, but, at the other end of the scale, it also possible – particularly in small and medium size enterprises (SMEs) – that multi-skilling is a de facto outcome of a series of largely unconscious/unplanned events.

Vocational education and training: the basis of multi-skilling

In the last decade, there has been increasing concern in Britain about the education and vocational training system (Finegold and Soskice, 1988). This concern has focused on two major issues, low post-16 participation rates among young people and the failure of the education and training system to provide enough sufficiently qualified and skilled workers for the needs of industry. The UK's weaknesses lie particularly in the area of basic and intermediate skills. In comparison to competitor nations the British system produces much fewer adults with qualifications up to intermediate levels[12] (DfEE, 1998a). Although the perception of the extent of the problem has varied among commentators with some, for example, in 1998 claiming that 15% of manufacturing firms expected a lack of skilled labour to limit output in the immediate prospect[13], and maintaining that 74% of manufacturers were experiencing recruitment difficulties (Skills and Enterprise Network, 1998b). It is still evident that there are difficulties in recruiting and retaining suitably skilled employees in the UK. For example, a survey by the West Wales Chamber of Commerce revealed that over 70% of respondents experienced difficulties in finding suitable staff, particularly concerning the recruitment of skilled manual and technical employees (*Western Mail*, 1998a).

In the UK fewer young people than in most other European countries continue in education and training after the age of 16 (Gorard et al, 1997a), with participation and qualification levels in Wales being especially low (ETAG, 1998). In 1998 about one in five 16-18-year-olds in Wales had no qualifications, one in nine pupils were leaving school without GCSEs, and one in three 19-year-olds did not have five or more GCSEs at Grade C and above or equivalent qualifications, with about a quarter of the adult population in Wales having no qualifications (Welsh Office, 1998). In contrast, only 10-14% of young adults in Germany do not have any formal qualifications (BMBF, 1996). The Welsh Office Green Paper *Learning is for everyone* (1998) maintains that the situation in Wales is characterised by an education and training divide:

> The country is divided between the relatively few whose education and training has been substantial, and the many for whom levels of both education and training, together with their fruits, have been much less. (Welsh Office, 1998, Chapter 1)

For many years, Germany's vocational training and education system has been presented by some commentators as the opposite of the British VET (Vocational Educational Training) system, as delivering high quality, highly skilled workers in sufficient numbers. However, recent research has shown that this does not reflect the true picture, and that a simple replication of features of the German training system in Britain is unlikely to be successful (Shackleton, 1997; Deissinger, 1997). Although the German system undoubtedly succeeds in producing highly qualified and skilled workers, in the last decade serious questions, particularly concerning issues such as cost-effectiveness and flexibility[14], have been raised. These and other issues relating to the German VET system and policies will not be discussed here since they have been rehearsed by the authors and other commentators in much detail elsewhere (for example Cockrill and Scott, 1997a; see also Shackleton, 1997; Bock and Timmermann, 1998; BMBF, 1998).

Objectives and methods

In light of the discussions above and the framework of the overall ESRC *Learning Society Programme*, this project was based on a number of objectives, which were addressed throughout our research, including:
- making a contribution to the exploration of a *learning society*, taking particular note of the possible role and significance at institutional and individual levels of socio-cultural interaction and cooperation;
- understanding the processes by which a learning culture develops and to benchmark the UK and Germany in some limited respects;

- investigating the contribution of particular government initiatives to the further development of the UK VET regime and to compare these with German programmes to meet needs for changing skill requirements; and
- evaluating the extent to which the British and the German VET systems can successfully deliver outcomes to employers seeking multi-skilled personnel in the engineering, construction and care sectors.

This research compares training systems, skill provision and multi-skilling in two German states and one British region (Northrhine Westphalia, Baden Wuerttemberg and South Wales) chosen on the basis of socio-economic similarities. In both Northrhine Westphalia and Wales, the coal and steel industries are in decline, but, in contrast, the automotive and electronics sectors are flourishing both in Baden Wuerttemberg and Wales. The study focuses on three industrial sectors: engineering, construction and care. These sectors were chosen to provide a view of a range of different economic activity. Although engineering and construction are similar, insofar as they are male-dominated and have reputations as manual industries, the care sector is structured in a totally different way and is far more heterogeneous. The latter sector was also chosen to introduce both public sector and gendered elements into the research, this sector consisting of a mixture of public and private organisations and, in contrast to construction and engineering, being female-dominated.

This sectoral approach can also be justified by the fact that at EU level, the sectoral dimension in education and training has become increasingly important. Warmerdam (1997) maintains that in several European countries economic sectors[15] or branches have organised separate systems for continuing training, with their own training agreements, training institutes, training policies and training provision and that these systems often play a key role in policies of national governments. This observation is certainly true for the German (and to a lesser extent for the British) side of this research, where the type of training, quality of provision and policies differ considerably between the sectors involved.

The methodological aim was to interview approximately 25 firms and/or organisations, categorised as small to medium enterprises (SMEs) in each of the three sectors in each country and 25 training providers, umbrella organisations and policy-making bodies. Access to such organisations turned out to be unproblematic in both countries. Success in gaining access to SMEs was more uneven, as Table 1 demonstrates.

Table 1: The achieved SME sample

	Wales	Germany
Engineering	24	22
Construction	25	15
Care	12	12

As measured by the number of directly employed staff these ranged in size from under 10 to approximately 850 employees. As Table 1 indicates, access to engineering firms was also relatively straightforward in both countries (there were only some very minor shortfalls in the numbers of these interviews due to last minute dropouts) and turned out to be unproblematic for construction firms in Wales and care homes. However, access to construction firms in Germany turned out to be more difficult. Sources and databases used to obtain appropriate contacts in Germany were often outdated and it required an inordinate amount of effort to arrange interviews. This was exacerbated by a considerable number of last minute dropouts. Due to the constraints of time and money, only 15 interviews with German construction firms were achieved. It was our intention to represent the care sector via research conducted in residences caring for young people and also for elderly people. This had to be adjusted in the light of investigations into allegations of child abuse which were taking place in Wales at the time of this research. That substantially inhibited cooperation by potential contacts. We attempted to overcome these difficulties by contacting appropriate personnel within a cross-section of South Wales local authorities. Research in the care sector therefore focused primarily on residential care for elderly people and this is represented in the somewhat lower figures in Table 1.

Findings

This project was particularly concerned with institutional, work-based learning and the initial training provided as a basis for such activities. There was also a special focus on finding out whether there was an increased demand for multi-skilled employees in the study sectors and how this potential increased demand might translate into learning experiences and thus contribute to the building of a *learning society*. Since the findings for the three sectors investigated in this research differed substantially, it assists clarity to present them in turn. Further accounts of results can be found elsewhere in more detailed reports of the results

(Cockrill, 1996a, 1996b, 1997c; Cockrill and Scott, 1997a–d; Scott, 1996a, 1996b; Scott and Cockrill, 1996, 1997).

Engineering

(For more details see Scott and Cockrill, 1996)

In many respects, the environments that Welsh and German engineering SMEs face are remarkably similar. Initial training at intermediate level was, in the mid-1990s, holding up quite well in the SMEs in both countries. It was undergoing a modest revival in Wales, while declining from a higher baseline in Germany. However, and this is a crucial point when talking about the building of a *learning society* and of improving organisational learning, further training within the production environment, although widespread in absolute terms, was mainly geared towards immediate, job-specific, and non-transferable skills rather than to longer-term development of either personal or organisational capability in both countries.

Consciously planned, strategic programmes of multi-skilling activity were relatively rare in both countries. Despite this, many of the SMEs in both countries had begun to develop initiatives to multi-skill their employees, although this process could be described as constituting a definite strategy in only a minority of the total number of cases, particularly in Germany. New quality assurance methods, especially ISO 9000 series registration, were responsible for perhaps the most wide-ranging skills enhancement throughout the various levels of firms and have uncovered barriers of inadequate basic skills at operative level in both countries. The devolution of quality management has resulted in a requirement for higher level skills among production staff. Organisational restructuring within firms has also played a significant role in the reconstitution of the occupational skill base in both countries. However, the impact has predominantly involved the additional assumption of tasks at a similar or lower level of skill and has had relatively fewer training implications than the above form of multi-skilling. In Germany this process has affected mainly skilled workers because of the shakeout of numbers of semi-skilled staff, while in Wales a perceived need to improve employees' ability to cover a larger proportion of production activities has been more significant. Much of what is called multi-skilling at present in Wales is essentially job enlargement and involved, in the main, 'downward vertical role integration'. Clearly, the training implications of such a process of increased flexibility between existing tasks are considerably more ambiguous. Several firms developed such flexibility in an ad hoc way that only rarely led to the award of externally certified qualifications. A proportion of the Welsh firms were admittedly trying deliberately to structure this process of expanding employees' repertoire within the existing total task base by means of monitoring and the use of skill matrices, although plenty of scope exists for further generalisation of such good practice.

Construction

(For more details see Cockrill and Scott, 1997b)

The differences between UK and German construction industries can be overstated. Both countries face difficulties in attracting a suitably motivated and qualified workforce; in both countries there is some unwillingness and a lack of ambition to venture beyond the boundaries of existing trades and occupations which limits strategically planned moves towards multi-skilling and, although it does occur widely on an ad hoc basis, relatively little formal further training is provided in a structured way. However, the German construction industry operates from a higher and more secure baseline than its UK equivalent and functions within a network of high-trust relationships. Our Germany-based research in SMEs and with employers' umbrella trade organisations suggests that the present 'stage training' system is still widely supported, despite some criticism of the vocational schools involved in this training (see Scott and Cockrill, 1998). The cooperation between SMEs and inter-company training centres has created a deeply rooted form of interactive learning and responsive further training provision at local level. This is especially important in view of the relatively higher technology methods utilised by the German construction industry, which might imply greater recourse to a need for rapid updating than many UK methods.

   Perhaps the most striking feature of the German construction industry and its training provision appeared to be the fact that a well performing training system was in place[16] but few willing and suitable candidates to use it. The UK also has a national body to provide guidance and advice for construction training, the Construction Industry Training Board. However, the industry does not have a training 'system' in the German sense and that is reflected in our Wales study. Many firms are forced to rely on knowledge of the extended local labour market in order to establish skill bases because, otherwise, the quality of recruits remains uncertain due to the haphazard provision of formal training. Traditional unstructured methods of skill formation are coupled with an emphasis on competition based on cost minimisation, leading to low-trust relations between contractors as well as between employers and employees. Reluctance in some cases to engage with the external training system hinders the revival of initial training, further training and the formal development of more broadly skilled workers. These factors are compounded by an overly complex training system, a lack of cooperation between funders, policy makers and training providers and a lack of qualifications with acceptable and recognised standards. Examples of collaborative learning by interaction between colleges and firms do exist but are far more limited than those established in Germany by inter-company training centres.

Some limited evidence of change was discovered. Perhaps one of the most useful immediate steps for firms of the type studied would be the expansion of the formal accreditation of workers through the Construction Skill Certification Schemes (CSCS). This would encourage and require both the transparency and transferability of skills and could provide formal building blocks to accredit workers' possession of skills outside of their main trade. However, the take-up of CSCS has been relatively limited thus far and is entirely voluntary at present.

Some form of multi-skilling was quite common in the Welsh SMEs studied. Twenty firms (80%) seem to have experienced some form of integration of roles, again in the direction of horizontal or downward vertical modes of integration. Multi-skilling had developed almost entirely without recourse to formal training, even in those companies actively engaged in training in other respects and with little apparent demand for such training. However, there is a considerable degree of scepticism about multi-skilling within large sections of the industry. The main objections were on economic grounds and included fears that multi-skilled workers would be slower and less competent than specialists, concerns about multi-skilled employees expecting higher wages and, paradoxically, craft workers themselves perceiving multi-skilling as dilution and 'down-skilling'.

In many ways, multi-skilling does not have the same importance in Germany as it has in Britain because, as Clarke and Wall (1996) maintain, the German training system effectively creates a workforce that is already multi-skilled because knowledge and expertise are not confined to single trades. The widespread use of apprenticeships and their broad-based curriculum provide workers with flexible, transferable skills. However, on site these skills often seem to remain underutilised. Indeed, it was found in the interviews that many employers were sceptical about the multi-skilling component of initial training.

Two opposing trends within the German construction industry were discovered. A number of companies claimed that there was both considerable need for and practice of multi-skilling at craft level as the result of customer demand for concentrating as many tasks as possible in the hands of one firm. Others frequently mentioned that multi-skilling was concerned with the learning of additional administrative or social skills. However, a smaller number of firms maintained that their workers only or mainly worked within the boundaries of their own occupation. This latter group also strongly opposed the broad training which characterised the first year of all related apprenticeships in the building trades. As in Britain, there was considerable resistance to any form of multi-skilling in this sector.

Care

(For more detail see Cockrill, 1997a and Cockrill and Scott, 1997c)
A very different picture concerning skills provision, training and multi-skilling emerges in the care sectors in Germany and Wales. One of the most striking differences between the two countries concerns the recruitment and selection of care personnel. In Germany skilled and qualified personnel, who are supported by auxiliary staff, largely conduct care functions. German managers in residential homes for the young usually employed staff fully qualified as *Erzieher* (educator)[17] or *Sozialpädagoge* (social pedagogy)[18] and in residential homes for elderly people, an *Altenpfleger* (carer for elderly people) or *Krankenpfleger* (nurse) qualification would usually be expected. In Britain unskilled or low-skilled employees who have experienced short-term training programmes provide the bulk of care. Some of these carers are trained to National Vocational Qualification (NVQ) Level 2. In our study however, nine of the 12 residential homes linked training and NVQs. Paradoxically this qualification was poorly regarded by the same organisations and criticised for being too basic. These different recruitment practices also imply a different labour market. Recruitment of suitably skilled and qualified personnel encounters difficulties in Germany, whereas in Britain there seems to be a plentiful supply of unskilled/low skilled staff to be drawn on.

It should be a matter of concern that in both countries there is considerable reluctance on the part of employees in this sector to undergo further training. The reasons for this were much alike, particularly a female-dominated workforce, many of whom are part-timers facing the multiple demands of family, home and work. In both countries a range of further and continuous training is offered whose extent did not seem to differ very much. However, in Germany there was heavy emphasis on supervisory and management skills in homes caring for elderly people; and on leisure skills and the ability to work with families in organisations caring for young people. It was in these two areas that skills shortages were most pronounced. This did not feature in Wales where the emphasis seemed to be on encouraging staff to take and complete NVQs at Level 2. There was also a marked lack of opportunities for internal advancement and of career progression in this sector.

The picture also varied between the two countries in regard to multi-skilling. Although there were problems with definitions in both countries, it was clear that in Germany multi-skilling of all types seemed to be far more widespread than in the Wales. In the latter region, such activities seemed to be largely limited to very small homes where the small number of staff necessitated interchangeability of staff. Undoubtedly these differences were the consequence of the different training backgrounds and skill levels of the care staff in the two countries. The more thorough initial training of German care staff enables German homes to utilise them in a wider range of functions. However, although multi-skilling was found to be of considerable importance, this does not seem to be the result of an active approach to multi-skilling per se but to be due to the demands and nature of the work in this sector. It does have to be said, however, that some German employers were actively recruiting staff with dual qualifications and were looking for staff with specific additional skills. It could be concluded that, certainly for Germany, this sector was the one in this study where most multi-skilling took place and where, in contrast to the other areas of this research, at least some of it was actively planned rather than on an ad hoc basis.

In the context of building a *learning society*, it is a sobering thought that one of the groups of employees with least status, career progression opportunities and pay are also those with least motivation for further training and development. This is a structural and societal problem: as long as the care sector is perceived as female, low-skilled and underpaid, there is little incentive to turn work in this sector into a career. However, it is exactly this professionalisation which is lacking, particularly in the

British case, although this is also true, albeit to a lesser extent, in the two German regions.

UK government initiatives: NVQs, Modern Apprenticeship, National Training and Education Targets and Investors in People

Engineering

Apprenticeship training at intermediate level in UK engineering appeared to be more resilient from the evidence of our survey than one might have expected. A small number of our respondents were participating in the Modern Apprenticeship (MA) scheme. These employers claimed satisfaction with it, on balance, although there were some concerns that the initial year was pitched at too low a level to enable trainees to become useful. It seems likely that at least some of those employers who do train apprentices have switched to MA specifically, or are considering doing so in the near future, primarily for financial reasons rather than out of any great expectations of this initiative. Our evidence suggests that the current schemes are being used as an alternative to satisfy the skill needs presently perceived and not as a means to enhance the level of skills utilised.

The further training offered by 18 of the 24 engineering firms (75%) only occasionally led to externally recognised qualifications. In this context, it was evident that NVQs have been important in enabling at least some continuing training to be externally validated, often for the first time. Over half of the firms were using NVQs in one form or other, although there was a definite undercurrent of concern that their standards are of questionable equivalence because of their assessment procedures and that the theoretical content of such qualifications is insufficient. These concerns also carry the implication that occupational standards cannot necessarily be guaranteed on either the internal or external labour markets. Most of those employers who are training to NVQs in engineering admitted that the qualifications parallel the training they would have been doing anyway but allow the employee the added bonus of a certificate as a motivational byproduct.

Construction

Of the construction firms surveyed, 40% were participating in the MA scheme, with trainees being selected and employed by the firm in most of these cases rather than being recruited via a Further Education (FE) college or the Construction Industry Training Board (CITB) as a managing agent and then placed with them. A number of the companies expressed the strong opinion that MA could only be successful if the firm had control in this way, as the element of company loyalty gained through direct selection and employment of the trainee was critical. On balance, the firms' evaluation of the MA scheme was broadly positive, although six (24%) noted disparagingly that trainees' motivation was poor, which led to problems such as non-attendance at college and high dropout rates. The other main area of employers' criticism was a perception that the depth of MA compared unfavourably with that of the traditional apprenticeship most of them had undergone. Many construction employers were simply unconvinced that the new system could produce a comparable capability.

The remainder of the criticism focused on the role of NVQ-based assessment within MA. There seemed to be a fairly widespread undercurrent of belief that overall standards of workmanship were in decline. For example, one firm found that apprentice carpenters were of insufficient standard after three years training to be sent to hang doors, an activity it expected of them. Trainees who had passed their college-based NVQ training were also subsequently failing basic CITB skill tests. Outcome-related funding was suspected of tempting colleges to perhaps pass trainees who were of inadequate standard. Furthermore, our evidence indicates that the practical difficulties of workplace-based assessment on construction sites have resulted in a large proportion of assessment being undertaken in college environments. An interviewee from one of the construction trade unions also indicated that some organisations have been trying to designate Level 2 of the NVQ system as equivalent to craft level rather than the normally accepted Level 3. This has also not aided the acceptance of NVQs.

Care

NVQs have had a bigger impact on the care sector than on the other two sectors investigated. Training in the form of NVQs was relatively widespread, and several homes have a member of managerial staff who has been (or is currently being) trained as an in-house NVQ assessor. However, none of the organisations were involved in the MA framework at NVQ Level 3 in care. In the view of professional and sectoral training bodies there was also the widely acknowledged problem that the MA scheme is geared at the age group 18-24, with an expected completion age of 25, which was generally considered far too young to develop the kind of maturity and life experience that are perceived to be particularly important for working within this sector.

Much of the impetus for NVQ-based training arose not only from the wish to motivate staff but rested on a desire on the part of employers that they possess certification which improved the chances of gaining client referrals from local authorities. Workplace-based qualifications have proven a popular route in a sector that is dominated numerically by small organisations lacking resources for staff training. Generally, it was clear from the interviews that, insofar as vocational training leads to externally recognised qualification, NVQs are by far the main contributor to this and have thus been very important in improving the levels of transferable certification.

Although five of the 12 homes in our study had managerial staff trained as an in-house NVQ assessor and one other used an outside training provider, on balance, the sector's perception of them as a form of qualification was remarkably poor. There were a number of significant barriers to the take-up of further training in general and of NVQs in particular. The dominant views were either that they made no difference or had become unpopular with staff because they were seen as too basic at NVQ Level 2 and embodying merely 'common sense', or items were impractical. Criticisms about the bureaucracy involved were also raised. As a result of these problems, some homes had rejected the NVQ route, either at the outset or in practice, when they found that staffs were reluctant to continue with the qualification. In this sector the situation was characterised by high usage of NVQs but they were not held in high esteem. In the firms where we conducted interviews very little use was made of the more advanced NVQ Level 3, which is less open to the criticism of over-simplicity that plagues NVQ Level 2. Only two homes had a member of staff who already possessed or was currently following the NVQ Level 3 standard of qualification.

Presently, awards in the care sector are being reviewed, with the intention of simplifying the structure via a system of core and additional options centred upon job-specific skills. This review is still under progress.

National Targets for Education and Training (NTETs) only played a very minor role in our research. They were only mentioned by training providers and policy-making organisations and seemed to have no impact at the work place. However, NTETS seem to have had the effect that at least some of the policy and training provision offered by Training and

Enterprise Councils (TECs) and FE colleges tended to be geared to meeting these national targets rather than providing regionally and locally responsive options. A fundamental flaw of these targets seems to be that they aim at increasing the levels of certification among the British population, using existing qualification networks without necessarily leading to increased skill levels. On the other hand, they may serve to raise the expectations of individuals about their career choices and opportunities.

Conclusion and policy recommendations

During the course of this research, the issues of 'lifelong learning' and a 'learning society' have become even more topical than they were at the outset. While terms have also been the focus of sustained commentary and critique (see Coffield, 1999; Rees et al, 1997) the present Labour government has embraced notions of lifelong learning and the establishment of a learning culture at the centre of its education and training policies. This increased awareness of and interest in issues connected with learning and education in the widest sense are reflected in the number of policy documents that have appeared and with the launch of several new initiatives. This emphasis on learning and the recognition that the present system of education and training and participation rates in it are unsatisfactory have not been evident at the regional level. So in April 1998 a Welsh Office Green Paper *Learning is for everyone*, which is wider in coverage and more detailed than its English counterpart *The Learning Age*, was presented to Parliament. It specified opportunities for national initiatives to be tailored to the circumstances in Wales, such as its distinctive pattern of post-16 education and training, bilingualism, the importance of provision for part-time learners, the needs of the regional economic fora and the need to prepare the ground for the time when the National Assembly took over responsibility for education and training in 1999 (Welsh Office, 1998).

It could be maintained that Wales is already well on the way to developing its own distinctive pattern of education, training and skills provision characterised not only by bilingualism but also by adaptation to local needs and developments[19]. Such regional factors are, for example, a different pattern of secondary education (Gorard, 1997) and a distinctive history of education and training (Rees, 1997a), as well the development of an all-Wales credit accumulation scheme for post-compulsory education (CREDIS). Other distinctive local characteristics include such features as very localised labour markets (Scott and Cockrill, 1996) and the role of regional institutions such as the Welsh Development Agency. More recently the establishment of the National Assembly has given new impetus to the development of a distinctively Welsh system of post-compulsory education and training. For example, the Assembly has created two committees to oversee the territorial provision of education and training, one concerned with pre- and compulsory education, and, for the first time, a committee responsible for post-compulsory education and training. The latter has already had an impact through its consideration of the rationalisation of school sixth forms and further education. The Territorial Schools' Inspectorate in Wales has been renamed Her Majesty's Inspectorate of Education and Training and, as its name suggests, its remit has been expanded to include the inspection of post-16 education and training provision. In addition, post-compulsory education and training targets are being established for Wales by the National Assembly but in consultation with local employers and training providers (see ETAG, 1998; Gorard et al, 1999). These developments suggest that the National Assembly is keen to develop further the post-compulsory system of education and training and to align it closely with the perceived needs of local labour markets and employers.

One of the objectives of this study was to contribute to the definition of the concept *learning society*. This project has produced some strong evidence that it is not sufficient to regard a learning society in terms of fostering access to learning in the form of education, training and/or qualifications. Whereas this type of access is undoubtedly an important element in the establishment of a learning society, such opportunities do not guarantee either that individuals are interested in or that there are not significant structural barriers to the uptake of such opportunities. There were indications, for example, of very localised labour markets in South Wales and Baden Wuerttemberg, geographical restrictions on taking up training and education opportunities and that there is no such thing as a learning society but, rather, that larger national learning societies consist of regional and even local ones and that it is these local, regional and national structures which define individual or class participation in and access to a 'learning society' (see also Macrae et al, 1997). The argument here, which is most powerfully documented in Gorard et al 1997b) is that opportunities for, and participation in, post-compulsory training and learning are strongly determined by the character, strength and history of local labour markets, local employers and patterns of employment. These claims were also evident in this study insofar as many employees in the care sector, as well as many older engineering and construction workers were very reluctant to undergo any further training. Even with increased political and societal pressures towards learning and training not all individuals can be convinced of its value or, even if they are, some face such significant barriers to participation that access to learning becomes virtually impossible. Therefore, the present UK government's focus on the creation of a 'learning age' or a 'learning society' is laudable but unrealistic as long as it remains in the realms of education and training policies alone. A much wider approach to changing societal structures and dismantling barriers is necessary. To a limited extent this problem has been recognised, for example, with the introduction of after-school clubs for children as an affordable childcare option. However, such attempts, to date, do not go far enough to address the issue of potential and actual exclusion from the *learning society*.

It is debatable whether the skill shortages in Britain and its 'low skills equilibrium' can be solved at policy level. The limited impact of such initiatives as NTETs suggests that imposing aims from above provide little incentive for individuals or organisations to attempt to reach these targets because they are perceived to be of little or no relevance to the individual or the enterprise. The need to make learning relevant is borne out by the results of the National Adult Learning Survey (Beinart and Smith, 1998). This investigation revealed that there is a strong link between learning and work, with 77% of the people described as learners[20] in paid work as opposed to only 39% of non-learners. This suggests that employment provides significant opportunities and incentives for learning. It appears that one of the most promising ways forward towards a 'learning society' might be to improve an individual's motivation to learn and train, rather than merely offering opportunities to do so.

On a regional level, the three most important barriers to learning found in this research were a physical lack of access to learning in terms of transport links, a lack of motivation arising from the absence or shortage of good job prospects, and the inevitability of unemployment or low skilled employment acting as powerful disincentives for learning. To address these issues would require a regional strategy not only in the area of education and training but addressing structural and societal difficulties as well. This has not gone unrecognised and there have been various policy initiatives addressing wider issues in Wales. However, so far, the practical implementation of these initiatives has not had the desired effect.

This might be due to the fact that real changes are unlikely as long as the national commitment to a *learning society* is largely restricted to the creation of a conceptual framework. Substantial financial commitment, unbureaucratic access to funds, particularly at regional level, and an emphasis on improving relationships between the potential social partners in learning processes (training providers, policy makers, employers and individual people) are necessary ingredients in any recipe for creating a learning society (Cockrill and Scott, 1997d).

As far as multi-skilling and work-based training are concerned, the findings of this research indicated that in both Wales and Germany a wide range of skills acquisition and learning happen in the workplace in all three sectors observed. However, much of it is of an ad hoc nature, designed to cover immediate skill shortages rather as part of long-term strategic planning. In the firms and organisations observed, multi-skilling or, indeed, any other form of work-based training, does not seem to be used as a tool to plan for the organisation's future to any great extent. However, the care sector, particularly in Germany, is an exception since in this area training was used extensively and at times with considerable thought for future organisational needs[21].

Among the firms that we investigated apprenticeship training was still relatively widespread and held in relatively high regard, even though there was an undercurrent of belief that the new system of MAs does not provide the same level of training as the old type of 'time-served' apprenticeships. The two most noticeable complaints about MA in the care sector were the age limitation to 25 years and concerns about its underlying NVQ structure. Problems with the bureaucracy and assessment procedures were among the most common complaints. However, it is not inconceivable that these problems could be overcome. The original idea of the NVQ system has much to offer, notably the encouragement to managers and employers to participate in schemes of on-the-job training attached to national awards. It may well be that its flaws have dissipated its strengths. The authors do not agree with some commentators like Sellin (1994), who maintain that modularisation of initial vocational training should only be a phase on the way to a comprehensive overhaul of the system.

Instead, we suggest that modular qualifications could be a successful device for initial vocational training but their strong points such as flexibility must be structured by a transparent national system of standards in order to encourage consistent training quality. Potential structures for such a system are already in place but so far they are not utilised effectively, for example there are indications that there are significant variations in the assessment of candidates between different NVQ assessment centres

(University of Sussex, 1996). Another unsolved problem area concerns comparability: how and by whom can it be determined which skills and knowledge in widely different occupations constitute, for example, NVQ Level 2? This issue has not yet been adequately addressed so that some NVQs of the same level appear to be considerably more demanding than others although time allowances for funding purposes are the same. It seems that as far as comparability is concerned, a considerable amount of work remains to be done by the Qualifications and Curriculum Authority[22].

Many of the problem areas identified both in MAs and NVQs have been addressed by Gordon Beaumont (1996) in his review of the 100 most used NVQs and SVQs. This review was carried out in 1995 at the same time as this research and the resulting recommendations were sent to the DfEE, the Northern Ireland Office, the Scottish Office and the Welsh Office. Beaumont addresses most of the problem areas identified in this research, particularly the need for simplification and reduction of the paperwork involved, the need for clearer guidance on assessment and the need for adjusting funding to qualifications. Time will tell if his recommendations are implemented and if NVQs can become the universally recognised, transferable qualifications that they were intended to be. It should be stressed at this point that the area with most potential use for NVQs appears to be not initial but further and continuous training. It is in this area that modular, specific qualifications could be particularly useful both as an incentive for further learning and as transferable proof of skills acquired in the work place.

Implications from this research are that, as far as SMEs in construction, engineering and residential care homes are concerned, there is a substantial amount of learning taking place within such firms but only a minority could be described as 'learning organisations' following conscious, deliberate routes in their employees' training and learning in the organisation. In 1998 many, if not most, of the organisations observed in this study were not truly contributing to a *learning society*. However, the picture emerging might have been different had the focus of the investigation been larger organisations and/or multi-national companies.

Notes

[1] We acknowledge funding under the ESRC *Learning Society Programme 'Training for multi-skilling: a comparison of British and German experience'* (grant no L123251020), awarded to a team from the Centre for Advanced Studies in the Social Sciences

and the School of Education, Cardiff University, under the direction of Professor Phil Cooke. Other members of the research team were Professor Brian Davies, Dr John Fitz, Dr Antje Cockrill and Dr Peter Scott. We are grateful to our 'user group' and for the contributions and comments of our interviewees.

[2] This is outlined in DfEE (1998a) chapter 4, section 2.

[3] For more on this see *Individual Learning News*, issue 5 (1998b) on the DfEE lifelong learning Internet site http:www.lifelonglearning.co.uk/iln5000/iln5109.htm. In Wales, the Welsh Office launched *Learning Direct* helplines in both English and Welsh in May 1998.

[4] For more on this see DfEE (1997a), the Government's consultation paper and for a discussion see Selwyn (1998).

[5] For an outline for the plans for the University for Industry see *Pathfinder Prospectus* (DfEE, 1998c) on the DfEE lifelong learning Internet site http://www.lifelonglearning.co.uk/ufi/index.htm

[6] For more see the DfEE (1998d).

[7] See note 3.

[8] See the way the present government has built its policies on the findings and recommendations of the report by Dearing (1996) and also Avis (1998).

[9] Introduction to section 2, http://www.lifelonglearning.co.uk/greenpaper/ch0002.htm

[10] For years it has been a policy in many countries to encourage early retirement and labour markets openly discriminated on grounds of age. However, several EU governments, including Germany, have now reversed the support they previously gave to early exit and are seeking ways of reducing the opportunities for and costs of early retirement. Similarly, employers and unions are reassessing their attitudes towards older workers (European Commission, 1998). The British government is in the process of establishing a voluntary code of practice aimed at reducing ageism at work. However, this code would not be legally binding (*Western Mail*, 1998b).

[11] This basic distinction originates in Kelly (1982).

[12] This does not hold true for degree holders. At this level the UK compares well with other nations.

[13] CBI Quarterly Industrial Trends Survey, April 1998, quoted in Skills and Enterprise Network (1998a).

[14] This debate is not limited to the VET system alone but concerns German manufacturing in general (Herrigel, 1997).

[15] Warmerdam also raises the issue of the definition of the term 'sector' which he identifies as having two different meanings: first, as a statistical or economic category as a designation of a specific 'collection' of economic activities; and second, as a social or sociopolitical category in which collective actors strive to promote their own particular interests (Warmerdam, 1997).

[16] It could be maintained that this system is under threat. Its functioning is dependent on the cooperation of the 'social partners', and increasingly this cooperation seems to be breaking down in the construction sector (Syben, 1998).

[17] 'Educator' – this occupation is that of a skilled and trained carer for children or young people in both residential and non-residential establishments including nurseries.

[18] 'Social pedagogy' or 'social education' – this is a graduate profession in the same field as *Erzieher*. *Sozialpädagogen* also work in residential and non-residential organisations caring for children and young people, although they usually do not work in nurseries.

[19] Delamont and Rees (1997) raise some useful questions concerning the distinctiveness and characteristics of these developments.

[20] The survey defines a learner as "a respondent who has left full-time continuous education, and has taken part in at least one [...] taught or non-taught learning activity within the three years prior to fieldwork or since leaving full-time continuous education (whichever period was shorter)" (Beinart and Smith, 1998, p 37).

[21] This might be partly the result of the different structure of the care sector. Some of the care homes visited were funded via charities and thus did not have to make a profit (although all had to recover their costs), which might decrease short-termism to some degree.

[22] In Wales, the Awdurdod Cymwysterau, Cwricwlwm ac Asesu Cymru (ACCAC), the Qualifications, Curriculum and Assessment Authority for Wales, is responsible for curriculum and assessment policy.

References

Atkinson, J. (1984) *Flexibility, uncertainty and manpower management*, Report No 89, Brighton: Institute of Manpower Studies.

Avis, J. (1998) '(Im)possible dream: post-Fordism, stakeholding and post-compulsory education', *Journal of Education Policy*, vol 13, no 2, pp 251-63.

Beaumont, G. (1996) *Review of 100 NVQs and SVQs*, London: NCVQ.

Beinart, S. and Smith, P. (1998) *National adult learning survey*, Research Report 49, London: DfEE.

BMBF (Bundesministerium für Bildung, Wissenschaft, Forschung und Technologie) (1996) *Berufsbildungsbericht*, Bonn: BMBF.

BMBF (1998) *Berufsbildungsbericht*, Bonn: BMBF.

Bock, K. and Timmermann, D. (1998) 'Education and employment in Germany: changing chances and risks for youth', *Education Economics*, vol 6, no 1, pp 71-92.

Brine, J. (1998) 'European education and training policy for under-educated unemployed people', *International Studies in Sociology of Education*, vol 7, no 2, pp 229-45.

Clarke, L. and Wall, C. (1996) *Skills and the construction process: A comparative study of vocational training and quality in social housebuilding*, Bristol: The Policy Press.

Cockrill, A. (1996a) *Towards a Learning Society: Iinitial and continuing vocational education and training*, ESRC Learning Society Initiative Project:'Training for multi-skilling – a comparison of British and German experience', Working Paper 1, Cardiff: CASS/School of Education, University of Wales Cardiff.

Cockrill, A. (1996b) *The care sector in Britain*, ESRC Learning Society Initiative Project: 'Training for multi-skilling – a comparison of British and German experience', Working Paper 3, Cardiff: CASS/School of Education, University of Wales Cardiff.

Cockrill, A. (1997a) *Residential care for the elderly in Germany: Training and multi-skilling*, ESRC Learning Society Initiative Project: 'Training for multi-skilling – a comparison of British and German experience', Working Paper 5, Cardiff: CASS/School of Education, University of Wales Cardiff.

Cockrill, A. (1997b) *Residential care in Germany: Training and multi-skilling in organisations caring for the young and the elderly: Caring for young people*, ESRC Learning Society Initiative Project:'Training for multi-skilling – a comparison of British and German experience', Working Paper 5b, Cardiff: CASS/School of Education, University of Wales Cardiff.

Cockrill, A. (1997c) 'Erfahrung zählt mehr als Qualifikation', *Position* 2, pp 23-4.

Cockrill, A. and Scott, P. (1997a) 'Vocational education and training in Germany: trends and issues', *Journal of Vocational Education and Training*, vol 49, no 3, pp 49-53.

Cockrill, A. and Scott, P. (1997b) *Training, skills provision and multi-skilling in the construction industry: A Welsh German comparison*, Regional Industrial Research Report 28, Cardiff: CASS: University of Wales Cardiff.

Cockrill, A. and Scott, P. (1997c) *Training for multi-skilling in residential care homes for the elderly: A Welsh German comparison*, Regional Industrial Research Report 27, Cardiff: CASS, University of Wales Cardiff.

Cockrill, A. and Scott, P. (1997d) 'Training providers, employers and trainees in Britain and Germany: the policy implications of differing needs, perceptions and attitudes', Paper presented at the International JVET Conference, University of Huddersfield, 16-18 July.

Cockrill, A., Cooke, P. and Schall, N. (2000: forthcoming) 'The Welsh perspective', in R. Sturm, G. Weinmann and O. Will (eds) *The information society and the regions in Europe: A British-German comparison*, Schriftenreihe des Europäischen Zentrums für Föderalismus-Forschung, Baden-Baden: Nomos (forthcoming).

Coffield, F. (1999) 'Introduction', in F. Coffield (ed) *Why's the beer always stronger up North? Studies of lifelong learning in Europe*, Bristol, The Policy Press, pp 1-11.

Cross, M. (1985) *Towards the flexible craftsman*, London: Technical Change Centre.

Dearing, R. (1996) *Review of qualifications for 16-19 year olds: full report*, Hayes: SCAA Publications.

Deissinger, T. (1997) 'The German dual system – a model for Europe', *Education and Training*, vol 39, no 8, pp 297-302.

Delamont, S. and Rees, G. (1997) *Understanding the Welsh education system: Does Wales need a separate 'policy sociology'?*, Working Paper 23, Cardiff: School of Education, University of Wales Cardiff.

DfEE (Department for Education and Employment) (1997) *Connecting the Learning Society*, London: DfEE.

DfEE (1998a) *The Learning Age: A renaissance for a new Britain*, Green Paper, downloaded from Internet site http://www.lifelonglearning.co.uk/greenpaper/index.htm.

DfEE (1998b) 'An update on direct learning', *Individual Learning News*, issue 5, downloaded from Internet site http://www.lifelonglearning.co.uk/iln5000/iln5109.htm.

DfEE (1998c) *University for Industry Pathfinder Prospectus*, downloaded from Internet site http://www.lifelonglearning.co.uk/ufi/index.htm.

DfEE (1998d) *Background strategic document on Individual Learning Accounts*, downloaded from Internet site http://www.lifelonglearning.co.uk/ila/index.htm.

ETAG (Education and Training Action Group for Wales) (1998) *An education and training action plan for Wales: A draft for consultation*, Cardiff: Manweb PLC.

European Commission (1998) *The ageing population and technology: Challenges and opportunities*, ETAN Working Paper prepared for the European Commission Directorate General XII Directorate AS-RTD Actions: Strategy and Coordination, Luxembourg: Office for Official Publications of the European Communities.

Finegold, D. and Soskice, D. (1988) 'The failure of training in Britain: analysis and prescription', *Oxford Review of Economic Policy*, vol 4, no 3, pp 128-39.

Fryer, R.H. (1997) *Learning for the twenty-first century: First report of the National Advisory Group for Continuing Education and Lifelong Learning*.

Fuller, A. and Unwin, L. (1998) 'Reconceptualising apprenticeship: exploring the relationship between work and learning', *Journal of Vocational Education and Training*, vol 50, no 2, pp 153-71.

Gorard, S. (1997) *A brief history of education and training in Wales 1900-1996*, Patterns of Participation in Adult Education and Training, Working Paper 5, Cardiff: School of Education, University of Wales Cardiff.

Gorard, S., Rees, G. and Selwyn, N. (1999) *Lifelong learning targets: A research review. A report prepared for the National Assembly for Wales*, Cardiff, Cardiff University School of Social Sciences, October.

Gorard, S., Furlong, J., Rees, G. and Fevre, R. (1997a) *The learning society*, Patterns of Participation in Adult Education and Training Working Paper 5, Cardiff: School of Education, University of Wales Cardiff.

Gorard, S., Furlong, J., Rees, G. and Fevre, R. (1997b) *How to spot a lifelong learner at 40 paces? The two components of determination*, Patterns of Participation in Adult Education and Training Working Paper 9, Cardiff: School of Education, University of Wales Cardiff.

Herrigel, G. (1997) 'The limits of German manufacturing flexibility', in L. Turner (ed) *Negotiating the new Germany*, Ithaca and London: ILR Press, pp 177-205.

IDS (Incomes Data Services) (1994) *Multi-skilling*, IDS Study 558, London: IDS.

Keep, E. (1993) 'Missing, presumed skilled: training policy in the UK', in R. Edwards, S. Sieminsky and D. Zeldin (eds) *Adult learning, education and training, Learning through Life 2*, London and New York, NY: Routledge.

Kelly, J. (1982) *Scientific management, job redesign and work performance*, London: Academic Press.

Kern, H. and Schumann, M. (1984) *Das Ende der Arbeitsteilung? Rationalisierung in der industriellen Produktion*, Munich: Verlag CH Beck.

Lindley, R. (1991) 'Interactions in the markets for education, training and labour: a European perspective on intermediate skills', in P. Ryan (ed) *International comparisons of vocational education and training for intermediate skills*, London: Falmer Press.

Lundvall, B. and Johnson, B. (1994) 'The learning economy', *Journal of Industry Studies*, vol 2, no 2, pp 23–42.

Macrae, S., Maguire, M. and Ball, S.J. (1997) 'Whose "Learning Society"? A tentative deconstruction', Paper presented at the BERA Conference held at the University of York, 11–14 September.

Piore, M. and Sabel, C. (1984) *The second industrial divide: Possibilities for prosperity*, New York, NY: Basic Books.

Rees, G. (1997a) 'Making a Learning Society: education and work in industrial South Wales', *The Welsh Journal of Education / Cylchgrawn addysg Cymry*, vol 6, no 2, pp 4–16.

Rees, G. (1997b) 'Vocational education and training and regional development: an analytical framework', *Journal of Education and Work*, vol 10, no 2, pp 141–9.

Rees, G., Fevre, R., Furlong, J. and Gorard, S. (1997) 'Notes towards a social theory of lifetime learning; history, place and The Learning Society', *Patterns of Participation in Adult Education and Training*, Working Paper 6, Cardiff: School of Education, University of Wales Cardiff.

Scott, P. (1996a) *From a skill-based to a competence-based labour market in the UK?*, ESRC Learning Society Project: 'Training for multi-skilling – a comparison of British and German experience', Working Paper 2, Cardiff: CASS/School of Education, University of Wales.

Scott, P. (1996b) *Leading by exhortation and by example, The National Training and Education Targets and Investor in People initiatives in the UK vocational training system*, ESRC Learning Society Project: 'Training for multi-skilling – a comparison of British and German experience', Working Paper 4. Cardiff: CASS/School of Education, University of Wales.

Scott, P. and Cockrill, A. (1996) *Training for multi-skilling in small and medium sized engineering companies: A Welsh German comparison*, Regional Industrial Research Report No 21, Cardiff: CASS, University of Wales.

Scott, P. and Cockrill, A. (1997) 'Multi-skilling in small- and medium-sized engineering firms: evidence from Wales and Germany', *International Journal of Human Resource Management*, vol 8, no 6, pp 807-25.

Scott, P. and Cockrill, A. (1998) 'Artisans in the making? Comparing construction training in Wales and Germany', in F. Coffield (ed) *Learning at Work*, Bristol, The Policy Press.

Sellin, B. (1994) *Vocational training in Europe: Towards a modular form?*, CEDEFOP Panorama Discussion Paper, Thessaloniki: CEDEFOP.

Selwyn, N. (1998) 'A grid for learning or a grid for earning? The significance of the Learning Grid initiative in UK', *Journal of Education Policy*, vol 13, no 3, pp 423-31.

Shackleton, J.R. (1992) *Training too much? A sceptical look at the economics of skill provision in the UK*, Hobart Paper 118, London: IEA.

Shackleton, J.R. (1997) 'Training in Germany: a view from abroad', *Education and Training*, vol 39, no 8, pp 303-8.

Skills and Enterprise Network (1998a) 'Bridging the skills gap', *Skills and Enterprise briefing*, issue 4, August.

Skills and Enterprise Network (1998b) *Labour market quarterly report August 1998*, Sheffield: DfEE.

Steedman, H. (1998) 'A decade of skill formation in Britain and Germany', *Journal of Education and Work*, vol 11, no 1, pp 77-94.

Syben, G. (1998) 'Winners and losers in the German construction industry', *CLR News*, vol 3, pp 13-17.

University of Sussex (1996) 'Quality of NVQs in doubt', *Bulletin*, Newsletter 6, December. downloaded from the Internet site http://www.sussex.ac.uk

Warmerdam, J. (1997) *Sektorale Ausbildungssysteme in der Wissenschaftsgesellschaft*, CEDEFOP Panorama Diskussionspapier, Thessaloniki: CEDEFOP.

Welsh Office (1998) *Learning is for everyone*, Green Paper, downloaded from Internet site http://www.wales.gov.uk/cgi-bin/hmappserv?tester2.mv+repost+16+1+1

Western Mail (1998a) 'Not enough skilled workers', 10 August, p 12.

Western Mail (1998b) 'Code to curb ageism in jobs will mostly not work, says TUC', 14 August, p 15.

SEVEN

Development of knowledge and skills at work

Michael Eraut, Jane Alderton, Gerald Cole and Peter Senker

Introduction

Our proposal argued that policy discourse about education and training is focused mainly on formalistic aspects of provision and achievement. Provision is defined in terms of how training is delivered or facilitated. Achievement is defined in terms of qualifications and credits with rather less attention to gains in knowledge, skills or capability which escape formal assessment. Hence, we chose to study learning at work without making any prior assumptions about its connection, or lack of connection, with education and training. Our three main questions were:

- What is being learned at work?
- How is learning taking place?
- What other factors affect the amount and direction of learning in the workplace?

Our focus was on employees at the professional/managerial and technical/supervisory levels in three occupational areas, engineering, business and healthcare.

This relatively un-researched domain posed several theoretical and practical problems, critical to developing and defining *The Learning Society*. Hence our aims emphasised the pioneering nature of the research, preparing the way for others to follow. These aims were:

- to collect and analyse evidence from three occupational areas about the learning of knowledge and skills in employment;
- to develop research methods for investigating learning in employment;

- to develop a theoretical framework for interpreting the findings and guiding future research in this area;
- to contribute to the development of thinking across *The Learning Society Programme*.

The primary purpose of this report is to describe and discuss the main findings of the project and their practical and theoretical implications for policy and research. For more detailed analyses of the various aspects of the project's work, readers are referred to project publications and our forthcoming book.

Theoretical foundation

The formalistic emphasis of education and training policy treats learning as a self-conscious, deliberate, goal-driven process which is planned and organised by 'providers' to yield outcomes that are easily described and measured. Our starting assumption was that, although a great deal of important learning is attributable to formal contexts and frameworks which fit these assumptions, this paradigm fails to capture much of the learning that occurs in the workplace. Yet challenging this dominant paradigm renders our research questions highly problematic. What is to count as knowledge if it is not defined in terms of the outcomes of education and training or research? How will one detect learning in non-formal settings if it is not planned, measured or talked about, possibly not even conscious?

In policy terms there has been some movement over the last 10 years to give more emphasis to practical knowledge, but the formalistic paradigm has ensured that, in order to be valued, practical knowledge has to be specified, assessed and codified in propositional form. Only book-based representations of practical knowledge can be accorded importance and status. Indeed the term 'knowledge' is often defined so that it refers only to what has been formally codified. To study learning in non-formal settings and also, we would argue, the unrecorded learning which takes place in formal settings, an alternative definition is needed. Thus, from the onset of the project we recognised two competing definitions of the term ' knowledge'. We were not in a position to impose the broader definition we favour because we had to be sensitive to the way the term was used by our respondents and the representatives of the organisations with whom we work.

Codified knowledge (C knowledge) is defined in terms of propositional knowledge, codified and stored in publications, libraries, databases and so on, subject to quality control by editors and peer review, and given foundational status by incorporation into examinations and qualifications. Under this definition, skills are regarded as separate from knowledge (although some of them, such as reading and reporting, are essential for acquiring knowledge and passing it on to others). Hence there is a potential problem when an educational system, which has evolved with propositional knowledge as its main focus, is also expected to deliver certain skills and competences.

Personal knowledge (P knowledge) is defined in terms of what people bring to practical situations that enables them to think and perform. Such personal knowledge is acquired not only through the use of public knowledge but is also constructed from personal experience and reflection. It includes propositional knowledge along with procedural and process knowledge, tacit knowledge and experiential knowledge in episodic memory. Under this definition, skills are treated as part of knowledge rather than as separate from it. This allows for representations of competence, capability or expertise in which the use of skills and propositional knowledge are closely integrated.

These two domains are not mutually exclusive. P knowledge incorporates a great deal of C knowledge, but in a personalised form whose resemblance to published forms will vary according to its history of use. Conversely, the creation and the use of C knowledge will depend on the development of the creators' or users' P knowledge.

The typology described by the project to handle responses to the question "What is being learned in the workplace?" is summarised in Table 1 below (a fuller version can be found in the Appendix of Eraut et al, 1998a). Only W3 and part of W4 can be described as C knowledge. Parts of W2 can be found in NVQs. The other forms of knowledge lie mainly outside the scope of the formalistic paradigm.

Our definition of learning as 'the process by which personal knowledge is acquired' is more satisfactory than one based on C knowledge, because learning is an essentially personal process which occurs within mainly social contexts whose multi-layered communications are only minimally receptive to codification. Moreover, our definition of P knowledge implies that extending the range of action contexts entails a corresponding increase, large or small, in personal knowledge; thus recognising that transfer is also a learning process, as emphasised in Eraut (1997a). Although the project initially focused on sources and contexts for learning in the workplace we later developed a second, rather different typology (Table

2) that focuses on the nature of learning in non–formal contexts. The most important theoretical issue is the level of awareness and attention, and there are also the important questions of the respective timing of the learning and the stimulus which gave rise to it.

Table 1: What is being learned?

W1	*Understanding*
	Understanding of situations and systems
	Understanding of colleagues and work unit
	Understanding of own organisation
	Understanding of self
	Strategic understanding
W2	*Skills*
	Technical skills
	Learning skills
	Interpersonal skills
	Thinking skills
W3	*Propositional knowledge*
	General knowledge taught during initial training for occupation
	Specialised occupational knowledge
	Firm-specific knowledge (technical)
	Knowledge of systems and procedures
W4	*Knowledge resources and how to access them*
	People in the department/work group
	People elsewhere in the organisation
	Internally available materials; manuals, records, databases, learning materials
	Networks of customers, competitors, suppliers
	Professional networks
	Higher Education institutions
	Local networks
	Previous employers
W5	*Judgement*
	Quality of work
	Evaluation
	Strategic decisions
	Staff issues
	Prioritising

Reber (1993) defined *implicit learning* as "the acquisition of knowledge independently of conscious attempts to learn and in the absence of explicit knowledge about what was learned"; and the primacy of the awareness issue is reflected in the title of Berry's (1997) book, *How implicit is implicit learning?* When analysing the data collected in our project, we found it useful to introduce one further category between implicit learning and deliberative learning to describe situations where the learning is explicit, but takes place almost spontaneously in response to recent, current or imminent situations without any time being specifically set aside for it. We call this *reactive learning*.

Table 2: A typology of non-formal learning

Time of stimulus	Implicit learning	Reactive learning	Deliberative learning
Past episode(s)	Implicit linkage of past memories with current experience	Brief near-spontaneous *reflection* on past episodes, communications, events, experiences	*Review* of past actions, communications, events, experiences
Current experience	A selection from experience enters the memory	*Incidental* noting of facts, opinions, impressions, ideas *Recognition of* learning opportunities	*Engagement* in decision making, problem solving, planned informal learning
Future behaviour	Unconscious effect of previous experiences	Being prepared for *emergent* learning opportunities	*Planned* learning goals *Planned* learning opportunities

The version of *reflection* used by Dewey (1933) and Kolb (1984) is deliberative and classified under *review* in our typology: Schön (1983) would describe it as "reflection-*on*-action". Schön's contrasting term "reflection-*in*-action" is more problematic because it could be construed either as a reactive learning response to an event in the immediate past or as referring to a metacognitive awareness that triggers learning or decision making but is not in itself a form of learning (Eraut, 1995). *Emergent* is the term used by Megginson (1996) to describe an alternative strategy to planning; but using an emergent strategy for defining goals need not prevent a deliberative rather than reactive approach when learning opportunities occur.

The concept of *implicit learning* is matched by that of *tacit knowledge*, first described by Polanyi (1967) when he claimed that "we can know more than we can tell" (p 3). The problem this poses for the researcher depends on whether knowledge is tacit because knowers are unaware of their knowledge due to its implicit acquisition; or because they cannot find a representation of it which might enable them to communicate it to others. If awareness is the problem, because the knowledge is used rarely or rapidly without thinking, it may be retrievable by triggering an appropriate memory. Otherwise the researcher will have to infer the existence of the knowledge from observations or accounts of the knower's behaviour. If representation is the problem, the researcher may also have difficulty in "telling". However, there are situations where a researcher with appropriate experience and knowledge of the literature may be able to suggest partial representations for approval, rejection or improvement. Similar respondent verifications are needed for inferences from behaviour. The process is likely to be more successful when the researcher is able to use a more ethnographic approach, so as to be able to ground conversations in concrete examples of events witnessed by both parties; but this was not feasible for our project because we felt we needed to operate with quite a large number of respondents in order to establish credibility with policy makers.

Methodology

The three occupational sectors (and the organisations within them) were chosen for their contrasting features. These include both public and private sectors, national (sometimes international) and local spheres of operation, production and service orientations, and varying levels of professional influence. Our original intention was to conduct two interviews, 6–12 months apart, with 15 respondents from nine organisations (three in each sector). However, it proved difficult to get 15 respondents from any one site, and one financial service organisation dropped out at the last minute. Thus we ended up with 120 respondents from 12 different organisations, of whom 88 were available for second interviews within the time span of the project. In nine organisations we were able to interview employees on a single site. As intended, our sample excluded small organisations, whose learning contexts are so different as to need a separate study. Details of the gender, age, occupational sector and status of the respondents are given in Table 3 below:

Table 3: Details of people interviewed

	Business	Engineering	Health	Total
Male	21	40	8	69
Female	15	7	29	51
Age				
20-29	17	13	10	40
30-39	12	26	12	50
40-49	5	4	6	15
50-59	2	4	9	15
Manager	8	20	9	37
Professional/team	6	21	15	42
Leader	22	6	13	41
Technician				
Graduate	17	22	3	42
HNC/HND	1	12	1	14
Prof/Man Qual	13	12	24	49
No Higher Qual	5	1	9	15
Total respondents	36	47	37	120

As explained earlier, the problems faced by researchers investigating non-formal learning are very considerable. Not only is implicit learning difficult to detect without prolonged observation, but reactive learning and some deliberative learning are unlikely to be consciously recalled unless there was an unusually dramatic outcome. Worse still, potential respondents are unaccustomed to talking about learning and may find it difficult to respond to a request to do so. If they do, they are more likely to refer to formal learning rather than non-formal learning. The latter is just part of their work: solving a problem at work is unlikely to be interpreted as a learning process unless an interviewer can home in on it in a particularly appropriate way. Given all these difficulties, it is not surprising that several research approaches have been tried; and these are briefly reviewed below. All use interviews, but they differ in the number of interviews (some used two interviews separated by several months), the structuring of the interviews and the kinds of questions asked. None asked vague, open-ended questions which rarely succeed in probing deeply in this particular type of inquiry.

Key lifetime events

The McCall et al (1988) study of 191 successful executives from six major US companies investigated how they learned from experience by asking them to talk about at least three key events or episodes in their career that led to *a lasting change* in their approach to management.

Learning projects

Tough (1971) developed the construct of a *learning project* to describe an extended piece of self-directed learning with a particular idea in mind; and used it to reveal much greater non-formal learning by adults than had been assumed previously. Gear et al (1994) asked a sample of professionals from several occupational sectors to list their learning projects in the previous three years and select one of them for discussion. Half of them had carried out between three and six such projects but less than 20% claimed to have unequivocally followed a pre-determined plan. A total of 80% had an idea of the outcome they wanted but followed an *emergent strategy* which took advantage of learning opportunities as they arose: the intent and the learning activity were deliberative, but the recognition of learning opportunities reactive.

Recent changes in your life or practice

Fox et al's (1989) study of 356 North American physicians began by asking 'What changes have you made or have occurred in your life or practice during the past year?' An average of 2.2 changes was reported for that year, although many had earlier antecedents. Their follow-up questions were 'What caused the change to occur?' and 'Did you learn anything in order to make this change?'

Situations where more knowledge or skill was needed

Slotnick et al (1997) asked doctors to identify situations where they needed more knowledge and skills, attending first to the nature of the circumstances giving rise to this need, then to how they sought and found the information and skill they needed, then to how they used the information and their thoughts about the whole learning episode. He has now extended this procedure (Slotnick, 1999) to include a second interview. The first interview now includes a current problem and plans to deal with it, while the second revisits the same problem to find out what actually happened. This procedure elicits information about factors leading to changes of plan or even the abandonment of the original learning goal.

Given our concern to include learning needed for, and arising from, taken-for-granted aspects of daily work, we returned to the questioning strategy, used by two of us in earlier research on the use of scientific knowledge by nurses and midwives (Eraut et al, 1995). This was adapted to focus on learning rather than knowledge use and promised to elicit a wider range of learning experiences than those 'captured' by the projects discussed above.

Our strategy for the first interviews was to ask first about the nature of the respondent's job, recent tasks, duties and problems; secondly to discuss the nature of the competence/expertise required to do it; then thirdly to ask how the necessary expertise was acquired and the extent to which it was changing. Finally, if it had not already become apparent, questions were asked about different sources of learning. Respondents were also encouraged to elaborate on salient learning episodes or to exemplify general statements about learning. Most of the interviews lasted between one and two hours, and many of those interviewed stated that they had found it a valuable experience which had stimulated their thinking about learning. They often yielded some evidence on the factors effecting learning, although we did not intend to introduce that question until our second interviews.

These first interviews were transcribed and provisionally analysed by the interviewer, then converted into interim reports on each occupational sector for discussion at a meeting with our organisational contacts. This discussion raised a number of questions to be addressed by further analysis, and was followed by a brainstorming session on categories to be included in our framework for analysing the data. These were then classified, checked for consistency and elaborated in certain areas to take account of other research findings. The draft framework was then sent to our contacts with a report of the meeting and used for further analysis of our interview transcripts. During this further analysis researchers also noted points needing elaboration in the second interview, and categories where the absence or paucity of information needed to be checked in case it had been an artefact of the interview situation. Transcripts were sent to respondents about a month before their second interview, with a request for suggested modifications and a list of questions arising from the first interview. Thus second interviews focused partly on elaboration of the first and partly on our third research question about factors affecting the amount and direction of their learning. Those who gave the richest first interviews usually gave equally rich second interviews, suggesting greater self-awareness in the area of learning.

This research approach enabled us to uncover more of the daily processes of learning than approaches focused only on critical events or self-directed, pre-planned initiatives. But as the research progressed, we also became aware that even this improved approach could elicit but a small proportion of the learning occurring in the workplace. Our developing theoretical understanding of non-formal learning from this and other research (Eraut, 2000) helped to put these methodological limitations in perspective. So our final verdict is that we made some progress in developing the methodology, but we were also expecting too much. Our main concern is that both policy makers and several other researchers in this area expect even more. These overoptimistic assumptions about the extent to which learning can be 'captured' owe more to wish fulfilment than demonstrated achievement; and their theoretical foundations are suspect.

How do people learn?

Our findings strongly support our hypothesis that a learning-focused perspective provides a radically different view of a learning society from that afforded by a training-focused perspective. For most of our respondents, formal education and training contribute to only a small proportion of learning at work. Our framework of learning contexts, summarised in Table 4, can be used in conjunction with our knowledge framework (Table 1) to map connections between what is learned at work and how it is learned. This indicates a different mix between formal and non-formal learning according to the kind of learning involved. For example, most of the knowledge classified as W1 is acquired mainly by non-formal approaches. There may also be significant implicit learning. Formal learning, if it occurs, is most likely to take the form of information about the organisation, theories which aid conceptualisation or methods for more systematic collection of information. In contrast most of the propositional knowledge classified as W3 is often acquired as the result of a substantial formal input. Even here, however, the role of non-formal learning in developing the capability to use that knowledge at work is much greater than commonly assumed. For the skills listed under W2, there will be considerable variation in the contribution of formal learning according to the skill, the learning opportunities and the learner's personal disposition. While many of our respondents expected some formal training in most technical skills, we did encounter a few who insisted on learning by doing with a small amount of additional questioning. In other skill areas people expected to learn mainly by practice with some informal feedback, although more formal contributions were usually welcomed.

Table 4: Contexts and sources for learning

H1	Working for qualifications
H2	Short courses
H3	Special events
H4	Materials
H5	Organised learning support
H6	Consultation and collaboration within the working group
H7	The challenge of the work itself
H8	Consultation outside the working group
H9	Life outside work

The most frequently discussed issues in *initial training for the professions* (H1) concern (a) the need for breadth or specialisation and (b) the balance and phasing of learning in education and workplace contexts. Our engineering respondents who took initial degrees favoured breadth – a good general grasp of technology and a good range of general skills; and also favoured periods of work-based learning during their degree course. Those who experienced apprenticeships with day release found them to be effective for technical learning. Initial training for most health professions incorporates extensive work placements. This concurrent approach is considered the most appropriate, but there is still much argument about the quantity, quality and timing of the service-based learning. Those who took banking examinations, albeit part-time after entering employment, saw them providing a useful foundation for later technical courses as well as broad banking knowledge. *Mid-career qualifications* were significant for nurses, radiographers and engineers. For nurses these were usually degree courses which gave them a wider view of their profession, for radiographers they were usually specialist qualifications linked to new techniques, while for engineers they were usually management-focused rather than profession-focused. For nurses and engineers, the major outcomes were usually an increase in confidence and self-knowledge, the development of a more analytic approach to problems and issues and increased organisational understanding derived from working with colleagues from other organisations. Similar findings were reported by the McCall et al (1988) study of top American executives!

The central finding of Eraut et al's (1995) study of nursing and midwifery education was that learning in education and practice settings could not be easily linked by most students unless they occurred within a fairly short period of time. Moreover, students' perceptions of the relevance of each segment of their formal teaching affected their attention and retention. Translated into the context of *short courses* (H2), this implies that the prior experience and orientation of participants will be important for learning and the early subsequent use of what they have learned will be important for retention. Typically a short course using a formal approach needs both prior and subsequent non-formal learning if it is to be effective. This is well documented in the area of teacher education (Steadman et al, 1995), and was confirmed by the comments of our respondents. Their judgements about short courses frequently referred to their timing. Did they have the necessary experience? Could they receive the course before having to learn what they needed by other, possibly more time-consuming, methods? Did they have the support and encouragement to sustain the necessary period of learning how to use the knowledge which the course had introduced? Many positive examples were cited of "Just-in-Time" courses and of coaching and mentoring after courses; and negative examples of courses coming too early or too late, or wasted through lack of follow-up. Some courses, however, had other important outcomes. They helped to establish networks, both across different parts of the same organisation and between people doing similar work in different organisations; and, like conferences, they provided an opportunity for people to discuss current changes and possible new developments, thus helping them to think and plan ahead.

A significant development in the banking and insurance sector was the transformation of what had previously been short courses of up to two weeks into distance learning packages, often computer-based or video-based, for flexible use in a workplace *learning centre*. While a few respondents welcomed this flexibility, most responded rather negatively. *Packaged training* (H4) reinforced the image of a distant, uncaring employer and was generally demotivating; whereas training courses were often positive occasions when they established contact with the wider organisation in a range of different ways. For example, networks were formed, greater awareness of the organisation developed; and it was possible to ask questions about the organisation's work which went well beyond the specific training objectives.

Other *materials* such as manuals and reference books were welcomed, as were materials linked to formal qualifications from professional bodies. Usage of *manuals*, however, appeared to be confined to a minority who thrived on learning from manuals; while the others did all they could to avoid them. The best response could be to make sure that manual readers are available where needed. One respondent reported how much easier she had found learning from materials when working in a pair; and this also merits further investigation. Others mentioned that a combination of materials with face-to-face teaching was often more effective than either method on its own. In contrast to physicians (Jennett et al, 1994), very little use of journals was reported by any of the groups we studied. A few engineers use trade journals, catalogues or the business sections of newspapers to maintain current awareness; but most relied on learning from other people.

The two modes of non-formal learning reported as important by nearly all our respondents were learning from *The challenge of the work itself* (H7) and *Learning from other people* (H6, H8). Either could involve reactive or deliberative learning, during or subsequent to a work activity or consultation. Very often both were involved, as consultations with other people were an accustomed and integral part of work-based problem-solving. Slotnick et al (1997) has recently identified two kinds of learning stimulus for doctors. Two thirds of the situations precipitating their reported learning episodes were patient problems, whose solution was part of their normal work. It would be misleading to attempt to separate working from learning during such episodes, nor could any part of the problem-solving process be described as 'not working' or 'not learning'. The other type of learning episode arose when the doctor recognised a need to acquire new knowledge and skills, which could be used with classes of patients rather than individual cases. These were usually advances in either diagnosis or treatment which the doctor could learn to use for the benefit of patients; and their acquisition normally involved both off-the-job and on-the-job learning. They fitted Tough's (1971) definition of a *learning project* (see above). Both types of learning were reported by our respondents; but there was also a significant difference in our research. Slotnick describes the learning of "independent professionals", whereas we studied people working in large organisations. While some personal learning projects were reported by our interviewees, most of the learning and working they described was organisationally situated.

The allocation of work is a critical factor in work-based learning. Lack of variation or lack of challenge lowers the rate of learning – a particular problem for the nursing assistants. Changes in work role and special assignments featured frequently in our interviews because they stimulated or necessitated new learning (this was also reported by McCall et al, 1988). Typical examples were acting up, being 'on call', becoming a mentor, joining a review or policy-making group, representing the work group and making presentations. The initial period in a new job could be as great a stimulus as a difficult problem or a critical incident. To Slotnick's client problems and learning projects, we have to add a third kind of learning stimulus – changes in a person's duties and expectations about work processes or outcomes. For many of our respondents this was the most important stimulus of all.

Those in leadership or management roles faced problems of a rather different kind. They still had a steady flow of critical incidents and problems hitting their desk, but they also had an ongoing challenge of a more strategic kind. They were expected to improve both the efficiency of their work unit and to improve the quality of its work, whether this goal was communicated to them through target-setting or through informal indications of expectation. In the healthcare sector this often took the form of reducing staffing and budget costs without any concomitant reduction in work to be done. Thus they required them to prioritise, to innovate and to frame problems whose solution might lead to improved performance. This demands not only analysis and imagination but also skills in managing change, consulting and using the resources of all members of their work group.

Another factor to be born in mind is that today's problems often become tomorrow's routines, especially in the technical domain. Novel problems demand a deliberative approach and possibly some trial and error; but once solved on a number of occasions, they cease to be novel and can be handled reactively by intuitive recognition of the situation and the application of a 'well-tested' solution. What begins as an overt deliberative process may end up as tacit knowledge. In retrospect people call this *learning from experience*, a term which is difficult to deconstruct. Only the most salient examples of problem solving are likely to be remembered, especially those involving memorable mistakes. Indeed learning from mistakes was given considerable emphasis by some of our respondents.

Much learning from other people is self-directed because it arises out of a person's work when they seek consultation and advice; but this can become almost incidental when people are in the habit of sharing their experiences and problems with colleagues and/or friends. There is also a significant amount of learning by peripheral participation (Lave and

Wenger, 1991), simply by seeing other people in action. Then finally learning can be initiated by another person offering feedback or advice about one's performance, one's role or even one's future prospects.

Our framework has classified learning from other people at work under three main headings: *Organised learning support* (H5), *Consultation and collaboration within the working group* (H6) and *Consultation outside the Working Group* (H8); and detailed examples to support and amplify the following analysis can be found in Eraut et al (1998b). We have defined a working group as a group of people who have regular contact with each other at work, some sense of shared purpose and no stronger allegiance elsewhere in the organisation. We also found it useful to distinguish between normal groups with a common leader or manager and special groups to which people may be allocated for a fixed period on a part-time or full-time basis.

Activities reported under *Organised learning support* include apprenticeships, trainee appointments, induction, mentoring, coaching, rotations, visits, shadowing and reference to experts. Though never subversive these activities were not necessarily organised in any official way, and knowledge of them was often confined to the immediate work unit. It was also possible to discern different assumptions about learning underpinning the selection and transaction of modes of learning support. Thus the practices we noted resulted from the interaction between:

- the prevailing level of formality and structure in the workplace;
- the initiator(s) – the learner, the organisation, the line manager or another (usually more experienced) colleague; and
- the assumptions about learning held (but not often overtly stated) by the parties involved.

Four main approaches to the facilitation of learning could be distinguished, which operated sometimes on their own and sometimes in combination.

Induction and integration focused primarily on people becoming effective members of their work unit and the organisation as a whole. The emphasis is on socialisation: understanding the purposes and goals of the unit and the organisation, their own roles and others' expectations of them; and fitting into the interpersonal nexus in which their work is embedded. The management approach can vary from laissez-faire and light monitoring to a succession of formal events, for example an induction course followed by other short courses.

Exposure and osmosis are frequently used to describe the process of learning by peripheral participation. Through observations and listening the exposed learner picks up information and know-how by a process of osmosis. The role of the manager is limited to that of enabling sufficient exposure to a diversity of contexts and situations; but otherwise remains passive. In contrast, the learner has not only to be alert and receptive but also to work out what he or she needs to know. Shadowing and certain types of rotation and visit are the usual methods employed.

Self-directed learning assumes that learners take a more active role, learning from doing the work and finding out on their own initiative what they need to know. Such an active role is more likely to be adopted if the work is appropriately chosen and learners encouraged in their learning. Like the first two approaches, managers' hopes that employees will be self-directed learners may not be realised if their own attitude is perceived as less than positively supportive.

Structured personal support for learning involves the use of supervisors, mentors or coaches. Sometimes this is an official process; sometimes the role is assumed by a manager or a more experienced colleague; sometimes a manager asks someone to provide help and advice; sometimes the learner is encouraged to seek advice from a particular colleague or group of colleagues. Whether officially organised or not, the climate of the workplace is likely to affect significantly the quality of learning support. We found both positive examples where organised support made an important contribution to learning and negative examples where lack of such support left people struggling and wasted a great deal of their time. What surprised us, however, was that very few of our positive examples resulted from organisation-wide strategies or initiatives. Most were relatively informal – initiated by middle managers, colleagues or the learners themselves.

In normal working groups we found three main types of learning situation: collaborative teamwork, ongoing mutual consultation and support, and observing others in action. We encountered several small teams of engineers with complementary skills working together on a succession of problems; and of cross-professional teams such as cardiologist and cardiac technician, radiographer and consultant. This helped people to recognise knowledge and skills which they did not themselves possess; and knowledge of tasks and situations was broadened by continuing contact with people who had different perspectives. The process of learning to work with other people was often mentioned as transferring to other, less intensive kinds of group situation.

Several situations were reported which raised the question of when a group becomes a team. Two factors in particular seemed to affect this:

the advent of a crisis and the strength of the affective dimension. Groups of individuals working in parallel with occasional consultation could become transformed into teams when confronted with a major problem or deadline; and sometimes this had a lasting effect as people began to recognise each other's contributions and group identity was strengthened. Gradual development of interpersonal support which extends beyond the workplace also contributed greatly to team feeling among certain working groups. This is more likely to happen when the work is emotionally demanding, as, for example, with a group of nurses on a ward.

When people spoke about collaborative teamwork, mutual learning tended to be assumed as an integral aspect of it. But with other types of working group, there was more overt discussion about learning from each other. Typically such consultations would entail a request for quick advice, seeking another perspective on a problem, help with a technical procedure or information on whom to ask for help on a particular issue. The way in which learning from colleagues happens can be very different in a new activity from the way it happens in an established one. In a start up activity, knowledge and skills are being acquired in a multitude of ways and can flow from person to person in several directions at once. In contrast, one person may acquire a large measure of the skills and knowledge needed directly from a predecessor in an established activity, perhaps by means of mentoring.

Membership of special groups charged with a specific task, for example review, audit, preparation of a decision or policy brief also generated significant learning, as did special assignments where people represented their working group in an external context. Another mode of learning, observing others in action, was frequently cited in relation to interpersonal skills; although many of the examples cited were negative rather than positive.

People outside the immediate working group can be usefully divided into three categories: those in what one might call an extended working group with whom there is regular contact; people in one's own organisation with whom contact has to be specially arranged, sometimes through a common acquaintance; and people outside the organisation altogether. Various reasons were cited for seeking help from people in parallel positions in one's organisation. For the newly arrived or newly promoted it was often practical help with common organisational procedures such as tendering or preparing specifications. For others it was keeping abreast of the micropolitics of the organisation, getting early information about changes of people or policies, getting advice about when, to whom and in what way to put forward a proposal. This nearly always took place in an informal setting, over lunch or in a bar, using networks created by people who used to work together or met on an in-house training course. These meetings were also used to get feedback about the work of one's own unit.

In several cases critical information for one's work had to be sought elsewhere in the organisation and this often required some initiative. For example, a service engineer we interviewed made considerable effort to be present wherever new services were being installed, in order to debrief people and see what went where. We also interviewed an installer who emphasised the need to go and talk to the people who designed the telecommunications equipment he was about to install. Sometimes people realised with considerable concern that an individual elsewhere in the organisation had unique knowledge which they needed. They would need to get him or her over for a day to brief them properly and save weeks of tinkering around. One company set up a special communication channel to encourage the flow of information between departments; but informal contact was still the preferred method and usually proved to be faster and more effective.

In the health sector, the working group was also extended by a rich variety of professional networks. But these networks were still largely dependent on personal contacts – A had previously worked or trained with B – often renewed by finding themselves on a course together or working for a common organisation. There was also some evidence of 'invisible colleges' in the health professions which extended beyond close personal contacts but also depended on occasional meetings for their sustenance.

The search for knowledge by some engineers is best described as entrepreneurial. We have already described a service engineer who went to great lengths to be present whenever something new was being installed. Another 'shortcircuited' a week's course by getting the materials, skimming through them, then spending a couple of hours with the in-house presenter – 4 hours instead of 40. Others sought to extract information from suppliers and/or customers, not just market information but also technical information. One sought to get the customer perspective on technical aspects of the equipment he installed. Another described how he had begun to acquire a more customer-oriented view of production and criticised his colleagues for giving this insufficient attention in their development of new products. A third found debriefing customers and suppliers a better way of keeping up to date than reading the journals!

Any theory of a learning organisation has to take account of the importance of informal learning. Our research shows how strongly this is situated in the work itself and in its social and organisational context. However, a major reason for the prevalence of learning from other people was that this knowledge was held by individuals rather than embedded in social activities. While some knowledge was firmly embedded in organisational activities, other knowledge was located only with a small number of individuals, often only one.

In most cases scarce knowledge was highly contextual in nature, either associated with a particular kind of software, equipment or installation, or else micropolitical and cultural, for example knowing how to access or develop relations with another department or organisation. It was difficult to conceive how it could have been acquired without working alongside or engaging in prolonged consultations with the 'expert'. As Fevre et al (2000) conclude from their parallel *Learning Society* project investigating the historical development of training in South Wales:

> It is very difficult to see how such knowledge and skills ('reading' the condition of the mine roof and making it safe) could have been imparted in a more formal manner.... They were not the sort of skills and knowledge that a formal standardised system of training could handle successfully. (Fevre et al, 2000, pp 65-6)

Factors affecting learning at work

Bandura's (1977) social learning theory views learning as resulting from the continuous, reciprocal, dynamic interaction among three elements: the attributes, attitudes and values of individuals; their behaviour; and environment or situational factors. Behaviour is construed by Bandura as a self-directed goal-setting activity; but his theory is still relevant to reactive as well as deliberative learning, provided that the work itself provides purpose and direction. As discussed above, learning at work more often results as a byproduct of the pursuit of work goals than from the pursuit of learning goals per se.

Confidence was frequently cited by our respondents as both the major outcome of a significant learning experience and a critical determinant of good performance at work. This applied to off-the-job learning, especially in mid-career, as well as to learning in the workplace. Sometimes it derived from the achievement of a good result or the solution of a problem, sometimes from the recognition that others were no less fallible than themselves. Confidence encouraged more ambitious goal setting and more risk taking, both leading to further learning. Usually it was fairly specific, relating to ability to execute a task or successfully perform a role, what Bandura calls *self-efficacy*. Bandura (1995) believes that such self-efficacy is a major determinant of the goals individuals will set and their motivation to achieve those goals.

Self-efficacy also depends on self-evaluation and how people view their capability. People may perceive an ability needed for some aspect of their current or anticipated future work either (a) as an acquirable skill or (b) as an inherent, possibly inherited, aptitude. The first view of capability is highly conducive to skills development as people judge themselves in terms of performance improvement and regard errors as a natural part of the learning process. The second, more conservative view constrains learning, especially when people compare themselves unfavourably with others – a behaviour strongly encouraged by the formal education system. The term *capability* neatly combines prior knowledge and skill, a critical factor in all learning, with expectations of achieving future goals.

Besides achievement, other sources of *motivation* reported in our interviews were self-development through learning, changing and proving oneself, career progression, an orientation towards outcomes for clients or the work group, and professionalism in the sense of pride in a job well done (and reported by technicians as much as 'professionals'!) – see also Mann and Ribble (1994). Dubin (1990) and McCauley et al (1994) report a strong relationship between challenge at work, self-development and on-the-job training for engineers and managers. In addition to these personal factors, our research identified two key situational factors, the *microculture of the workplace* and *how a person is managed*.

The merits of a *continuous-learning work environment* have been promoted by writers in learning organisations, focusing mainly on learning being a taken-for-granted part of the job, supported by social interaction and work relationships, on formal systems that reinforce achievement and provide opportunities for personal development, and an emphasis on innovation and competition (Rosow and Zager, 1988; Dubin, 1990). However, empirical research has concentrated on the more restricted construct of a 'transfer of training climate', finding evidence in favour of various uses and forms of feedback. Tracey et al (1995) examined the effect of factors associated with both the *learning culture* and *transfer climate* constructs on 505 newly trained supermarket managers. They found that the most influential group in shaping these constructs was the small self-selected work group, and that both constructs had significant positive effects on managers' performance. For both training climate and learning culture the scale with the greatest effect was the one most closely related to the social support system.

Our own analysis of the impact on learning of these situational factors (Alderton, 1999) can be summarised in terms of a triangular relationship between confidence, challenge and support. Offering support to an individual, particularly at critical junctures, leads to them developing confidence in their capabilities. Increasing confidence enables them to better manage more challenging work which, if successfully achieved, increases confidence further. A virtuous circle of positive development is established. A confident practitioner is better able to offer support to others in the workplace. The interactions between challenge, support and confidence are reciprocal, each reinforcing and being conditional on the other.

Recent literature on human resource management has highlighted the role of the manager as staff developer, which is conceived in terms of appraisal and target setting, planned development opportunities, mentoring and even coaching. Managers are expected to assess the needs of those they manage, preferably in collaboration with them, and jointly prepare personal development plans. While the range of methods for supported learning has widened, the underpinning concept is still based on learning goals being clearly specified and learning opportunities being planned. We found several positive examples of this in our research. But we also found situations where appraisal had minimal impact or missed out people who needed it. Several organisations had recognised this problem and were currently working with appraisers to improve the quality. Mentoring by managers was rare, although many respondents were prepared to apply the label retrospectively to previous formative relationships. Coaching was rarer still, largely confined to small technical departments.

Our general findings about learning suggest that this move towards seeing managers as staff developers needs reassessment; because so much of the non-formal learning described in our interviews was neither clearly specified nor planned, indeed it was not easily separated out from the flux of daily living and working. For many people learning arose out of the challenges posed by their work – solving problems, improving quality and/or productivity, getting things done, coping with change – and out of social interactions in the workplace with colleagues and customers/clients. This learning was either facilitated or constrained by (a) the organisation and allocation of work and (b) the social climate of the work environment. While our methodological approach led to a greater emphasis on positive evidence of learning, our respondents not only volunteered negative evidence but implicitly provided it when they compared their personal experiences of different work contexts. The clear implication, sometimes explicitly stated, was that important learning opportunities were missed in certain kinds of work situation, with negative consequences for the quality and speed of work. These claims about missed opportunities were based either on self-evident misses ('it would have saved a lot of time', 'if only I had known ...') or on comparisons with other, more learning-friendly work environments. Thus they were credible assessments of what was feasible in those contexts, not untested aspirations driven by hypothetical models of a 'learning organisation'. Some respondents may have been more cognitively aware of, and positively disposed towards, recognising and using learning opportunities at work; but they still had to know whom to ask and to feel that their requests would be positively received. An important corollary would be an orientation towards offering help rather than waiting to be asked. The positive effect on confidence and performance of being consulted by colleagues should also be noted. Thus a major factor affecting a person's learning at work is the personality, interpersonal skills, knowledge and learning orientation of their manager.

It follows that of all the mechanisms used at organisational level to promote learning the most significant is likely to be the appointment and development of its managers (Eraut et al, 1999). However, while approaches to management development normally emphasise motivation, productivity and appraisal, comparatively little attention is given to supporting the learning of subordinates, allocating and organising work, and creating a climate which promotes informal learning. This imbalance may result from ignorance about how much learning does (and how much more learning might) take place on the job. There are also implications for the selection of people for management roles. In most organisations the practical implications of strengthening informal learning for developing the individual and collective capabilities of employees are not yet widely understood.

From a manager's perspective organisational policies can appear as dominant, enabling or disinterested. Taking courses as an example, centralised provision of in-house or bought-in courses is quite common. Such policies may be guided by perceptions of organisational weaknesses, strategies for building up particular future capabilities, the need for technical or legal updating, ongoing programmes of skill development and management development. Whether or not middle managers are consulted, there is an assumption of needs being similar across the organisation which is sometimes true and sometimes false. More problematic is the difficulty inherent in a central system of timing courses appropriately. Our evidence suggests that timing is often a critical feature in learning from courses. In particular, courses need to relate to participants' current concerns, whether they are present or future orientated. The advantages of central provision, not always realised in practice, are economies of scale, relevance for the organisation and control over the quality of provision. But economies of scale need to be counterbalanced by diversity of need; and relevance is difficult to achieve in fast-changing situations. Enabling strategies provide support in the form of funds and advice, to managers seeking to meet the needs of their subordinates or directly to individual employees. In either case the initiative is more likely to come from the employee, and with it more motivation and commitment. The manager's role is to ensure relevance to needs which have been properly assessed and discussed; but with some managers this degenerates to 'laissez-faire'. There is also a danger under either dominant or enabling regimes that too much emphasis is given to courses.

All four of the financial organisations in the study had performance managements systems, but these differed according to:

- frequency of formal meetings;
- approaches to performance criteria and target setting;
- use of generic skills and competencies;
- linkage to pay;
- balance between performance evaluation and personal development.

A few respondents tried to reconcile these systems with their own personal philosophies of management, demonstrating the tension between *performance management systems*, which focus on short term results and key activities which directly affect 'the bottom line', and a *human resource development* approach focused on the development of staff capability over a longer time scale (Eraut, 1997a). Reconciling these two approaches depends on the skills of the manager. But even the most skilful managers are constrained (a) when stakes are high because of possible promotions or contingent financial benefits; and (b) when their authority to make developmental responses to employees' learning needs is limited by finance and/or flexibility. Professional bodies played a small role in financial organisations through their provision of initial qualifications, and only affected a small minority of engineers for whom membership of the appropriate Institute was an important source of information and opportunities for Continuing Professional Development (CPD). In the health care sector, however, their influence was very considerable both through their CPD policies and by providing networks which were important sources of learning for their members

Theoretical development

While not engaging in an ethnographic approach, the project nevertheless collected abundant evidence to support theories of situated learning. The organisation of work, social relations in the workplace, the effect of challenge and support on individual competence, self-efficacy and risk taking were key factors affecting the level and the direction of the learning which occurred. However, the situations we encountered were rarely static: a high proportion of work contexts were in a process of rapid change, and the people in them also came and went quite frequently. Not many work groups could be described as settled working communities. Thus the 'community of practice' metaphor (Lave and Wenger, 1991) can be profoundly misleading; what many of our older respondents reported was the break-up of working communities. The closest analogue to a community of practice would be the health professions, but even they might be better described as networks. Networks do not necessarily have the same degree of continuity as communities, and are more interpersonal than collective in their mode of operation. Within organisations, we found that networks across work units, and sometimes also including suppliers and customers facilitated the linkage of different types of information and expertise more effectively than formal mechanisms. Learning from other people was triggered by one-to-one relationships and participation in temporary groups (see below) as much as by membership of an ongoing work group.

This suggests a different picture of a work group from that eulogised in some recent social psychological literature. The group comprises a changing set of individuals who spend varying periods of time within it. These individuals come from and go on to other groups, sometimes within the same organisation, sometimes not. Each has a distinctive learning career which can be traced through a sequence of work groups: in some groups it flourishes, in others it stagnates or regresses. This depends on how much group members learn from each other, to what extent individuals of the whole group respond to the challenges of their work and support each other, and what additional learning opportunities for the group are located and developed. Typically, groups do not spend time, indeed often they strongly discourage, finding out about the knowledge resources and networks of new members; they regard external contacts and learning opportunities as diversions from the work of the group; and they do not seek to learn from diversity of experience or perspective. Our analysis suggests that a group climate for learning has to be created, sustained and recreated at regular intervals; and this has to be a management responsibility. The learning of individuals and work groups has to be high on managers' agendas, and managers have to be educated and supported in this role. Few groups are sufficiently stable and coherent for corporate leadership to develop spontaneously.

An additional strategy for developing learning is the creation of, or participation in, a temporary group. Short courses can be usefully construed as temporary groups whose overt purpose is a concentrated period of learning (Eraut, 1994, Chapter 5). But other groups, whose titles suggest a different purpose, may equally depend on learning for their success, for example an audit group, a quality improvement group, a liaison group, a problem-solving working party. These groups may draw their membership from a single unit, or several units in the same organisation. For many groups, a review of the knowledge resources of their members is a neglected first step; but nevertheless the temporary nature of the group gives opportunities for interpersonal learning that might be unlikely to occur in more permanent groups with settled pecking orders and agendas. All these groups are intended to affect the working practices of their participants' work-group(s) or organisation. Hence accomplishing their goals will depend on their relevance to their members' work, the briefing and preparation of participants and ongoing interactions between the temporary group and the normal work settings of its members. These concerns rarely occupy as much of the groups' time as they should. Short courses in particular often fail to articulate properly the participants' work: bad timing, lack of preparation, lack of follow-up, can lead to their potential contribution being wasted. The more distant they are from the workplace, the more likely they are to fail to connect with its current priorities, whatever their merits. Thus the management of courses and other temporary groups is an important aspect of learning in the workplace, one which often impinges on organisational as well as work unit strategies for priority learning and improving the quality of performance.

When one combines the above analysis with the typology of non-formal learning developed by the project (Table 2) several conclusions may be drawn:

- the emphasis given to deliberative learning often results in reactive learning and implicit learning being ignored;
- nevertheless, deliberative learning is important and still needs promotion and support within the workplace;
- the deliberative learning activities listed in Table 2 could form the basis of a group learning agenda for a work team or unit;
- important episodes of reactive learning depend on individuals or groups noticing and taking advantage of learning opportunities as and when they occur. This may require more than a positive learning climate, it may need to become part of a working routine. What did we learn from that customer, that visit, that mishap, that success, that discussion, that difference in opinion, our new colleague, and so on?

Finally we return to the role of implicit learning and tacit knowledge, which are discussed in depth in Eraut (2000). The relevant areas of research literature are those of professional expertise (Eraut, 1994) and decision making in naturalistic settings (Klein et al, 1993), both of which conclude that situational understanding is often the most important factor in the quality of decisions. They also suggest that important aspects of situational understanding are based on tacit knowledge, especially when decisions are rapid and complex and made under conditions of pressure and uncertainty. Preparation for such decisions may be significantly enhanced by incorporating multiple perspectives and sources of information, but these sources may also find difficulty in explaining what they know because of the tacit nature of part of their knowledge. The issue of how much knowledge is tacit and how far it can be made explicit is of considerable practical importance.

Much of the literature on tacit knowledge is rather confusing on this issue. For example, the widely quoted book by Nonaka and Takeuchi (1995) attributes a series of high profile successes by Japanese manufacturers to the companies' ability to convert the tacit knowledge of their employees into explicit knowledge. However, careful reading suggests that the knowledge they describe is explicit, personal knowledge which had not previously been considered relevant or shared with others. They had no problem in 'telling' once corporate relevance had been established. There are also a few examples of important sudden insights of the kind popularised by Gestalt psychologists, but this is knowledge creation not knowledge elicitation. Of greater theoretical interest, perhaps, are attempts to infer maxims or principles of action from observational or interview data. Implicit in this work is the assumption that codification which derives C knowledge from P knowledge encapsulates the essence of that P knowledge: it does not become 'knowledge' until it has been codified. However, knowledge of these principles alone does not improve performance; because performance also depends on knowing when and how to use the principle, situational understanding and skilful activity. Our own interpretation is that 'thick' tacit versions of this knowledge co-exist alongside 'thin' explicit versions: the thick version is used in practice, the thin version for justifying that practice.

The limits to making tacit knowledge explicit have yet to be explored, and progress will be slow. Nevertheless this is an important area of research to pursue because of the many practical benefits. These include:

- improving the quality of a person's or a team's performance;
- improving communication between co-workers;
- constructing aids to decision making;
- enabling people to review their actions and to keep them more under critical control even when they are not easily described;
- possible creation of new knowledge.

Policy implications

One of the most interesting aspects of this research project has been that its theoretical development of frameworks for thinking about non-formal learning and workplace learning has clear and significant practical implications. The way people think about learning affects their practice, whether that practice is policy making, managing or learning at work. We would argue that there is nothing esoteric about our framework and our findings: people can recognise many features of it in their own experience. However, articulating it and clarifying it makes it possible to bring that experience to situations from which it would previously have been excluded. If those kinds of learning are important, and that is how they are most often triggered and sustained, then the actions needed to promote learning in the workplace are different from what we had previously assumed. Simplistic assumptions about the dominance of codified knowledge and learning in formal education and training have to be abandoned. Moreover, by locating much important learning in workplace settings and emphasising the influence of social relations within those settings and the influence of managers and the microculture of the workplace, the symbiotic relationship between working and learning becomes apparent.

We would also suggest that many features of our framework apply also to learning in community contexts. The knowledge typology (Table 1) might need a little adjustment, but that would be unlikely to weaken its validity for work contexts. The typology of non-formal learning (Table 2) is equally valid for community contexts. The list of knowledge contexts and sources (Table 4) would need changing to reflect the rather different kinds of groups, networks and activities in community contexts. In less managed community contexts, social relations would become even more important and microcultures critical. Informal induction and mentoring arrangements may and probably do play a significant role in facilitating learning.

Implications for managers seeking to promote learning at the organisational or work unit level were discussed above; and in Eraut et al (1998b) and (1999) we have provided a wealth of detailed examples of workplace learning which may suggest or stimulate a range of new ideas about the facilitation of learning in a wide range of contexts. Alderton's (1999) paper complements these chapters with an analysis of workplace learning from an individual worker's perspective and the role of the manager in developing people's capability through providing an appropriate balance of challenge and support. There is enough material here to provide the foundation for a learning facilitation strand within a management development programme. Since the project is recommending that the introduction of such a strand, with an appropriate follow-up, should be given top priority in any organisation's policy for promoting learning in the workplace, it has been important to provide this more detailed guidance.

Adopting this approach to improving on-the-job learning will have important positive effects on off-the-job learning. Off-the-job learning has an important role to play in bringing new knowledge and perspectives into an organisation and developing its capability to respond to its changing environment (Eraut, 1997a). Neither off-the-job learning nor on-the-job learning can compensate for weaknesses in the other. But our research confirms that the use of off-the-job learning is highly dependent on consequent on-the-job learning, whether personal or collective. Without further on-the-job learning there will be little mutual accommodation between new knowledge and working practices, the knowledge will be branded as irrelevant and practice will stagnate. Conversely, if on-the-job learning and networking lead to an awareness of particular needs, relevant off-the-job learning can be located, prepared for and properly used. When off-the-job learning fails to produce the desired effect, it is usually because no such needs assessment from the work setting(s) has been provided. Hence education and training policies which focus only on off-the-job learning are doomed to be ineffective.

For government, there are clear messages from our research about the nature of lifelong learning and policies which might facilitate it or constrain it. While it is much easier for government to influence formal education and training, policies for formal learning should be formulated in full knowledge of the significance of non-formal learning and checked out for possible effects upon it. For psychological reasons, the term 'non-learner' should be banned from government publications as a description of non-participants in formal education. Policies for post-qualification education and training should be reviewed for their congruency with the promotion of lifelong learning by both formal and non-formal means, especially policies pertaining to funding and qualifications.

There are also important implications for the education system. We have shown that learning in the workplace is very different in kind from learning in school or college. Thus learning in one context will not easily transfer to the other. Nor will knowledge and skill transfer without being resituated in the new context, which will require significant further learning. We would argue for greater use of a wider variety of learning contexts for all learners from the age of 14 onwards, if lifelong learning is to be seriously promoted (Eraut, 1997b). The attributes and dispositions required for lifelong learning in the workplace cannot be acquired outside the workplace; and a significant amount of preparation for work can only be undertaken in employment. To pretend otherwise would be to deceive the public and limit the quality of the outcomes of both general and vocational education.

References

Alderton, J. (1999) *Factors which facilitate workplace learning: Confidence, challenge and support*, AERA Conference Paper, Montreal, April.

Bandura, A. (1977) *Social learning theory*, Englewood-Cliffs, NJ: Prentice-Hall.

Bandura, A. (1995) *Self-efficacy in changing societies*, Cambridge: Cambridge University Press.

Berry, D.C. (ed) (1997) *How implicit is implicit learning?*, Oxford: Oxford University Press.

Dewey, J. (1933) *How we think – A restatement of the relation of reflective thinking to the educative process*, Boston, MA: Heath.

Dubin, S.S. (1990) 'Maintaining competence through updating', in S.L. Willis and S.S. Dubin (eds) *Maintaining professional competence*, San Francisco, CA: Jossey-Bass.

Eraut, M. (1994) *Developing professional knowledge and competence*, London: Falmer Press.

Eraut, M. (1995) 'Schön Shock: a case for reframing reflection-in-action?', *Teachers and Teaching*, vol 1, no 1, pp 9-22.

Eraut, M. (1997a) 'Perspectives on defining "The Learning Society"', *Journal of Educational Policy*, vol 12, no 6, pp 551-8.

Eraut, M. (1997b) 'Curriculum frameworks and assumptions in 16-19 education', *Research in Post-Compulsory Education*, vol 2, no 3, pp 281-97.

Eraut, M. (2000) 'Non-formal learning, implicit learning and tacit knowledge', in F. Coffield (ed) *The necessity of informal learning*, Bristol: The Policy Press, pp 12-31.

Eraut, M., Alderton, J., Boylan, A. and Wraight, A. (1995) *Learning to use scientific knowledge in education and practice settings*, London: English National Board for Nursing, Midwifery and Health Visiting.

Eraut, M., Alderton, J., Cole, G. and Senker, P. (1998a) *Development of knowledge and skills in employment*, Research Report 5, University of Sussex, Institute of Education.

Eraut, M., Alderton, J., Cole, G. and Senker, P. (1998b) 'Learning from other people at work', in F. Coffield (ed) *Learning at work*, Bristol: The Policy Press, pp 37-48.

Eraut, M., Alderton, J., Cole, G. and Senker, P. (1999) 'The impact of the manager on learning in the workplace', in F. Coffield (ed) *Speaking truth to power: Research and policy on lifelong learning*, Bristol: The Policy Press, pp 19-29.

Fevre, R., Gorard, S. and Rees, G. (2000) 'Necessary and unnecessary learning: the acquisition of knowledge and skills in and outside employment in South Wales in the 20th century', in F. Coffield (ed) *The necessity of informal learning*, Bristol: The Policy Press, pp 64-80.

Fox, R.D., Mazmanian, P.E. and Putnam, R.W. (1989) *Changing and learning in the lives of physicians*, New York, NY: Praeger.

Gear, J., Mcintosh, A. and Squires, G. (1994) *Informal leaning in the professions,* University of Hull School of Education.

Jennett, P., Jones, D., Mask, T., Egan, K. and Hotvedt, M. (1994) 'The characteristics of self-directed learning', in D.A. Davis and R.D. Fox (eds) *The physician as learner*, Chicago, IL: American Medical Association, pp 40-65.

Klein, G.A., Oranasu, J., Calderwood, R. and Zsambok, C.E. (eds) (1993) *Decision making in action, models and methods*, Norwood, NJ: Ablex.

Kolb, D. (1984) *Experiential learning*, Englewood Cliffs, NJ: Prentice-Hall.

Lave, J. and Wenger E. (1991) *Situated learning: Legitimate peripheral participation*, Cambridge: Cambridge University Press.

McCall, M.W., Lombardo, M.M. and Morrison, A.M. (1988) *The lessons of experience: How successful executives develop on the job*, Lexington, MA: Lexington Books.

McCauley, C.D., Ruderman, M.N., Ohlott, P.J. and Morrow, J.E. (1994) 'Assessing the Development and Components of Managerial Jobs', *Journal of Applied Psychology*, vol 79, no 4, pp 544-60.

Mann, K. and Ribble, J. (1994) 'The rule of motivation in self-directed learning', in D.A. Davis and R.D. Fox (eds) *The physician as learner*, Chicago, IL: American Medical Association, pp 67-90.

Megginson, D. (1996) 'Planned and emergent learning: consequences for development', *Management Learning*, vol 27, no 4, pp 411-28.

Nonaka, I. and Takeuchi, H. (1995) *The knowledge creating company*, Oxford: Oxford University Press.

Polanyi, M. (1967) *The tacit dimension*, Garden City, NY: Doubleday.

Reber, A.S. (1993) *Implicit learning and tacit knowledge: An essay on the cognitive unconscious*, Oxford: Oxford University Press.

Rosow, J. M. and Zager, R. (1988) *Training: The competitive edge*, San Francisco, CA: Jossey-Bass.

Schön, D. (1983) *The reflective practitioner: How professionals think in action*, New York, NY: Basic Books.

Slotnick, H.B. (1999) *How doctors learn in the medical workplace*, AERA Conference Paper, Montreal, April.

Slotnick, H.B., Kristjanson, A.F., Raszkowski, R.R. and Moravec, R. (1997) *How doctors learn: Mechanisms of action*, AERA Conference Paper, Chicago, March.

Steadman, S., Eraut, M., Fielding, F. and Horton, A. (1995) *Making school-based INSET effective*, University of Sussex Institute of Education, Research Report No 2.

Tough, A.M. (1971) *The adult's learning projects*, Toronto, Canada: Ontario Institute for Studies in Education.

Tracey, J.B., Tannenbaum, S.I. and Kavanagh, M.J. (1995) 'Bridging trained skills on the job: the importance of the work environment', *Journal of Applied Psychology*, vol 80, no 2, pp 239-52.

Index

W

Y

The Learning Society series

The neccesity of informal learning

Edited by Frank Coffield

The ESRC's programme of research into The
Learning Society did not set out to study
informal learning, but it quickly became clear to
project after project within the Programme that
the importance of informal learning in the
formation of knowledge and skills had been
underestimated. Policies to widen and deepen
participation in learning need to concern
themselves not only with increasing access and
appreciating the different contexts in which
learning takes place, but also with the different
forms of learning. Formal learning in institutions
is only the tip of the iceberg and this report
constitutes an exploratory study of the
submerged mass of learning, which takes place
informally and implicitly.

Contents: *Introduction: The structure below the
surface: reassessing the significance of informal
learning* **Frank Coffield;** *Non-formal learning,
implicit learning and tacit knowledge in professional
work* **Michael Eraut;** *Informal learning and social
capital* **John Field and Lynda Spence;** *Implicit
knowledge, phenomenology and learning difficulties*
**Stephen Baron, Alastair Wilson and Sheila
Riddell;** *Formalising learning: the impact of
accreditation* **Pat Davies;** *Necessary and
unnecessary learning: the acquisition of knowledge
and 'skills' in and outside employment in South
Wales in the 20th century* **Ralph Fevre, Stephen
Gorard and Gareth Rees.**

Paperback £13.99 (US$25.00) ISBN 1 86134 152 0
297x210mm 88 pages January 2000

Speaking truth to power: Research and policy on lifelong learning

Edited by Frank Coffield

In this collection of essays researchers discuss the implications of their findings for policy. They make positive recommendations for policy makers and those concerned to improve the quality of learning at work. Findings are also presented for the first time from a major new survey, commissioned by The Learning Society Programme, which examined the skills of a representative sample of British workers.

Contents: *Introduction: Past failures, present differences and possible futures for research, policy and practice* **Frank Coffield;** *The impact of research on policy* **Maurice Kogan;** *The impact of the manager on learning in the workplace* **Michael Eraut, Jane Alderton, Gerald Cole and Peter Senker;** *Young lives at risk in the 'Futures' market: some policy concerns from ongoing research* **Stephen Ball, Sheila Macrae and Meg Maguire;** *The costs of learning: the policy implications of changes in continuing education for NHS staff* **Therese Dowswell, Bobbie Millar and Jenny Hewison;** *Skill trends in Britain: trajectories over the last decade* **Alan Felstead, David Ashton, Brendan Burchill and Francis Green;** *Adult guidance services for a learning society? Evidence from England* **Will Bartlett and Teresa Rees.**

Paperback £13.99 (US$25.00) ISBN 1 86134 147 4
297x210mm 76 pages July 1999

Why's the beer always stronger up North?: Studies of lifelong learning in Europe

Edited by Frank Coffield

This edited report offers a fresh approach on lifelong learning and attacks the consensual rhetoric which has become dominant in the English-speaking world over the last 20 years. It provides a more convincing explanation of the high levels of non-participation in continuous learning, and sees lifelong learning as a new moral obligation and a new form of social control. The report suggests that lifelong learning may be better viewed as contested terrain between employers, unions and the state than as the new wonder drug which will solve a wide range of economic, social and political problems.

Contents: *Introduction: lifelong learning as a new form of social control?* **Frank Coffield;** *Lifelong learning: learning for life? Some cross-national observations* **Walter Heinz;** *Models of guidance services in the learning society: the case of the Netherlands* **Teresa Rees and Will Bartlett;** *The comparative dimension in continuous vocational training: a preliminary framework* **Isabelle Darmon, Carlos Frade and Kari Hadjivassiliou;** *Inclusion and exclusion: credits and unités capitalisables compared* **Pat Davies;** *Using 'social capital' to compare performance in continuing education* **Tom Schuller and Andrew Burns;** *Issues in a 'home international' comparison of policy strategies: the experience of the Unified Learning Project* **David Raffe, Cathy Howieson, Ken Spours and Michael Young;** *Planning, implementation and practical issues in cross-national comparative research* **Antje Cockriill, Peter Scott and John Fitz.**

Paperback £13.99 (US$25.00) ISBN 1 86134 131 8
297x210mm 88 pages January 1999

Learning at work

Edited by Frank Coffield

Learning at work is important in helping to
transform fashionable phrases such as 'the
learning organisation' or 'lifelong learning' into
practical ideas and methods which could enhance
the quality of learning in British firms. It examines
the key processes of learning, as embedded in
particular workplaces, in organisational structures
and in specific social practices.

Contents: *Introduction: new forms of learning in the
workplace* **Frank Coffield;** *Artisans in the making?
Comparing construction training in Wales and
Germany* **Peter Scott and Antje Cockrill;**
*Jobrotation: combining skills formation and active
labour market policy* **Reiner Siebert;** *Continuing
vocational training: key issues* **Isabelle Darmon,
Kari Hadjivassiliou, Elisabeth Sommerlad, Elliot
Stern, Jill Turbin with Dominique Danau;** *Learning
from other people at work* **Michael Eraut, Jane
Alderton, Gerald Cole and Peter Senker;** *The
Learning Society: the highest stage of human
capitalism?* **Stephen Baron, Kirsten Stalker,
Heather Wilkinson and Sheila Riddell;** *Skill
formation: redirecting the research agenda* **David
Ashton.**

Paperback £13.99 (US$25.00) ISBN 1 86134 123 7
297x210mm 76 pages September 1998

Other related titles from The Policy Press

Researching education: Themes in teaching-and-learning

Harold Silver

Recent criticisms of research on education have largely missed the point. By focusing on schools, they have failed to take note of the enormous range of research on teaching and learning in education defined more broadly.

This highly topical report looks across the traditional education system and wherever else teaching and learning takes place. It looks at schools, colleges and universities on the one hand, and industrial training, nurse and student mentoring, professional development and lifelong learning/learning society on the other.

The report illuminates the current intensive debates at government, quasi-government and research community levels about the nature and status of research in 'education'. Conceived from a refreshingly wide angle, *Researching education* is an essential review of the field of educational research.

Contents: *Prologue; Points of entry; 'Teaching'; Research and dissemination; Motivation and learning; Organisation and change; Outside 'the system'; Communication and information technology (CIT); Skills; Learning for futures; Directions.*

Paperback £15.99 (US$29.00) ISBN 1 86134 177 6
234x156mm 88 pages July 1999

Forthcoming

Adult guidance services and The Learning Society:
Emerging policies in the European Union
Will Bartlett, Teresa Rees and A.G. Watts

Adult guidance services, the 'brokers' between individuals and the labour and learning markets, take on a new significance in the context of The Learning Society and the end of the 'job for life'. This unique book analyses contrasting approaches to the delivery of guidance services in the UK, Germany, Netherlands, Italy and France, focusing on the effects of marketisation and the impact on European Union policies.

Paperback £14.99 (US$25.00) TBC ISBN 1 86134 153 9 297x210mm
72 pages TBC October 2000 TBC

Differing visions of a Learning Society: Research Findings Volume 2
Edited by Frank Coffield

The conclusions from The Learning Society Programme are brought together in this second volume, and suggest very different ways of thinking about a learning society and very different policies from those introduced by the present government and earlier administrations.

Paperback £16.99 (US$31.00) TBC ISBN 1 86134 247 0
Hardback £45.00 (US$81.00) TBC ISBN 1 86134 248 9
216x148mm 160 pages TBC October 2000 TBC

The learning society and people with learning difficulties
Sheila Riddell, Stephen Baron and Alistair Wilson
Paperback £15.99 (US$26.99) TBC ISBN 1 86134 223 3
234x156mm 176 pages TBC January 2001 TBC

Learn to succeed: The benefits of a skills revolution
Mike Campbell
Paperback £15.99 (US$26.99) TBC ISBN 1 86134 269 1
234x156mm 144 pages TBC May 2001 TBC

Creating a learning society? Learning careers and their relevance for policies
of lifelong learning
Stephen Gorad, Gareth Rees, Ralph Fevre and John Furlong
Paperback £15.99 (US$26.99) TBC ISBN 1 86134 286 1
234x156mm 224 pages TBC June 2001 TBC